HOMECRAFT

HOMECRAFT

A STUDENT'S INTRODUCTION TO
THE MODERN FAMILY AND HOME

THIRD EDITION

MARGARET CLARK

SENIOR ADVISER FOR HOME ECONOMICS FOR
DERBYSHIRE

ROUTLEDGE & KEGAN PAUL   LONDON

First published in 1966
by Routledge & Kegan Paul Ltd
Broadway House, 68–74 Carter Lane
London EC4V 5EL

Printed in Great Britain
by Richard Clay (The Chaucer Press) Ltd
Bungay, Suffolk

© *Margaret Clark 1966, 1975*

No part of this book may be reproduced
in any form without permission from
the publisher, except for the quotation
of brief passages in criticism

Reprinted February 1967
Reprinted September 1967
Reprinted November 1968
Second edition 1971
Reprinted 1972 and 1974
Third edition 1975

ISBN 0 7100 7948 6 (C)
ISBN 0 7100 7951 6 (P)
ISBN 0 7100 7960 5 (L)

CONTENTS

PREFACE *page* xi

ACKNOWLEDGEMENTS xiii

SECTION I   MONEY MANAGEMENT

CHAPTER 1   SHOPPING AND SPENDING   3
Supermarkets — Smaller or family shops —
Mail order firms — Consumer protection —
The legal side of protection — Care labelling

CHAPTER 2   BUDGETING   29
Planning your spending — Compulsory
deductions (income tax, V.A.T., National
Insurance contributions, superannuation,
union fees)

CHAPTER 3   SAVINGS OF ALL KINDS   39
Post Office — Banks — Insurance — Hire
purchase — Saving with the Co-op

SECTION II HOMES AND PEOPLE

CHAPTER 4 LIVING ACCOMMODATION: TO SHARE, TO RENT, TO BUY 63
'Digs' — Hostels — Furnished rooms and flats — Buying a house — Estate agents — The solicitor

CHAPTER 5 GETTING ON WITH PEOPLE 87
Friends and neighbours — The family — Your friends — The older generation — The role of the host or hostess — Leisure — Serving the community

CHAPTER 6 THE HOUSE (1) 103
Daily chores — Weekly chores — The right equipment — Equipment for the removal of dust, dirt and grease — Doing the washing — Stain removal and dry cleaning — Types of stains and how to treat them — Simple repairs — Electrical repairs — Aids to the housewife — Paint — Painting — Wallpaper — Wallpapering — Floor surfaces — Working surfaces — Furniture and furnishings

CHAPTER 7 THE HOUSE (2) 145
The kitchen — Orders of work — Kitchen equipment — Kitchen implements — Refuse disposal — Heating — Comparative costs — Hot water — Ventilation — Lighting

SECTION III HEALTH AND SAFEGUARDS FOR YOU AND YOUR FAMILY

CHAPTER 8 HYGIENE FOR YOUNG PEOPLE 179
How about you? — Sleep — Food — Cleanliness — Cosmetics

CHAPTER 9 CHILD CARE 195
Health — Causes of ill health — Prevention of ill health — Infectious diseases

CONTENTS

CHAPTER 10	FIRST AID A few facts about accidents — Simple treatment — Accidents in the home	213
CHAPTER 11	WHEN AND WHERE TO GO FOR HELP — OFFICIAL ORGANISATIONS The National Health Service — The Department of Health and Social Security — The Police — The Fire Service — Trade unions	229
CHAPTER 12	WHEN AND WHERE TO GO FOR HELP — UNOFFICIAL ORGANISATIONS Voluntary organisations — The Citizens' Advice Bureaux — The Women's Royal Voluntary Service — The British Red Cross Society — The Order of St. John — The N.S.P.C.C. — The National Marriage Guidance Council — The Samaritans — The R.S.P.C.A.	251

SECTION IV TEENS, TWENTIES, MARRIAGE AND MOTHERHOOD

CHAPTER 13	TEENS TO TWENTIES Puberty — Growing up	271
CHAPTER 14	MARRIAGE Your own marriage — What is marriage? — The 'working wife' — Your baby — Your example — Your responsibility	283
CHAPTER 15	THE MATERNITY SERVICES The expectant mother — Where to have the baby — Post-natal treatment — Health Visitors — Play is a child's 'work' — Day Nurseries — Nursery classes — The dentist — Financial help — Special laws relating to children	297

SOME BOOKS WHICH MIGHT INTEREST YOU … 311

INDEX … 315

ILLUSTRATIONS

Drawings by Robert Hammal and G. T. Hughes

1. The happy toddler filled her basket	page 7
2. It is difficult to put up a tent with the postman at the door	12
3. The Kitemark of the British Standards Institution	13
4. The Gas Council's mark	13
5. The B.E.A.B. sign	13
6. The C.U.C. sign	13
7. A Teltag	13
8. 'I wish I'd tried them on before I bought them!'	15
9. The Food and Drugs Act protects us now	20
10. Obey the maker's instructions	25
11. Where does it go?	34
12. Never forget to save	39
13. An open cheque	44
14. A crossed cheque	45
15. 'Excellent for lagging the pipes, madam'	54
16. *Some* landladies will allow you to use the kitchen sink . . .	67
17. Sharing a bathroom with your friends may not be good fun	71
18. Choose your flat carefully	76
19. Television—the hostile intruder	88
20. Too occupied to listen	90

ILLUSTRATIONS

21.	A blind and deaf shopper gets a special market report tapped out on her hand by her cadet escort (The British Red Cross Society)	97
22.	Don't let routine dominate your life	105
23.	A cartridge fuse	121
24.	What a toddler can do in 5 minutes	126
25.	The Design Centre sign	138
26.	Order of kitchen equipment	146
27.	Positioning of equipment	146
28.	Positioning of equipment	147
29.	Positioning of equipment	147
30.	Kitchen plan	148
31.	Heights are important, too	150
32.	Drawers should be shallow	151
33.	The U-bend	159
34.	A pivot-hung window	171
35.	A sash window	172
36.	Casement window with pivot upper window	172
37.	Be 'with it' with milk (Pupils of Manor School, Chesterfield. Photograph by Derek Jones)	183
38.	A child needs to know that he is loved	195
39.	In one hour one bacterium becomes eight	202
40.	As flies feed they both vomit and excrete	204
41.	A typical mantelpiece	221
42.	Would *you* dress *your* child in inflammable materials? (Crown Copyright—C.O.I.)	222
43.	What a moment's thought could so easily prevent (Crown Copyright—C.O.I.)	224
44.	A medical card (Crown Copyright—C.O.I.)	232
45.	What the rates help to pay for	240
46.	A Woman Special Constable (Crown Copyright—C.O.I.)	243
47.	A nineteenth-century chimney sweep	244
48.	The sign of the Citizens' Advice Bureau	252
49.	The sign of the Women's Royal Voluntary Service	253
50.	The sign of the Red Cross	254
51.	The Junior Red Cross Club in Ottershaw (The British Red Cross Society)	255
52.	The sign of the Order of St. John	256

ILLUSTRATIONS

53. St. John Ambulance at work (St. John Ambulance Association) — 257
54. The sign of the N.S.P.C.C. — 258
55. *You* can help prevent suffering like this (N.S.P.C.C.) — 260
56. The sign of the R.S.P.C.A. — 264
57. Will *you* try to stop such cruelty? (Kent County Constabulary) — 265
58. Menstruation — 275
59. Don't make the most of it— — 277
60. —make the best of it — 278
61. Probably consideration is the greatest asset in a husband — 281
62. 'His' and 'Hers'—all right for towels, but not for wage packets or salary cheques — 287
63. Just scoop up the spider and drop it out of the window — 293
64. Milk at school (Glass Manufacturers' Federation) — 303

PREFACE

Home Economics has now broadened its scope in Education. Recognising, as it does, the wide use of convenience foods and labour saving devices, it can now concentrate less on the practical skills, which used to occupy most of its time, and more on the complexities of learning to live. An integral part of this is Homecraft which is as vitally important to the school leaver at any age as it is to the student studying for an examination. Homecraft is not simply concerned with the day-to-day business of running a house and family. It is also very much to do with ourselves, our health, our happiness and with how we get on with other people—our friends, shopkeepers and, most important of all, those *within* our own family: at the moment our parents and, in time, our husbands and children. These are matters carefully introduced by Mrs. Margaret Clark, the author of this book.

She also looks outside the home to the social services on which we all rely for the running of our households, for education, health and help in times of difficulty.

Mrs. Clark has children of her own. She has a Home Economics training and has, in fact, taught in every type of school with one exception—that of a 'boys only' establishment—over the past twenty years! She is at present Senior Adviser for Home Economics for Derbyshire. She was, moreover, a member of the Certificate of Secondary Education Homecraft Panel on the East Midlands Examinations Board.

So, if you are working for an examination, you will find this book of practical help, for the author knows exactly what the young student requires. You will also find it useful in a much wider sense, in your own life, for your future home and family.

The information is set out clearly and with ample illustration. Special care has been taken to explain technical matters as straightforwardly as possible, and there are many helpful suggestions for practical and written work.

Note

Measurements have been given in metric units in fields where metrication has already been introduced, e.g. the building trade. Other measurements have been given in non-metric units.

ACKNOWLEDGEMENTS

The form for the basic principles of first aid has been taken from the booklet *Golden Rules of First Aid* and has been reproduced in this book by kind permission of the British Red Cross Society.

Permission of the Controller of Her Majesty's Stationery Office has been obtained to print illustrations 42, 43, 44 and 46. Permission of The National Westminster Bank Ltd. was kindly given to print illustrations 13 and 14.

SECTION I · MONEY MANAGEMENT

CHAPTER 1 · SHOPPING AND SPENDING

Why start a book on homecraft by talking about money? Is it the most important foundation on which to build a home? Certainly not! Wrongly used it may buy just possessions rather than contributing towards happiness. But to begin by discussing spending makes a good opening because here we all have something in common. All of us go shopping and choose our purchases whether they are clothes, records or the family groceries. Because the amount of money we have to spend is limited, how we spend it is important, whether we are at school, at work or running a home. We must plan what we want to buy in order to avoid waste and get the best value.

Make a list

Before we go shopping we should work out exactly what we can spend, otherwise we may find ourselves short of money for essentials. When we start to run a home we will probably have a tight budget and careful planning is required to make the money go round. Shopping wisely or unwisely can make a vast difference, so always make a list of the items you need. Not only will this save you unnecessary extra journeys for forgotten items but it will help to prevent you buying things you do not really need.

Value and service

What should we look for when choosing where to shop?

Value We need to be sure we are paying a fair price, comparable with prices for similar goods elsewhere. It is sensible to note down the average prices of the essentials you buy every week. Then you will know if you are really getting a cut-price bargain or paying a little extra. We also must be sure that the goods supplied by the shop are of a consistently high standard. We must be sure of accurately totalled bills, of correct change and of fair weighing.

Service We must look for high standards of cleanliness, both in the shop premises and among the assistants. We need to be served promptly, yet in turn. If the shop arranges deliveries we must be sure that the goods arrive on time. If the shop promises to order goods for us or to put items on one side we must be sure that the promise will be kept. The opening and closing times should be regular and reliable. The staff should be well trained and show fairness and consideration to each customer, whether old or young, irrespective of how much they spend. Guided by the example of a shop owner or manager of integrity, they should receive genuine complaints, deal with them and put them right promptly and without resentment.

Shopping around

If you are out at work, or very busy in the home, it is easiest if you do all your shopping in a single shop, perhaps a supermarket where the prices are reasonable and the service good. If, however, you have more time to spend you will be able to 'shop around' and take advantage of the various cut-price offers which are made in different shops. You will notice that many of the smaller family shops are being replaced by large supermarkets. Which type of shop gives the better value, the better service and is more pleasing to deal with?

Supermarkets

Perhaps the most important thing to realise about supermarkets is that they are designed to get you to spend as much as possible, and it is necessary for you to be on your guard about the ways in which you may be persuaded to spend. Forewarned, you can take full advantage of the convenience and economies of supermarket shopping.

First, learn to find your way about the shop, so that time is not wasted in searching for goods. The manager will not usually keep altering his layout, for he is anxious for you to find your way about. His first concern is to persuade you to spend as freely as possible. At the same time he wants you to enjoy your shopping and to leave his shop a satisfied customer. He provides everything he can to attract you into his store and to make your visit as profitable to him as possible. You are greeted by an atmosphere of warmth and colour, sometimes accompanied by soft background music, by attractive displays and a tremendous variety of goods, 5,000 different items in some! Large trolleys help you to gather your purchases and the smooth glide and weightlessness of these are intended to help you to forget just how much you have collected.

Bargain offers, advertised in the windows in huge letters, of '1p or 2p off' or 'A free towel with this soap' are placed near the door to draw customers in. More bargain offers are placed carefully round the store, so that it becomes necessary for you to tour the whole shop to take advantage of all the bargains. Have you ever wondered why the vital goods such as tea, sugar and flour are often right at the back of the store? Think of all the other goods you have to walk past and cannot fail to notice on your way to collect them. When buying potatoes recently we found them at the far end of the supermarket on a small circular stand. Propped against the front were inflatable plastic cushions—very gay and attractive—against the back were gilt and black magazine racks filled with artificial flowers, and at each end were bags of liquorice allsorts and fruit drops. I wonder how many of these tempting extras accompanied potatoes into the baskets and trolleys?

Luxury goods are sometimes accessible at eye or basket level, or even in front of essential but cheaper ones. So, as the housewife bends down for her bread, she cannot help but notice the expensive salmon or chicken spreads just near them. Perhaps she falls for the jar of cream, taped to the tin of fruit she needed, or the gay beakers surrounding the orange squash; or why not just one pretty tea towel as it happens to be draped over her usual brand of detergent? How many of these *link goods* have you noticed—egg cups with eggs, shakers near the salt and pepper, etc.? Have you or your mother ever come home with an extra piece of kitchen ware when you only meant to buy food? This is known as *impulse buying* and the supermarket manager relies on the high profit from this to keep his other prices low. A survey in American supermarkets showed that only three out of each ten shoppers had prepared a shopping list before entering the store. The other seven decided on their purchases once inside the store and bought their goods on impulse. It was calculated that 25% of their money could have been saved had they prepared and kept to shopping lists. The same survey showed that there was only half as much impulse buying in shops where assistants were waiting to serve the customers. Husbands—sent just for a loaf of bread—fall easy victims to these impulse buys, so the cashiers tell us, and often leave the store laden with both luxuries and a guilty conscience!

At the cash desk, you nearly always have to wait, unless you have chosen an off-peak time, such as the morning. As you wait you cannot help noticing the many little luxuries grouped round the cash desk, for example, sweets and cosmetics, and the temptation to pop one into your basket is sometimes overwhelming. Cigarettes are usually there too, but this is partly to make sure that they do not get slipped into pockets.

Watch your reactions next time you queue at the cash desk—which of the items surrounding it would you like to add to your purchases? Are there any you do, in fact, put into your basket at the last minute? Your time would be better spent in adding up the cost of the items in your basket. This will help you to budget and to remember the prices of the essential everyday goods. A recent survey showed that not many more than half the women questioned while shopping in a supermarket, had any idea of the prices of their basic goods—sugar, flour, fats, etc. So when packets were labelled '1p off' they had no idea what they should be charged or if they were really getting good value for money. One firm tried out toddler baskets to entertain the youngsters while mother shopped. The happy toddler filled her basket with the gay novelties placed just at her level, and only when the cash desk was finally reached did the intention of the plan become clear. Often the harassed mother had a horror of being shown-up by a weeping child and would sadly pay for the expensive little items collected in this way.

The music, warmth and air of luxury are carefully designed to create a dreamlike atmosphere, and a general sense of well-being is intended to make you forget your budget and indulge yourself and your family. It has been observed that some customers go from shelf to shelf in a semi-trance, and then have a rude awakening at the cash desk! Yet it also has been proved that up to 20 minutes in

SUPERMARKETS

1 *The happy toddler filled her basket*

the hour, and 8½p in the pound, can be saved, by carefully planned use of these stores.

How to plan

1 Always take a shopping list with you, and stick to it!

2 Know exactly how much you can afford for extra treats, and do not exceed it.

3 If time allows, jot down the prices against the articles on your list, and see if your total agrees with the cashier's.

4 Do not be afraid to query items, or to reject those that prove too dear. You will be respected for this, and the goods will be returned to the shelves for you, usually without complaint.

5 Remember you may have to carry home all that you have bought. Is this going to be possible? If you have spent a considerable sum, some supermarkets will deliver the groceries for you—this, of course, means a short wait.

Remembering these points will give you confidence and help you to enjoy using a supermarket. It has a wonderful variety of goods to offer, all of which are on display so that you can study the price and quality as you choose. No one will hurry you on, or press you to buy; you have time to decide. Because everything is on display, the standard of freshness and cleanliness of goods is usually very high. No one is going to *choose* a soggy lettuce, so there is no point in displaying one. If you select carefully, taking advantage of genuine bargains and cut-price necessities, you really can save money. The supermarket manager buys in bulk, which is always cheaper, and has fewer assistants to pay because the customers do so much of the work in his shop. So he can afford to offer many genuine bargains.

Possibly you will have to stand in one queue—unless you have shopped sensibly in off-peak hours—but you may have avoided queuing in each of several smaller shops.

Smaller or family shops

Here the advantages and disadvantages of using such a shop are more obvious. These shops have none of the cunningly clever organisation of the supermarket. Nevertheless they too must make a profit. They have expenses to meet and staff wages to pay.

Advantages of using a small shop

1 *Personal service* You quickly become known by your name, by your likes and dislikes and even by the time when you usually shop. You will be made to feel welcome in an atmosphere that is friendly and familiar.

2 Special items may be kept for you, special joints cut or large packets of goods halved. If the shop does not stock items you wish to try, they may order them just for you.

3 You may be given credit and allowed to pay at the end of each week or even monthly.

4 For the lonely person who longs for a chat, for the old one who needs to sit as she orders, or for the busy mother who sends a child

with a note, this type of shop is ideal. For the blind or disabled it is essential. The shopper does no work; all the fetching and carrying is done for her.

5 Frequently the shop is near at hand, saving the shopper time and bus fares, and, of course, the long carrying of heavy baskets.

6 Because small shops sell to a limited number of customers they can often buy really fresh eggs, fruit or vegetables from local farms and market gardens.

7 You can usually order the exact amount that you require of such things as bacon, ham and cheese, instead of having to select from ready wrapped packages of a fixed size.

8 When an assistant is waiting to serve you, eye-catching displays do not tempt you to buy on impulse the luxury goods you may later regret.

9 The small shop-keeper cannot afford to lose your custom, so he will usually give you very good service.

Disadvantages

1 Of course the shop-keeper gives the same 'personal service' to all his customers, not just to you. So while he is giving careful individual attention to those in front of you in the queue, you will be waiting—and waiting—and this may happen in several of the small shops you visit.

2 You may find prices slightly higher than in a larger store and bargains will be fewer. This is because the cut-prices available to the buyer of huge quantities of merchandise—or bulk-buying as it is called—are not available to the smaller shop-keeper. Some shop-keepers are now beginning to get together to order in bulk for their shops, to help to reduce their prices.

3 Small shops cannot stock all sizes, in all brands, of all goods. They have to decide which they think their customers will choose. So choice and variety is bound to be smaller than in a supermarket.

4 Weighing is sometimes casual—you are told it is 'a bit over', but the coppers added on to your bill may be far greater than the value of the bit extra that you did not really want.

5 It is not always possible to examine what you are buying—to see the fatty 'other' side of the joint at the butcher's, or how many marble-sized potatoes go into your bag from the back of a pile at

the greengrocer's. You often do not like to fuss when people are waiting to be served behind you, and arguing with a shop-keeper you know well can be embarrassing.

6 Once you have started to be served you have little time to reflect on your order, or to change your mind. You cannot wander round the shop trying to remember items, unless you go to the end of the queue again.

7 Standards of hygiene vary. What is on show is usually clean, but because of limited space your goods may be fetched from a hut at the back, an attic or even a cellar. These too may be spotless, but can you really be sure?

8 Some small shops cannot afford the refrigerated facilities, the deep freeze or the air conditioning we take for granted at larger shops. Dogs are often allowed in, or a cat sits on the counter.

Summing up

Remember that it is the job of the shop—of whatever size—to get you to spend as much as possible, even though this means you buy more than you want. It is your job to see that you resist this temptation. Remember that supermarkets have made this an art. Their impersonal service saves them from worrying about your problems; but a kindly shop-keeper, anxious to keep your custom, may help you to keep within your budget.

Trading stamps

These are used by all types of shops to encourage trade, and to make sure that you keep returning to the same shop to get the same sort of stamps. A 'Free Gift' catalogue shows you the wide choice of products you can get in exchange for your filled book or books of stamps. But are you really getting something for nothing?

Something for nothing?

These are some of the facts. There are 1,280 stamp spaces in one type of well-known book. You must spend £32 and save every stamp you receive with your goods to fill this book. Providing you do all your family's shopping at stores selling these stamps, you can fill your book in 6–7 weeks. The cash value of your book is then about 80p. In other words you can change it for a 'gift' of about that value which can be chosen from a catalogue or a special shop. You are really getting $2\frac{1}{2}\%$, or $2\frac{1}{2}$p in the £1, discount on your purchases. The owner of the shop bought the stamps from a Trading Stamp Company. He has had to pay for them and must recover his money somehow. At first he may get it back by gaining extra customers who want the stamps he is offering. But if, in the future, nearly all shops give away these stamps, fewer customers will make changes to obtain them and so fewer customers will be gained. How will the shop-keeper then recover his money (sometimes 2–3% of his turnover)? He will either have to raise his prices or cut his costs, and this may mean poorer service and restrictions on the quantity and quality of his goods. In other words you may be paying for the stamps.

If you enjoy saving them, and changing them for goods of your choice, the pleasure they give is of value to you. Since the Trading Stamps Act, 1964, the filled books can be exchanged for cash. This usually is less in value than the gift you could choose instead. Research shows that only 2% of shoppers take advantage of this. Which would you prefer? Do you think that Trading Stamps are of value to the housewife? Remember if you do not want to save them it is a good idea to send them to Oxfam or other charities who change them for warm blankets, etc., for people less fortunate than you are.

The first supermarket was really the ordinary British village store which sold everything from prams to postage stamps. What it could not stock it ordered, showing catalogues of goods for the customers to choose from. It was, and often still is, the heart or focal point of village life. As such shops disappear, however, the catalogues they used to use increase steadily. They are issued by:

Mail order firms

If you wish to shop through mail order firms there are one or two points worth considering. There are vitally important safeguards that should always be looked for because you can neither examine nor try on the article before ordering it. Choose a well-known firm, not one you have never heard of. Read the description of the article carefully; make sure it is of the size, colour and material you want. Such terms as 'Government Surplus', 'Export Reject' or 'Seconds' often mean that goods are imperfect or second-hand. Ask for an explanation of any such terms which you do not understand. Study the catalogue and order personally from it rather than through neighbours. This way you cannot be coaxed into buying, misunderstandings do not arise, and if free gifts are offered with the purchase, they should be yours not someone else's.

The term 'Cash on Delivery' does not offer the protection it seems to. It is difficult to try on tights or to put up a tent with the postman standing waiting at the door! Yet both must be of the right size and both must suit your requirements. Though the same laws protect you when shopping in person or by post, it is sometimes more difficult to get satisfaction over a long distance, and it might also be more expensive.

2   *It is difficult to put up a tent with the postman at the door*

Consumer protection

We the customers—or buyers—of goods are protected in several ways. We do not have to accept shoddy goods, and we should be able to change them even after they have been paid for, and in some cases, after they have been worn or used. But we can only do this if we know what protection we are entitled to, and in what forms we can find this protection.

1   We can look for *recognised approval marks* on the goods we buy. Here are five well-known, reliable marks:

CONSUMER PROTECTION 13

3 *The Kitemark of the British Standards Institution*

4 *The Gas Council's mark*

5 *The B.E.A.B. sign*   6 *The C.U.C. sign*

7 *A Teltag*

(i) *The Kitemark of the British Standards Institution.* This mark shows that the goods bearing it have been carefully tested for safety, suitability, reliability and quality. Moreover, these goods are continually retested to make sure that a high standard is maintained by each new batch of articles manufactured. Saucepans, babies' cots and step ladders are a few of a huge range of goods tested in this way.

(ii) *The Gas Council's mark.* All appliances bought from the gas showrooms bear this mark, and show that each article has been thoroughly tested.

(iii) *The B.E.A.B. sign* which actually contains the kitemark is the symbol of the British Electrical Approvals Board, guaranteeing that electrical equipment such as hair dryers, electric blankets, vacuum cleaners, has been thoroughly tested.

(iv) *Teltags.* These are the result of the Consumer Council's recommendation to manufacturers to label their products with factual and useful information. The scheme started in 1967 and more and more goods are now carrying Teltags, e.g. electric kettles and carpets. The information given includes details of the product's composition and performance, and of how it stood up to an impartial test carried out by the British Standards Institution. Look out for Teltags: they represent real value for money.

If the goods we wish to buy do not carry a known, dependable mark then try some of the other ways of judging quality.

2 Look to see what label there is. A good make of clothes should carry the manufacturer's name, and care labels should tell you what material the garment is made from, how to wash it and if it will 'drip dry'. There is a special section on care labels at the end of this chapter. You should be warned if the garment must be dry cleaned and will not wash. Remember how expensive regular dry cleaning can be if you do not have a self-service dry-cleaners in your district. The size as well as the price should be clearly marked. Watch to see that the top and trousers of pyjamas are the same size and that slippers match. When buying tights, for example, there are at least six things to look for—the size, the colour, the denier (or sheerness), the cost, the leg length and whether ladder proof or not!

3 Make sure you ask the important questions; and if you are buying something expensive, take someone with you to help you in your choice. You will then also have a witness if the salesgirl misleads you. If she cannot answer your queries always ask for the manager; if he cannot, the goods are a doubtful buy. It takes courage to complain about faulty goods, and to ask for the manager. It takes tremendous courage the *first* time you do it. But when you are older and well-known to your shop-keeper, a severe look is often enough should you be offered goods of poor quality! Although the shopping you have done so far may not have involved much money or responsibility, remember that in a few years' time you may be shopping for your own family. You will then be responsible for making the money go round, and so now you must learn to shop with foresight, common sense and courage. There is never any need to become aggressive. Remember to be firm yet remain polite.

Such questions as these are worth asking.

CONSUMER PROTECTION

'Will the colours run?'	(perhaps for a swimsuit)
'Will it shrink—or stretch?'	(a sweater)
'Can it be dry cleaned?'	(a raincoat)
'How can I clean it?'	(a leather jacket)
'Is it heat resisting?'	(a tabletop)
'Is it inflammable?'	(a nightdress)
'Is it unbreakable?'	(plastic toys)
'Is it non-toxic—or non-poisonous?'	(a rattle)
'Does it pour without dripping?'	(a teapot)
'How do I look after it?'	(a potted plant)
'Has it a safety cut-out device?'	(an electric kettle)
'Will you change it if it does not fit?'	(clothes bought as presents)

4 When you go shopping know exactly what you want. Have your own measurements, and carefully check those of small children you cannot take with you. Take samples to match colours. Buy dress patterns before you buy the material, and measure such things as hot plates before you buy saucepans to fit on them.

5 Tell the assistant what you can afford to pay and look at articles in that price range. Often large shops have 'Budget Clothes' which are worth looking at.

6 Always try on articles such as shoes and hats. You cannot possibly tell if they suit or fit you without doing so. If possible try on all clothes. The large stores which have no facilities for doing this usually allow you to change your purchases without question.

8 *'I wish I'd tried them on before I bought them!'*

One very famous store, Marks & Spencer's, does this even if you buy the garment in one of their London branches and take it back to a Liverpool branch, even if your reason is simply that you did not like it when you got it home! If you have worn the article, of course, you must have a much better reason for wanting to change it—such as showing a fault that has developed in it. Then it will be readily changed or the money refunded. You will find a branch of this store in every large and most small towns. They are worth trying! Very few other firms are willing to refund money; but many will give credit notes. Some ask to see receipts before changing anything, so keep them carefully.

7 Watch to see that you are being served with the goods you have chosen, and not some you are told are identical but which you have not had a chance to examine. Look at the finish of clothes, the undersides of carpets, the insides of drawers, the fasteners on necklaces, and see whether lids fit where they should. Inspect all foodstuffs for freshness and do not buy at a shop where you cannot do this—what are they hiding? In several of the Continental countries you can pick out your fruit and greengrocery from the display counter or stall. You then hand it to the assistant to be wrapped. You are often offered cherries or grapes, or even pieces of cheese to taste before making your selection. In England we rarely, if ever, find this service. Usually we are only expected to look, without touching. But you should ask to be shown the other side of expensive fruits like melons or pineapples. Baskets of soft fruits, such as strawberries, should be turned out as soon as possible after purchase. If the fruit underneath is not of the same standard as the fruit on top, you have been misled. If any of it is bad the shop-keeper must exchange it, providing you have only just bought it. The cellophane wrapped packets at a supermarket make handling foods easy and hygienic.

8 Find out what to look for when buying food: the cut off the joint suitable for your purpose, the vegetables free from heavily weighing mud, or decay. Learn from your cookery book how to tell if perishable foods are fresh, and insist on having the fish or fruit *you* have chosen. Do not accept some from the back of the pile, and if you suspect that a bruised apple or open-ended banana has gone into your bag, return it to the shop-keeper. He is legally bound to sell you goods fit for the purpose for which he has sold them, if they are unfit he must exchange them.

CONSUMER PROTECTION

9 During sales, in fairs or markets, or while away on holiday, when the light-hearted atmosphere of the surroundings may make you less careful than usual, watch to see that you are getting value for your money. If you choose goods which are specially marked down in price you must often be prepared to accept less than the best, but you can get really good bargains at sales or in a market if you have your wits about you.

10 Read carefully price and size tickets. Three $7\frac{1}{2}$p tins of peas for 22p may sound a bargain, but how much are you really saving? Do you want *three* tins in any case? The $9\frac{1}{2}$p label on a cup and saucer may just apply to the cup. Look to see if food prices are per lb. or per $\frac{1}{2}$ lb. They do vary—mushrooms which are usually $7\frac{1}{2}$p to 9p per $\frac{1}{4}$ lb. may, in a glut, cost as little as 15p per lb.

Look at the weight on a tin or packet in comparison with the cost. Since 31 July 1965, it has been illegal to sell any food unless the container clearly states the net weight, which is calculated by a standardised weight or quantity measure. A 13 oz. tin at 11p is dearer than a 16 oz. one at 13p. Two packets of cereals, one tall and one squat, may contain the same weight of cereals, but be very differently priced. The Act which makes this compulsory is described later in the chapter. Size tickets are also gradually being standardised, but at present a size 14 in one make of dress may be the same as a size 16 in another make. E fittings in one brand of shoes are sometimes the same as D fittings in another. This is why the trying on of clothes is so important.

11 The need for such standardisation has been brought to the public's notice by such organisations as *The Consumer Council*. This was set up in March 1963 by the Board of Trade as a result of a report on Consumer Protection. This has now been replaced by the Ministry for Trade and Consumer Affairs. The Minister responsible for this department is advised by an experienced and non-political committee, who together look after consumer interests. He has the power to lay an order before Parliament prohibiting or controlling any trade practice he considers to be against the consumers' economic interest. This means quite simply that if, for example, some firms are found to be making too much profit on any of their goods, they can be made to lower their prices. Or if several firms wished to join together to form one large company so that they could control prices or a range of goods against the public's interest, they could be prevented from doing this.

12 Guidance on the choice between different makes of articles is printed in the magazine *Which?* This magazine is available at most public libraries or can be sent to each subscriber personally by the publishers, the Consumers' Association. The Consumers' Association is independent of the Government and takes no money from manufacturers or sellers of goods. Members of the Consumers' Association's governing body are not in business and the Association buys its goods for testing, in the shops; it does not accept them as gifts from the makers. Because the Association is independent, *Which?* is impartial. It publishes reports on all sorts of goods from cars to cosmetics, from record players to pork sausages, which have been tested by the Association. General advice on what to look for in buying a certain article is given and usually several 'best buys' from the point of view of quality and price are selected. All badly designed, unsafe or unreliable makes are rejected. The magazine can be a great help to shoppers, though one should remember that the design and features of many products, such as fridges, change yearly, so it is important to make sure that the reports are not too out of date. Information can also be found in consumer features in certain magazines and newspapers.

The legal side of protection

In 1893 the *Sale of Goods Act* was made law. By this the customer is entitled to hand back anything not fit for sale, or as the law puts it—'goods must be of merchantable quality' or they must not be sold. Moreover, this law requires that goods must be suitable for the purpose for which the customer buys them. If you buy an electric light bulb and then find it will not light up, the shop-keeper must change it. This is why he usually tests it before it leaves his shop. It is a good idea to keep all receipts in case the shop-keeper refuses to acknowledge your purchase, if faulty, as having been bought in his shop.

A 13-year-old recently took her Gondola basket back to a supermarket following a talk by her teacher on 'Consumer Rights'. She told the assistant that the handle had come apart after only one week's use. She was telling the truth, but the assistant did not treat the complaint seriously. So she plucked up courage and asked to see the manager. The shop assistant immediately exchanged the faulty basket! Encouraged by this her small brother aged 8 took back to a shop an egg-timer he had saved for and given to his mother for her birthday. He explained that the sand ran through in 2½ minutes and so his mother could not use it. He received the reply, 'Well there's nothing I can do about that, is there?' But his sister, full of her success at the supermarket, marched him back to the shop. She informed them that the timer did not do the job for which it had been sold. . . . She did not have to say any more; it was obvious that she knew her rights, and the money was refunded. A very happy small boy was then able to buy a box of chocolates on his way home instead!

Read any instruction labels attached to your purchase and follow their advice. If you are silly enough to buy a delicate coffee table which breaks because you place a heavy television set on it, you have no claim against the shop—unless you explained at the time that you wished to use it as a television table and received the shop-keeper's assurance that it would be strong enough. Even so, it is wise to have a witness to this assurance. If you do buy a properly designed television table and while adjusting your set the table breaks and crushes your foot, you can claim not only for a new table, but for damages for the injuries to yourself. You claim for these injuries under 'Common Law' and all shoppers are protected by both this and the Sale of Goods Act, provided that they:

(a) tell the shop-keeper what they want the goods for, and are then guided by him;

(b) use the goods for the purpose they are stated to be made for; and

(c) read and obey all instructions on the manufacturer's labels.

Remember the shop-keeper must keep the law, and should change faulty goods or refund your money. Some will tell you it is not their responsibility, but the manufacturer's. This is not the case and they are acting illegally. If you cannot make them face up to this and the faulty article was expensive you can go to your Citizens' Advice Bureau or your Local Consumer Group for support. These two groups will help you if the shop-keeper will not listen to you and tries to bully you out of the shop. Unscrupulous ones have been known to do this, but the well-known shops will usually give you a fair deal. They are only too anxious to keep their good reputations.

Since 1887 several other acts have also been passed for our protection. One is the *Merchandise Marks Act* which makes it an offence to offer for sale goods with a written description or label which is in any way untrue. Between 1887 and 1956 six of these Marks Acts have been passed, and they now cover advertisements, as well as labels.

The maker's name and address must be genuine. A 'Fresh Dairy Cream Cake' must only have real cream in it. 'Pure silk' must not be a mixture, and plastic goods must not be called leather. Once again, this emphasises how very worth while it is to read labels properly. Do not ignore, or lose them.

The Consumer Protection Act 1961 followed several nasty accidents caused by faulty oil heaters. It lays down standards of safety which these, together with electric and gas fires and heaters, must keep to. It was passed very quickly following considerable public concern about the danger of such stoves. In 1964 the Home Secretary used his powers under this Act to impose new regulations. Again in response to public pressure, and with advice from the Consumer Council, he prohibited the sale of inflammable nightdresses for children.

The Hire Purchase Acts, 1932–54 The protections afforded by these Acts are dealt with fully in Chapter 6.

The Food and Drugs Act, 1955 This Act states the minimum amount of a food that must be contained in a food product before it can be sold by that name. For example, if a jar is labelled 'Salmon Paste' it must by law contain 70% salmon. But if it is labelled 'Fish Paste Salmon' it need only contain 25% salmon and the other 75% may be made up of some other fish plus other ingredients. Jam must contain between 25% and 40% of the named fruit, butter may not contain more than 16% of water and 'cream' soups must have $3\frac{1}{2}$% of butter fat. There are no regulations for sausages or sweets. It also protects us against the use of harmful flavourings, colourings and additions. In the last century the whitening agent used in flour was found to be poisonous!

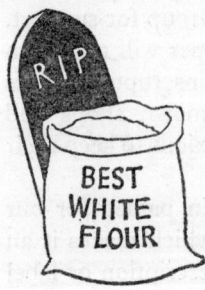

9 *The Food and Drugs Act protects us now*

THE LEGAL SIDE OF PROTECTION

The Trade Descriptions Act, 1968 This Act makes it illegal not only for labels and advertisements to mislead customers, but also for oral statements to do so. It is more far reaching than previous Acts; for example, a boarding house recommended as being '3 minutes from the sea' must in fact be this near; or a sale garment at '50p marked down from 75p' must have been displayed at the higher price for at least 28 days out of the previous six months.

The Weights and Measures Act, 1965 This brings up to date several previous Acts dating from 1878. There are three main sections. The first provides for inspectors to see that weights and measures are accurate and standardised. They visit dairies and public houses and check pint and half pint measures. They check ounce and pound weights used in shops against exact standard weights which they carry with them. Even as far back as the Magna Carta in the thirteenth century efforts were made to standardise in this way. It was laid down in this ancient document that—'One measure of Wine shall be throughout our Realm, and one measure of Ale, and one measure of Corn'. The second section of the modern Act lays down penalties for giving short weight or measure, and the third makes it necessary by law for the *net* weight of all pre-packed foods to be stated on the packet. This means we will know the weight of the goods contained, quite apart from the tin or jar or packet in which they are packed. If the weight of these containers is added to that of the contents then this is called the *gross* weight.

The Labelling of Food Order, 1970 This Act is being brought into force gradually. By 1 January 1973, most of its regulations were being carried out. These included:

1 An order by which all pre-packaged food must bear the common name by which the food is known, so that if a brand name such as 'Home Pride' is used this must be closely followed by the word 'flour'.

2 If a food comes under any special regulation—e.g. milk—a label such as 'skimmed with non-fat' must say precisely what the milk consists of.

3 The size and position of print used on labels is now controlled, so that nothing can be hidden away or written so minutely that it cannot be read.

4 A full list of the ingredients must appear on pre-packed foods and this must be in the order of importance as far as bulk is concerned, so for that a chocolate blancmange powder containing a little sugar, chocolate, colouring, etc., the list must start off with the main ingredient CORNFLOUR and then all the other ingredients must be listed in descending order of weight.

5 By 1975 all pre-packed food must be date-stamped to help the customer to judge its freshness. Some firms such as Marks & Spencers do this already.

6 By 1976 all food, not just pre-packed food, must come under these regulations.

7 The name and address of the seller, or importer, or packer, or labeller must appear clearly on the label. Previously only a name or trade mark was used as an identification.

The Fair Trading Bill, 1.12.72 This was the bill giving the Minister for Trade and Consumer Affairs the powers to act in the way that has been described in Section 11 under Consumer Protection.

The Supply of Goods (Implied Terms) Act, 1973 This is a most important Act which helps to reinforce the Sale of Goods Act. It prohibits anything in a contract or guarantee concerned with the sale of goods, which releases the retailer from his legal obligation to supply goods:

(*a*) which are of merchantable quality (fit for sale),

(*b*) which meet the description applied to them,

(*c*) which are fit for the purpose for which they were sold.

Previously some guarantees had assisted shoppers to get value for money by making sure that faulty goods were repaired or replaced free of charge, but other guarantees contained 'exclusion clauses' which took away the shopper's legal rights. Now these exclusion clauses, although they will continue to appear in guarantees for some time yet, are illegal. No one can take away your rights.

A good guarantee is still worth having. As *Which?*, the Consumers' Association magazine, for June 1973, says,

In practice it [a good guarantee] may well be the quickest way of getting your faulty equipment put right without argument. A guarantee like this for instance, adds to your normal legal rights, without taking anything away.

'We guarantee that should this Automatic Washing Machine prove to be defective by reason of faulty workmanship or material within 12 months of the date of purchase or commencement of hire purchase, we will repair, or at our option, replace the defective part free of any charge for labour or for materials or for carriage. . . .'

No matter what the guarantee says you should never be charged for labour or carriage, etc. *Which?* goes on to say:

Don't worry about any small print on a guarantee or order form for goods you buy now. The seller is legally responsible, no matter what it says on the order form, guarantee, or what have you—

insist that the seller puts right faults, and don't be fobbed off with suggestions that you should contact the manufacturer, or anyone else—

claim for additional expenses that you incur through getting a faulty article. But remember you have to keep the expenses down to a reasonable level, and that only expenses which are direct and predictable can be claimed (see Shoddy goods and the law, *Which?*, December 1972)—

be reasonable, patient and understanding with the retailer—

be firm and confident about your legal position regarding faults.

Almost the very last words spoken during the passage of the new law through Parliament were said by Mr. Arthur Davidson, M.P. for Accrington, and a member of CA's council, in the House of Commons on 4 April last: 'The public should know that a buyer can go to the seller and say "It may not be your fault, but it is your responsibility and I hold you to your bargain."' That is it in a nutshell.

So read your guarantee before signing it; note the period of time it covers. Is it fair? Does this period cover the whole or only part of the article? A refrigerator unit may be covered for 5 years while its cabinet is only covered for 1 year.

Is the guarantee 'transferable'? If not it is only of any use if the article is kept by its buyer, and this would raise problems if you had bought it as a present for someone else.

Remember:

to get the best value for your money stop and think before you buy.

1 Buy goods made by a reliable firm, but remember that the best advice is usually obtained from an independent source, not from advertisements issued by the makers whose job it is to sell the goods.

2 Examine everything you buy, allow yourself plenty of time to choose, and try on clothing if possible.

3 Read price, size and care labels carefully.

4 Study all the information given about the article. If none is available, consult the shop assistant or manager.

5 Read all guarantees slowly and thoroughly. Make sure you understand them before buying the article.

6 Remember your rights under the Consumer Protection Laws, and under Common Law.

7 Know where to go for advice if the shop selling you faulty goods will not act upon your complaint.

8 Keep all receipts and instruction labels. Carefully obey the maker's instructions.

9 Do not be afraid to return shoddy articles to the shop.

10 The shop-keeper or retailer should deal with your complaint. He is responsible to you, the manufacturer, in turn, is responsible to him. If you have signed a guarantee, the retailer is not freed from his responsibility, and he must still deal with your complaint.

11 *Learn by your own, and other people's mistakes.*

Care labelling

The International Textile Care Labelling Code was accepted and published in January 1974. Care labels should be looked for, studied and understood, preferably before buying a garment, always before washing it or having it dry-cleaned.

The code is the result of dividing all textiles into ten groups each of which needs a different washing programme. It should be noted that temperatures are all given in centigrade. This matches programmes on automatic washing machines. The temperatures given are the highest at which each category can be washed with safety. They should never be ignored as combined heat, pressure or spin-drying can ruin some textiles. Here are the ten categories clearly explained in the following care labels.

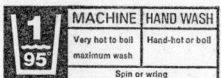
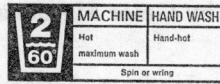

10 Obey the maker's instructions

The ironing symbols are now agreed by the International Standards Organisation. They are clear and self-explanatory and must be obeyed.

This symbol means 'do not wash'

This one means 'the garment can be dry-cleaned'

Further reading

You and Your Shopping, by Gilda Lund, published by Mills and Boon Ltd. at 52½p

You and Your Clothes, by Grace Macdonald, from the same publishers at £1·25

Is it legal?, issued by the Institute of Practitioners in Advertising, 44 Belgrave Square, London, at £1

Which? on Consumer Affairs, January 1973

Which? on Date Stamping, March/April 1973

Which? on Food Labelling, March 1973

Which? on Small Print, February 1973

Which? on Supply of Goods Act, June 1973

Getting Your Money's Worth, by Jane Probyn, published by Stanley Paul at 80p

The Family in the Community, by Phyllis Davidson, published by Longmans at 75p

Practical work

1 Next time you visit a supermarket notice which goods are at eye level, and which cannot be seen so easily. How many stands of bargain offers are there, and where are they placed? Suggest why the goods are arranged as they are.

2 See if you can count a dozen 'impulse buys'. Which goods are they placed near? Are these impulse buys of good value? Make three columns: (*a*) for the impulse buys; (*b*) for the goods they have been placed near; and (*c*) your idea of their quality.

3 Carry out a 'Time and Money' test with a friend when buying what you need for your Cookery lesson. You go to several small shops to buy your goods and let her buy identical items from one supermarket. Then compare the time you both took and how much money you spent. Also compare the quality of your purchases.

4 Repeat the last experiment at an off-peak shopping period and at a busy shopping period.

5 Look at the '$\frac{1}{2}$p off' and '1p off' bargains. What was their price before the offer and what is it now? Is the size of the packet the same as it was before the reduction in price?

6 Choose one commodity, note the prices and weights of small,

medium, large and giant or family sizes. Which packet is the best buy?

7   You are buying a set of saucepans for an electric cooker. Think out all the questions you need to ask before making your choice. Try out these questions on a friend who is acting as a shop assistant and is not at first being very helpful. Then reverse the roles and let her 'buy' something different from you, perhaps a transistor radio.

8   You have both been sold faulty goods. Practise on one another the correct method of complaint.

Questions

1   Make out the list you would take to a supermarket for a week's groceries for two people. Include perishable fruit, vegetables, meat or fish for two days. Allow yourself three luxury items, and finish the list with the cleaning materials you would need for that one week.

2   An old, arthritic lady of 70 is getting her food for 3 days. Where should she shop and why? Make out her bill, remembering that she is living on a pension.

3   You are sending a 7-year-old to a local shop for items just for tea. Write out: (*a*) the instructions you would give the child, and (*b*) the note you would send with her.

4   You are buying a record player for which you have saved for years. Where would you seek advice before going to the shop, and what would you look for once you got there?

5   Your raincoat labelled 'Washable' came apart at the seams the first time you washed it. What can you do about this?

CHAPTER 2 · BUDGETING

The last chapter was concerned with shopping. How can we tackle the problem of being able to afford the things that we really *need*, and also the things we would like to buy? This is a problem we have no option but to solve, so we might as well take a cool, calculating look at our income and our expenditure and decide how best to do it. This is called budgeting. Once a year the Government has to do this, and usually in March or April the Chancellor of the Exchequer, whose responsibility it is as the head of the Treasury, tells the country how he has arranged to do it for the forthcoming year. Once he has made his plan and Parliament has accepted it on our behalf, he has only got to stick to it and at the end of the year all should be well. We too would be wise to make this sort of long term plan. Wars or national disasters—such as floods, or earthquakes—might upset the Chancellor's plans, illness, or unemployment, might upset ours, but on the whole if you make a carefully thought-out plan, only emergencies upset it.

Planning your spending

Strangely enough this gives you more freedom and pleasure in spending, not less. You cannot really enjoy buying new items in the *hope* that you can afford them. It is all far too risky and worrying.

If you *know*, because you have budgeted, just how much you can afford to spend, you then have the pleasure of being free to spend. You must allow for the essential items first, and the following plan is generally accepted as one which works for most people.

Division of total income

Rent	$\frac{1}{5}$
Household expenses	$\frac{1}{5}$
Personal expenses	$\frac{1}{5}$
Clothes	$\frac{1}{10}$
Food	$\frac{3}{10}$

We shall see how this can be adapted to suit various situations. If you were earning £8 a week clear, you would probably be living at home, in which case you would be paying one lump sum for rent, household expenses and food. For this you should be charged about £5·60 but most mothers indulge their family's new wage-earners by either charging them less, or by 'subbing' it back again by the end of the week! But whether you are earning £8 or £12 or £18, the budget plan remains more or less the same. What do the five divisions really mean?

Rent We have allowed one-fifth of your income for this. However, rents today are often so high that you may need more, perhaps up to a quarter. More than this would make it very difficult to live in the place you have managed to rent. Local authorities and mortgage companies will not allow you to take on the buying of a property, the repayments for which are more than a quarter of your income. It is not in their interests for you to get into debt and not be able to keep up your repayments. If you are buying, remember you have rates to allow for as well. Sometimes if your rent includes such extras as central heating it is possible to cut down on one of your other divisions of expense, but not by much, as you will see.

Household expenses This will absorb another fifth of your income. It includes the expenses of lighting, heating and cooking and this may mean three bills, coal, gas and electricity. Your purchases for the household, your hire purchase instalments, your replacements (electric light bulbs, etc.), your cleaning materials, household insurance and laundry bills if any, should come out of this.

Personal expenses These include entertainment, meals out, tea and coffee breaks, sweets, toilet accessories, personal insurance, hair-dos, fares, savings for holidays and so on. Another fifth of your income will be needed here.

Food One-fifth is not enough in this section. Of all the sections this one must never be neglected. If your health is poor, your earning power will be poor. You will need a certain amount for meals at work, either at the canteen or the nearest snack bar. Packed lunches are not as inexpensive as I expect you imagined them to be when your mother made them for you. There may even come a day when you look back in amazement at the bargain you got in return for your 12p dinner money! You'll never get value for money like that again. You may, however, be lucky enough to get luncheon vouchers from your firm, but remember that these are really part of your wages. At home there is the milkman, baker, grocer, greengrocer, butcher and fishmonger to pay. Will you make your three-tenths income cover it?

Clothes We can only spare the remaining one-tenth for this, even though tights are expensive, shoes need repairing and dry cleaning must be allowed for.

What are these fractions in actual terms of money? Let us take two examples—you at 18 years, a well-qualified shorthand typist earning £15 clear. Then you again at 21 years, after a year of marriage, settling down to wait for the arrival of your first baby, with a young husband earning £25 clear. What is meant by 'clear'? This means your *net* income, what is actually handed to you to spend as you wish. Your total or *gross* income is usually slightly higher, but from it certain compulsory—and perhaps also some voluntary—deductions will also have been made. These will be dealt with later in the chapter.

Wages—Shorthand typist	EXPENSES	£
Net weekly income £15	Rent	3·00
	Household expenses	3·00
	Personal expenses	3·00
	Clothes	1·50
	Food	4·50
		15·00

Your husband's wages	EXPENSES	£
Net weekly income £25·00	Rent	5·00
	Household expenses	5·00
	Personal expenses	5·00
	Clothes	2·50
	Food	7·50
		25·00

Both of these budgets are worked out to follow the general plan. Now let us see how realistic they are. First, your wages as a shorthand typist.

You will be very lucky to find a place to rent as cheaply as £3·00 even if you are sharing with two or three others. You will probably need to borrow another £1 from another section to pay your rent. If you are sharing you can, I expect, get it from the household expenses section. It costs the same to keep the fire going for four as it does for one, so your final bills will be less. You will certainly need the £1·50 a week for clothes and if you deduct 30p or so a day from your food bill for a canteen lunch you will only have £3·00 left for morning and evening meals and the weekend. You will need every penny of this. Let us examine the personal expenses in detail and see how this works out.

	£
Entertainment (dance or cinema or concert, and fares) minimum	0·60
Meals out (even fish and chips and tea or 1 coffee and a salad)	0·35
Tea and coffee breaks—2 a day @ 3p	0·30
1 hair-do *or* new lipstick, lacquer or deodorant, etc.	0·75
Personal insurance and/or savings	0·35
	2·35

This leaves 65p for your fares to and from work. Let us hope your expenses are less and your savings more: 35p per week isn't going to help you much on a rainy day or give you much of a holiday. You must learn to budget and to stick to it so that when you have responsibilities you can manage. How well can you make your husband's wages go round? Let us look at them.

Rent £5   If the actual rent was £4·25 to £4·50 the rates would absorb the balance.

Household expenses Your fuel bills, especially in winter, would probably be £1·25 a week or more. Then there would be repayments on at least one sizeable item such as the cooker. Your increase in family means more furniture and more blankets. You will probably be spending about 30p a week for cleaning materials and you will need to insure the contents of the house. As you are at home all day you will probably have no laundry bills, but you will need part of the house heated all day in the winter, and there are extra meals to cook at home.

Personal expenses These soar when you stay at home because though you may not seek so much outside entertainment, there will be the licence and repayments or rentals on your television, record player and radio. You may have a paper bill. Your holidays will become more important and you will need to save because you now have very real responsibilities.

Food Here you may be able to save a little because if you have time and patience you can make nutritious dishes more easily than you could in the days when you rushed home from the office, grabbed a meal and rushed off to a dance. Also it doesn't cost twice as much to make a pot of tea for two as it does for one! Your food bill may look like this:

	£
Milk 2 pints per day	0·77
Husband's mid-day meals	1·50
Butcher and fishmonger	1·50
Greengrocer	0·60
Bread	0·35
Grocery	2·75
	7·47

Many, many families manage on far less, though of all economies it is most foolish to economise on food and milk.

Note Prices in London tend to be higher than those elsewhere and wherever you live you will find that they are rising all the time!

Compulsory deductions

Your gross income is what you actually earn, though as we have seen you do not receive it all. Where does it go?

1 INCOME TAX By levying this tax the Government raises part of the money it needs to run the country. Though we grumble about income tax it is, on the whole, fair, taking less from those with small incomes and more from those with large ones. It also takes the wage-earner's responsibilities and commitments into consideration. For example, various allowances are made for a wife and for children, for certain expenses involved with work, such as protective clothing or union fees, and for insurance premiums. The rate of taxation and the allowances made may, however, vary with each budget.

11 *Where does it go?*

2 V.A.T. This means Value Added Tax. It replaces Purchase Tax and is added to nearly all goods and services that you buy. It has only one rate, 8%, but some items are zero-rated, i.e. tax free. These include food, children's shoes and clothing, books, fuel and medicines on prescription. Some services are also exempt, such as postal charges, education, doctors' or dental charges.

3 NATIONAL INSURANCE CONTRIBUTIONS Everyone in the country must be protected by his own or someone else's contributions. Wives and children are covered by their husband's or parents', and retired people by the contributions they have made earlier in their lives. The rates of contribution vary with age and sex and are different for employed persons, self-employed persons and those who do not wish to work. All classes are not entitled to the same benefits. The non-employed cannot seek unemployment or sickness benefit when they do not lose pay for either remaining unemployed or for being ill.

COMPULSORY DEDUCTIONS

How is it paid? Usually the employer keeps the Insurance card and each week deducts the employee's contribution towards the Insurance stamp from his wages. He then contributes his own share, buys the stamp and sticks it on the card. Self-employed and non-employed contributors do this for themselves. Where the employers pay part of the contribution, their share is almost as large as the employee's. This is because the firm is usually making a profit through that person's work.

Who is exempted? If you are sick or unemployed you do not pay the contributions, temporarily. A married woman need not pay, providing her husband is paying his contribution, but she must if she is employed, pay the Industrial Injuries part of her contribution which will cost her $2\frac{1}{2}$p a week. Her employer still has to pay the full amount of his share. Children and students in training also need not contribute. Nor need widows receiving pensions.

What do you receive?

(i) Sickness benefit. Not payable for spells of less than three days' illness.

(ii) Unemployment benefit. To qualify for this the unemployed person must go to the Labour Exchange and prove that his loss of employment was not due to his own misconduct, or that he left the job without good reason.

(iii) Maternity benefit. See Chapter 15.

(iv) Retirement pensions. These are awarded to men over the age of 65 and to women over the age of 60. They are only a minimum pension, and really need supplementing with a graduated pension or a superannuation scheme of some kind.

(v) Widow's benefit.

(vi) Death grant. This is a sum paid on the death of an insured person to the next of kin. It is to help with funeral expenses and to see the family over the difficult period.

(vii) Industrial injuries benefit.

(viii) National Health Service. This is financed in three ways, mostly by taxation, partly by National Insurance contributions and, to a small extent, by the rates.

4 SUPERANNUATION This often constitutes about 5–6% of the salary or wage, and is again deducted entirely for the employee's benefit. (It provides a lump sum on retirement or a higher pension.) On leaving some jobs and professions it can be withdrawn, i.e. when the woman who has been paying it retires to marry and have children.

5 UNION FEES The first Trade Unions were formed to protect the workers from ill-usage by their employers. They have the same function today. To finance these Unions, the members pay fees, called dues. These average from $12\frac{1}{2}$p to 15p a week. Sometimes in a 'closed shop' the dues are deducted from the wage packet before it is received, but usually it is a voluntary contribution made regularly by the worker. Professional associations charge their members £6 to £9 a year. The cost of offices, conferences, administration, printing and the salaries of full-time officials has to be met and large sums are also put aside to support workers and their families should a strike be necessary. Union dues pay for all this.

Further reading

A Citizen of Today, by Michael Hansen, published by Oxford University Press at 40p

Your Own Home, by M. J. Joyce, published by Harrap and Co. Ltd. at $42\frac{1}{2}$p

Buying a House, published by the Citizens' Advice Bureau at $7\frac{1}{2}$p

Making Ends Meet, published by the National Marriage Guidance Council, 58 Queen Anne St., W.1, at $12\frac{1}{2}$p plus $2\frac{1}{2}$p postage

Money Matters, published by the National Savings Committee, and is free on application to Alexandria House, W.C.2

Managing the Home, published by the Education Dept., Co-operative Union Ltd., Holyoake House, Hanover St., Manchester, 4, at 15p plus $2\frac{1}{2}$p postage

Practical work

1 Compare your actual pocket money, plus all the casual earnings

you receive, with that of your friends. If you don't get much for this purpose invent an average amount! Now calculate a four-week total, and then list your approximate spending for four weeks. Can you balance your budget? Do you have a little over in your account? Often you find you have, because you haven't noted down the pennies you fritter away. Now try getting through the month without frittering—and then enjoy your nest egg at the end. Or, at your age, is it more fun to fritter?

2 Find out the average starting wage or salary of the job you hope to do. Are you going to be able to afford to: (*a*) live at home, (*b*) live in a hostel or digs, or (*c*) share a flat? Plan the spending of your first week's pay. How are you going to make it go round?

A question

Assume your husband earns £30·25 net a week and that you have two children. Will you have any other automatic source of income? Work out your weekly budget, remembering all the family's pocket money, repayments, rates and rent.

CHAPTER 3 · SAVINGS OF ALL KINDS

Planning our spending often shows us how little, at various times of our lives, we have left over for saving. Yet there are at least two very good reasons for saving, not for any specific purpose such as Christmas or a holiday, but for less obvious reasons. Firstly, we cannot completely guide our own destinies. We gamble with our lives when we cross roads, and we gamble with our health when we miss meals, smoke or wear silly shoes! We do need a reserve, Welfare State or no Welfare State, should accidents or illness befall ourselves or our dependants. Looking on the brighter side, we do not know what treats there are in store for us—from a day

Never forget to save

out, to a six weeks' holiday, from the offer of a puppy that needs a home, to fostering a small unwanted child. What a pity if that small reserve for an extra bed, care for the puppy, clothes for the holiday, or the fare for the trip did not exist.

Saving can be a habit learned through a piggy bank from the very youngest days. If a young child is encouraged to save it is most important that his efforts are soon rewarded by being able to see the results of his saving. Do not expect to hold his interest in saving if he cannot watch the money grow and share in the pleasure of what it has bought. Later he will save for the sake of it—once he has seen the point of it all!

Later you too should find a more mature way of saving than in a piggy bank; there are so many ways there is sure to be one to suit you. Let us examine some of them.

Post Office

1 *National Savings Stamps*

These are sold at the one price of 10p. They can be purchased at almost any Post Office, and stuck in books which are free of charge. The filled book may be cashed or used to:

(i) make a deposit in a savings account;

(ii) buy a Savings Certificate;

(iii) buy a British Savings Bond;

(iv) buy a Premium Bond.

Savings Groups are often formed either as a street or neighbourhood group, connected with a church or institute or at a school or college. Here the group secretary sells the stamps and acts as an intermediary between the buyer and the Post Office.

2 *Post Office Savings Bank*

Any one over the age of 7 can open a Savings Account. You go to the Post Office, pay a 25p deposit and make a specimen signature. You are then given a receipt for your 25p. When you receive your savings book a few days later you will see that this money has been credited to your account. Of course, you can deposit more than 25p initially if you wish. Once you have received your book you can make a deposit at any time, and each deposit is carefully recorded in the book and at the Post Office when you do so. You can open an account for a child under 7. Often parents do this when their children are born and then money is paid in on behalf of the child. No withdrawals can be made until the child, at the age of 7, can sign the withdrawal slip personally.

Withdrawals You can withdraw a sum of up to £20 on demand. Take your book to the Post Office and state that you wish to make a withdrawal. They retain the book while you fill in the appropriate slip, which you then hand over. Your signature on the slip is compared with that in the book, and provided that your book shows you have previously deposited sufficient funds to cover the amount you now wish to withdraw, the money is handed over. Four clear working days must elapse between the deposit and withdrawal of the same sum of money, or eight days in the case of a cheque. You must always leave at least 5p in the book to keep your account open. This system has three great advantages:

(i) If you leave your money in, it will increase because it will earn interest for you at the rate of 4p per £1 per year, or 4%. This is most important, since the value of money is more often than not on the decrease. Therefore, in order to have the same value in savings after a few years, interest is a necessity.

(ii) Your money, once paid in, is safe.

(iii) You can withdraw at any Post Office, and Post Offices are widely spread and have long opening hours.

3 *Savings Certificates*

There have been many issues of these certificates. At present they can be purchased in units of £1, £2, £3, £4, £5, £10, £20, £50, £100 and £200. They may be held for four years from the date of purchase. At the end of the four years 25p interest has been 'earned' by each unit of £1. No one may purchase more than 1,500 units, because the money invested in this way is free from income tax.

4 *Premium Savings Bonds*

These are a quite different sort of encouragement to save. They are like the other five methods mentioned, a form of Government security. But they earn no interest. Instead they offer the chance of winning a tax-free cash prize.

Buying Children under 16 cannot buy Premium Bonds, but a parent or guardian may buy some on their behalf. You buy them in the following denominations, £2, £3, £4, £5, £10 and £25, then in £10 or multiples of £10 up to £100, then in multiples of £100 up to £500. The maximum holding is £2,000 per person. Each unit of £2 gives you two chances to win a prize. If you had one £2 bond, one £4 and one £3 bond, this would give you nine chances of winning; if you had one £10 bond this would give you ten chances of winning. Each £2 bond has two numbers on it and a £3 bond therefore has three numbers.

The draw When you have held your bonds for 3 months they become part of a monthly draw. The winning numbers are selected by a computer, originally nicknamed 'Ernie' (Electronic Random Number Indicator Equipment). If your bonds do not win they go back into the following month's draw and so on. You cannot lose them. They continue to give you a chance to win until you choose to cash them. If the number on your bond does come up, you will be notified and the numbers (not owner's names) are published. The prizes range from £75,000 to £25.

To withdraw If you wish to withdraw your bonds, you receive exactly the same money for them as you paid for them. You must fill in a form at the Post Office and send it to the Premium Savings Bond Office (address on the form). After six days you will receive a warrant which the Post Office will cash for you. Banks will also sell you these bonds.

5 *British Savings Bonds*

These bonds can be bought at any bank or Savings Bank Post Office. They are sold in amounts of £5 or multiples of £5, and up to £10,000 worth can be bought. They earn $8\frac{1}{2}\%$ interest which is paid twice a year in March and September.

Banks

More and more people each year have their wages or salaries paid by cheque instead of cash. There are two reasons why this has not happened before and why there is still considerable prejudice against it. Firstly, the use some employers made in the past of paying their employees in kind was often an abuse, bringing much misery with it. Employees were paid in goods rather than in money. Potatoes, corn and bread were their wages. These were often mouldy, but the employees had no option but to accept them. Some employers used to issue credit notes which had to be spent in their own shops, and thus they received the money back. They could then charge what they liked for the essential goods and the employees were exploited that way too. No wonder they began to demand 'cash and nothing but cash'.

Secondly, some employees found the system of cheques representing money difficult to understand, especially as it meant that they could not spend part of their wages then and there on their way home on pay day, as many liked to do. The better educated salary earners first realised the advantages of a bank account and accepted this method of receiving their salary. Now more and more people are beginning to appreciate these advantages. How does a current bank account work? There are four main national banks:

Barclays
Lloyds
Midland
National Westminster

Then there are several smaller but important banks such as Williams and Glyn's Bank. There are also banks which work slightly differently, such as the Trustees Savings Bank and the Co-operative Bank.

Having chosen your bank you deposit a certain sum of money to open your account—usually from £3 to £5 as a minimum. Banking works partly on trust and so your Bank Manager will want to know something about you. Certainly, he will want to know your address, who your employer is, and he will want a copy of your usual signature as a reference. If he knows nothing at all about you he may ask for another reference from a friend of yours who is a customer at his bank, or from a well-known person in the area who will vouch for your reliability. He will then issue you with a cheque book and sometimes a paying-in book as well.

Paying money in Each time you pay money in, you write your name and the amount in the paying-in book in two places, firstly on the slip you tear out to hand over the counter with the money, and secondly on the counterfoil which remains in the book for your own reference.

Withdrawals When you wish to draw out some of the money you have deposited you make out a cheque, again writing on the counterfoil as well as on the cheque. Here is a cheque made out to yourself so that when you have handed it to the bank clerk you will receive the cash. You can put Pay *Self* or Pay *Cash*.

13 *An open cheque*

The bank clerk will glance at your account if he does not know you, to make sure that your account holds the sum of money you wish to withdraw. He will also check to see that the signature you have used is your usual one. If he knows you—and one visit is usually enough for this—he will hand the money over straight away in return for your cheque. Write how much you have drawn out on the counterfoil, so that you will know how much you have left in your account. However, if you do get muddled the bank will send you a *statement* when you wish. This will show you how much you have paid in, how much you have drawn out and the balance remaining. If by accident you have drawn out *more* than you have deposited the balance will be labelled D for debit or perhaps OD for overdrawn and you will receive an instruction to put the matter right straight away! You are not allowed to overdraw, but if you are temporarily in trouble, and you ask the bank manager, explaining how you can pay off the overdraft (or money owing), he may permit you to do so. For instance, perhaps you have arranged to pay hire-purchase instalments on a motor scooter which you had been promised by the firm in 3 months time. You know you can manage this because you are due for a rise in salary in 6 weeks. However, due to a speeded up delivery you suddenly find yourself landed with the scooter and the payments, before your rise in salary enables you to meet them. Here your bank manager will probably be only too pleased to help, provided you can prove you are going to receive a salary rise, and provided he is sure you are reliable. He may also help if he sees that owning a scooter will help you to get a better job, or save you considerable travel expenses. Borrowing money from the bank is expensive. You will have to repay the original sum borrowed plus interest.

You can have a *statement* sent regularly either monthly, quarterly or half yearly or just have one when you ask for one.

14 *A crossed cheque*

This cheque has been made out to a firm; perhaps it is to pay the monthly instalment on your scooter. It can go safely through the post because it is of use only to the person whose name you have put on it. Moreover, it is a crossed cheque. The two slanting lines across it on which you have written '& Co.' mean that the person to whom you have made it out cannot cash it for money. Instead he must pay it into a bank account. This stops a dishonest person from opening the letter and trying to cash your cheque. If desired, the Bank will issue you with a book of cheques already crossed. If you are forgetful and afraid you will miss a month's payment on your scooter you can ask your bank to handle all the repayments for you. This is known as a *Standing Order*. You fill in a form instructing your bank to pay J. R. Smith the sum of £2·50 on the third day of each month for the next 24 months. Your bank won't forget! Many people pay the rent, rates or insurance premiums in this way. It saves time and worry. The bank will charge you a small sum, a bank charge, for this service.

Your employer will probably like to pay you in this way too, telling you on a slip how much money he has paid by a standing order straight into your bank account. So you do not even have to go to the trouble of taking your pay cheque and depositing it in your bank. Now you will see some of the

Advantages of having a bank account

1 You need not carry large sums of money about with you, just small sums for small items and your cheque book.

2 Firms do not need to hold large sums in safes and fear robberies; all they need is a large cheque book or a series of standing orders.

3 You have less reason to fear robbery. But keep your cheque book safe—someone might steal it and use it to buy goods. Report a loss immediately to your bank manager. He will know the numbers your cheques bear and will be able to stop them from being used to draw money from your account. You would then be issued with another cheque book.

4 You can make payments easily and regularly.

5 On holiday you need not worry about money. Merely ask your local bank manager to make arrangements for you to cash cheques at the holiday resorts you are visiting.

6 Your bank will also arrange for you to have foreign currency and travellers' cheques for you if you go abroad.

7 In times of need the bank manager may prove a very good friend.

8 Valuables may be stored at the bank.

Large stores such as Marks & Spencers, allow you to collect your purchases from several different departments. When they are all assembled at the cash desk you can then pay by one cheque for all of them. You will be asked to put your address on the back of the cheque, if you are not known at the store, and also possibly to show some identification.

Considerations in having a bank account

1 The opening times of a bank are from 9.30–3.30 on week days plus a 2-hour session on one evening only in some areas. It may mean that part of your dinner hour is spent visiting the bank. In other countries banks have longer hours of opening.

2 You have to pay bank charges for any services which the bank gives. Students who keep a sensible bank account are not charged for services.

3 Money in a current account earns you no interest; in a deposit account it earns you the normal bank rate of about 5–6%. A bank rate of 5% means that if you deposit £100, you will get another £5 at the end of the year. Similarly, if you deposit £50, you will have £2·50 more, £25 deposit will give you £1·25 and so on.

As we have seen, banks will help to make payments for you; insurance and hire-purchase payments are frequently paid this way.

Insurance

This can be a way to save. Endowment policies are taken out by making a small payment. These payments are repeated, weekly or monthly, for an agreed number of years—perhaps 15 or 25. The policy then 'matures' and you receive back what you paid in plus interest. But sometimes you use it to buy security for your family, your car, your house and its contents. Insurance is considered so important that the Government makes it compulsory for us all to buy ourselves, through weekly National Insurance stamps, social security. But as we have also seen, the amounts this insurance scheme brings us are very small. Most of us, as soon as we can afford it, buy extra security through clubs or insurance policies. Clubs are mainly run on a small scale to help people to save for various events. Christmas clubs are still popular; if you pay in 5p a week for the whole year this helps with the Christmas grocery bill. Provident clubs will advance money to members who then pay back 5p a week for every £1 they have borrowed and the whole sum must be cleared in twenty weeks. Insurance policies can also be used as securities if you wish to borrow money, and you can receive income-tax allowances on life insurance policies.

Life Insurance

Most working men are anxious not to leave their wives unprovided for, especially if they have young children dependent upon them. The plight of a young wife, perhaps with three children under 5, and involved in paying off a heavy house mortgage and furniture repayments, is a sad one. It is difficult for her to work. If she pays someone to mind the children this takes such a slice of her earnings that there is probably not enough left to keep up payments on the house and furniture. It is difficult for her to find rented accommodation with young children. She won't be on a 'housing list', and if she sells the house she and her husband have only just started to buy, she will lose financially.

A wise husband will have taken out a Life Assurance for at least as much as they owe on the house, so in case of accident at least the wife will have the security of owning her own home. If they owe £2,500 he should take out a policy for this amount with a reputable firm of Insurance Brokers—a bank manager will advise on this. The premiums or repayments will be about £3–4 a month, about the same amount the average man spends each month on cigarettes. In the same way, if a widow can afford to insure her own life to provide for her children they will be in a much better position should they be orphaned.

House insurance

The company who have lent the money to buy a house will rightly insist that the building is insured against fire. They are not going to lend the money for something which 24 hours later may be a heap of ashes. Such policies usually also cover theft, tempests, floods, earthquakes, etc.

Contents You will be wise to insure the contents—furniture, fixtures, clothes and jewellery—against all these accidents. This usually costs about 50p–£2 a year for each £1,000 worth of contents. Don't forget to raise your contents' insurance if you buy another £500 worth of furniture.

Car insurance

You are not allowed to take a powered vehicle of any kind on to the road unless it is insured against damage to a 'third party'. This is a very sound law because you may injure or kill the breadwinner of a family. Then your Third Party Insurance will enable you to compensate that family for its loss with a payment of money. Recently a widow with two children was awarded £14,000 damages against a driver who ran over her husband. On your own you could never pay such a sum, but your insurance company would have to pay this for you. It costs about £8–£12 a year for third party cover for the average car, and more if you can extend this cover to include fire and theft.

Endowment Policies

Here you take out a policy to bring you in a certain sum a definite number of years ahead. For example you may decide that on retirement you would like to be able to count on £500 for a really enjoyable cruise or holiday. Or you may simply feel that you would like to supplement your pension with your savings. If you decide this at 20 and so have 40 years in which to pay, your payments will be small, spread over a long time. If you do not start to pay until you are 35, of course your payments will be bigger. Although the value of money may have dropped during the years, nevertheless your £500 will have been collecting profits for you and you may find you collect a sum nearer £600 than £500.

Hire purchase

This is spending, not saving, but often we have to resort to buying vital goods on credit when our families are in the greatest need of them. Buying a house by obtaining a mortgage is really buying it on credit and few people would ever own their house if they didn't do this. It is foolish to take on more monetary liabilities than you and your family can manage with ease. But it is far from foolish to buy a warm coat and wear it through the winter as you buy it, rather than to let your health suffer through cold and misery. Perhaps, though, it would have been even wiser to save up for it first! It is not so wise, however, to have a holiday which may or may not turn out successfully, and then when it is over, to have to go on paying for it week after week. You will still have the coat after you have finished paying for it, but not the holiday.

How does hire purchase work? You see an article you want—perhaps bunk beds for the children who have grown out of their cots. The cost is perhaps £25·79 and you ask to buy it on extended credit (or hire purchase). Sometimes the shop runs its own hire-purchase system. Co-operative Stores do, and you will be asked to fill in a form at once. You will be asked for a 20% deposit. You can pay more if you like, but the regulations of 1972 lay down that 10% is the minimum for furniture, and $33\frac{1}{3}\%$ for all other goods. You are then given the choice of spreading your payments over a certain number of months, usually 6, 12, 18 up to 24 months only. Obviously the more months you take to pay, the smaller will be your individual payments, but on the other hand the more interest on the loan you will be asked to pay. This interest varies from 5% to 25% of the purchase price, depending on the amount borrowed and for how long.

	£	
In the case of the bunk beds the cost was	25·79	
Less deposit	5·15	
Amount of loan	20·64	
Interest charged	2·06	
Balance to pay	22·70	at 25p a week

for 2 years. The rate of interest you are being charged is about 10%. You are, in other words, paying £2·06 more than you would have to if you could afford to pay cash. On the other hand if, during the two years the price of beds increased, the price of your bed won't, as you have already bought it at a fixed price. Had you saved 25p steadily for 2 years you might well find that you could not buy bunk beds for £25·79 and would have to find about the extra £2·06 anyway. So hire purchase sounds an economical arrangement. Is it really?

The advantages of hire purchase

1 You can obtain goods when you need them by paying $\frac{1}{10}$ or more of their price and promising to pay off the balance at a fixed rate in a fixed time.

2 You can buy goods which you might never be able to afford in any other way.

3 You can buy goods to enable you to earn money, e.g. a sewing machine, an electric guitar, taxi-cab or window-cleaning equipment.

The disadvantages of hire purchase

1 You always pay more in instalments for goods than you would if you had paid cash outright. Sometimes, even, the cash price is reduced if you are able to pay cash on the spot, instead of asking for extended credit.

2 Weekly or monthly payments are a nuisance. Sometimes you cannot risk changing jobs because you need to be sure of a steady income to meet your hire-purchase commitments.

3 It is easy to overcommit yourself when your wages increase with overtime, etc. Down go your 'small' initial payments easily enough. But how are you going to keep them up if bad times lie ahead?

4 The burden of repayments is particularly hard to bear if the article you are paying for is broken, lost or worn out before it is fully paid for.

Rules to observe to help you guard against these pitfalls:

1 Only buy what you really need, not what you can do without, by hire purchase.

2 Calculate what you can afford in the way of commitments when your pay is at its lowest and your ordinary expenses at their *highest*—e.g. allow for heating in winter.

3 Do not take a wife's earnings into consideration if she may be giving up work.

4 Read the hire-purchase agreement forms through very carefully before you pay your deposit and sign anything. Take your

time, do not be jostled and hurried into anything. Not all firms are as honest as they might be.

5 Buy from a well-known and reputable firm, and enquire about any guarantee your goods carry (see Chapter 1).

6 Know your *rights* under the Hire-Purchase Acts.

The Hire-Purchase Acts

Sixty-five per cent of all hire-purchase agreements are made between the customer called the hirer, and a *Finance Company*. Often the hirer thinks he is dealing with the shop or store where he buys the goods. At one time when fewer transactions were carried out in this way, shops and stores could extend all the credit their customers needed. Now the number of transactions is far too great and finance companies often provide the credit, an example of these is United Dominions Trust Company. The shop usually deals with one finance company which pays him a commission on the number of deals he forwards to it for action. The customer comes to the shop to plan his purchase, to pay his deposit and to fill up his hire-purchase form. The shop provides the goods, retains the deposit and sends off the agreement to the finance company. The finance company pays him the balance owing on the goods, plus commission and then deals directly with the hirer (or customer). The finance company becomes the owner of the goods until the hirer has paid his final instalment.

If a hirer under a hire-purchase agreement cannot keep up his instalments he is protected to some extent by the Hire-Purchase Acts 1938 which state the following:

1 If the total sum to be paid for the goods is under £300, and one-third of this has been paid, the owners of the goods (the finance company or shop) cannot repossess the goods without the consent of the hirer, or without a court order. Until 1938 this was known as the 'snatch back' and sometimes even today disreputable firms take back goods just before one-third of the purchase price has been paid. On goods costing over £300 you have no such protection so always use a reputable firm, read your agreements carefully and do not fail to pay any instalments. Be especially careful when you purchase second-hand goods over the cost of £300. They are not even covered by the protection of the Sale of Goods

Act. (See last chapter.) The White Paper on the Reform of the Law on Consumer Credit, 1973 suggests that if the hirer cannot keep up his payments, i.e. he defaults, he must be informed of the position in writing and told how much he owes. He must also be given time, i.e. 7 days, in which to pay. He must be warned what will happen if he fails to pay and how he can remedy the situation —all of this clearly and in writing.

2 If the matter is brought to court the judge may decide to give the hirer a longer time with smaller instalments in which to pay off his debts.

3 If half the cost of the goods (if this total cost is less than £300) has been paid, the hirer may end the agreement by surrendering the goods and paying no more instalments. He must, however, pay for any damage the goods have sustained if he has not taken 'reasonable' care of them. If the sum for damage cannot be agreed upon, the owners can sue him for damage.

4 If the hirer wishes to end the agreement before paying the full cost he may do so and surrender the goods. He must also pay for damages if any. He cannot, however, end his agreement until 18 months since the purchase date have passed.

5 These figures—also the total cost of the goods (*a*) as a cash deal and (*b*) as an extended credit deal—clearly showing the difference—must appear on the hire-purchase agreement so that the hirer is clearly aware of them.

6 Under the Advertisements (Hire Purchase) Act, 1957 the hirer must also be shown the terms he is expected to pay if he buys the goods advertised by hire purchase. The advertisements must not mislead or try to hide the hire-purchase charges. Such advertisements as this are deemed misleading

BUNK BED FOR ONLY £2·60 *deposit*

PAYMENTS ONLY 25p A WEEK *for* 104 *weeks*

An advertiser trying to mislead in this way can be prosecuted and fined.

7 A Bill is about to be passed to give the hirer further protection. This will allow him 4 days in which to change his mind and opt out of the agreement altogether, providing he has not signed the agreement at a shop, showroom or office of a finance company. It

only applies to credit sales of over £30. If you have signed an agreement and paid a deposit, you are entitled to a refund of the deposit paid upon cancelling the agreement. If you have given any goods in part exchange, those goods, or their value, must be returned to you. If neither deposit nor goods have been returned, you are entitled to keep any goods already delivered by the company—and they must collect them at their own expense. This has been made necessary by the pressure put upon potential customers by door-to-door salesmen.

Credit-sale agreements

Under a credit-sale agreement, the goods at once become the property of the customer. There is no question either of the trader having any right to take the goods away if he does not pay, or of his being able to hand the goods back if he does not want to go through with the agreement. A sale has been made; the goods are his and if he does not pay, the trader's only remedy is to sue for the money owed.

Door-to-door salesmen These come in all shapes and sizes, nationalities and ages. Many are reputable and genuine. Some

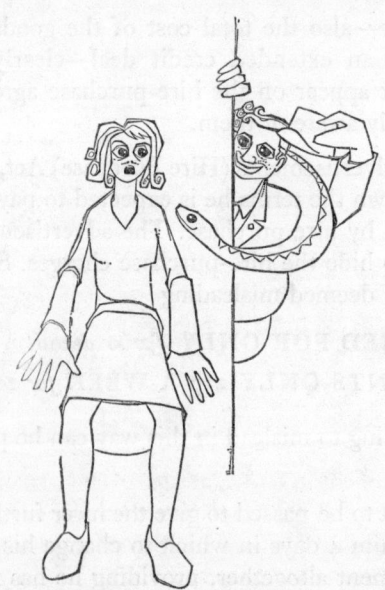

15 *'Excellent for lagging the pipes, madam'*

firms carry out their entire business this way, so avoiding the costs of renting and staffing shops. Some are such rogues that special measures are now being taken to protect the public, especially housewives, from being misled by them.

The Consumer Council did much valuable work to this end, and published a special survey of their activities. They summarised the four main ways in which disreputable doorstep salesmen work.

1 Mobile firms, taking cash from the public, have disappeared from the area when complaints have arisen. Examples are firms selling sub-standard carpets.

2 Switch selling: where a poor quality or virtually non-existent product is advertised at a low price as bait to effect a sale of a much higher-priced product.

3 Misrepresentation: examples are the educational book salesmen who say they are engaged on a social research survey; salesmen posing as Commonwealth students seeking points from sales of magazine subscriptions to obtain scholarships to universities; salesmen of central heating systems said to qualify for local authority grants, but which do not and are both more expensive than those bought at established dealers and inadequate in cold weather.

4 Advertisements for home-workers aimed at potential buyers of knitting machines and offering the inducement of high earnings through sale of work. Once a bond or hire-purchase agreement for the machine is secured the company frequently refuses, on various excuses, to accept the articles produced.

All four methods are those of salesmen trained to defraud, and these facts have partly been revealed by ex-salesmen who have been disgusted by the whole business.

The sub-standard carpets referred to in 1 are usually cotton made to look like wool, or have a pile specially and very temporarily fluffed up, or are rayon made to resemble nylon. The salesmen sometimes claim that the carpets are being sold cheaply by saying that they have come from a wrecked ship or bankrupt hotel. The switch selling of 2 has been widespread in washing machines and sewing machines. Often the higher-priced machine that the customer is bulldozed into buying is inferior to those of a similar price on sale in a normal shop.

The so-called educational book salesman of 3 exerts what is nothing short of blackmail. He suggests that your neighbours—who, of course, love their children and want their children to get on—have bought the books, often encyclopaedias, he is selling. So you start to feel that you, too, must buy the books to prove that you are a good parent as well! Often the plight of those caught by number 4 is the worst. Here you have people, perhaps handicapped in some way, anxious to earn at home. They contract to buy an expensive piece of equipment which they could not otherwise hope to afford because they believe all their work will be purchased and they will gradually earn a steady income. They find they are left with heavy hire-purchase commitments and goods that no one wants to buy. How can *you* be sure you will never be caught?

1 Never even listen to a salesman unless he is offering something you have already decided to buy.

2 Always ask to see his credentials, if he has not a printed card or letter of introduction have nothing to do with him. If he has, see if you can find the name of the firm on the card or letter he has shown you in the telephone directory. Check him carefully.

3 If what he is trying to sell sounds: (*a*) just what you want; (*b*) is reasonably priced; (*c*) is reputably guaranteed, ask him to call back when you will have a second opinion on the premises, from a husband or mother and father.

4 In the meantime check down the road to see what your neighbours think (they may know the representative) and find out the price of a similar object from a local firm, and their terms.

5 Have the prospective purchase demonstrated at your leisure, when you and your second opinion have time to watch, listen and think. If it is a vacuum cleaner that polishes, scrubs, etc., ask to see it do all these things, not just clean your carpet, which was probably clean anyway!

6 Ask about the hire-purchase terms, cash sale price and guarantee. If these are not handed to you in writing, write them all down. Ask to see a copy of the hire-purchase agreement.

7 If you are still interested send the representative away for long enough to give you a chance to think, work out the cost and talk it over. The cooling-off period of 4 days now being made law, only applies to cash or credit sales over £30.

8 If you finally decide to buy, make sure you get a new unused model, not one which has been demonstrated to the whole neighbourhood. If your local shops offer part exchange for your old machine make sure you get as good an offer from this salesman.

Finally Never be sorry for a door-step salesman. Some claim to be hard-up students working for their education; others deliberately develop 'asthma', etc., to win your pity. He has chosen that way of life.

Never be afraid to say 'No' even if he has visited you three times, cleaned four carpets and talked for five hours. He has chosen to do this.

Never interview a salesman alone in your house. Remember those from disreputable firms are trained to bamboozle you.

Never believe what they say about your neighbours—'the whole street is buying them'—Rubbish!

Never tell them anything about your neighbours. They may ask you for names, the ages of their children, etc. When they call on your neighbours, they may pretend to represent some authority or other.

If anyone tries to sell you anything over the 'phone, just replace the receiver. This is a real infringement of personal privacy. One firm I know of gives £7·50 to the representative for every vacuum cleaner he sells. Sometimes he earns this for 30 minutes' work, but, of course, he has got more sense than to go from house to house looking prosperous or driving his best car! Even the reputable firms selling such things as brushes charge far more than you would pay at a shop. They count on your not knowing comparable prices. If you need a brush, see what is offered, judge the quality and offer to buy next time, when you have had a chance to compare prices.

Saving with the Co-op

At one time the only hope many people had of saving was through Co-op dividends.

The Co-op movement was started in England about 120 years ago when the conditions of the working classes were almost unbelievably bad. In the industrial areas where the houses were often back-to-back with one lavatory serving twenty persons, children of 9 or 10 years were working perhaps a 10-hour day. The parents themselves often worked an 18-hour day and were desperate, for the pittance they earned was below subsistence level. From this misery the Co-op movement was born. The principles included open membership, democratic control, fixed and limited interest on capital and distribution of the surplus in dividend to members, in proportion to their purchases, pure and unadulterated food and the education of members. In such places as Rochdale and Nottingham, for the very first time, the working class began to get value for money.

We used not to question our right to value for money. We accepted the Co-operative dividends as standard practice and often tended to look on shopping at the Co-op as not very 'with it'. It is true that a few Co-ops seem old-fashioned; but many have opened up-to-date supermarkets. It is not true that only Co-op brands are stocked in Co-op shops. Nor is it true that a ½p or 1p is put on to help pay the dividend. The modern Co-op has just as many bargain offers as its fellow stores, but perhaps it is not as flamboyant about them. It is partly our fault if our local Co-op is a bit of a 'fuddy duddy'. We can be members, and if we are not satisfied, *we* should complain and make *constructive* suggestions, as, indeed, we should at all the shops we use. In 1970 Dividend stamps were introduced. One is given for each five pence spent in any department except for travel, hairdressing and milk delivery. A full book of stamps can be exchanged for 40p in cash or 50p in goods other than food, or paid into a share book. After one year the paid-in book will increase in value to 60p. So the Dividend stamp has now replaced nearly all the other methods of paying dividends.

Remember poor Mr. Micawber's warning, *Receipts* £1 *Spending* £1·01 *Result*—Misery. *Receipts* £1 *Spending* 99p *Result*—Bliss!

Further reading

A Citizen Today, by Michael Hansen, published by Oxford University Press at 40p

Post Office Guide, available from the larger Post Offices or from Her Majesty's Stationery Office, Cornwall House, Stamford St., S.E.1 at 20p

Door-Step Selling and *Hire Purchase* are free leaflets in the 'Consumer Contexts' series published by the Consumer Council, 3 Cornwall Terrace, N.W.1

National Savings Leaflets are free from any Post Office

The Consumer, Society and the Law, by Cole and Diamond, published by the Co-operative Union Ltd., Holyoake House, Hanover St., Manchester, 4, at $17\frac{1}{2}$p plus $2\frac{1}{2}$p postage

The Law for Consumers, published by the Consumers' Association, 14 Buckingham St., W.C.2, at 40p

Your Money in the Bank, a free leaflet from the National Westminster Bank Ltd.

Practical work

1 Collect leaflets from your G.P.O. on the various ways of saving. New ones are often introduced; keep up to date with them.

2 Make a list of the things you think are really worth saving for—compare it with your friends' lists. What would you really be prepared to go without in order to save for the things you have listed?

3 Which banks have you got in your city, town or village? Where are they? When do they open? Ask for leaflets concerning the work of the bank. What is a night safe?

4 Is your family, or are any friends, involved in any savings or insurance schemes? Do you, or your mother, pay into clubs? Find out all you can about them, pool your information in class and discuss which seem to be of most use.

5 Are you or any members of your family involved in any hire-purchase transactions? Ask if you could read the agreement form. Can you work out what rates of interest you are paying?

6 Go and have a look at your local Co-op. Compare the prices with other shops. List the good points and your criticisms. What other services does the Co-op offer in your area?

Bread delivery? Snack bars?
Milk delivery? Supermarket?
Laundry? Theatre or arts club?
Dry-cleaning? Youth club?
Shoe repairs? Scholarships for further training?
Coal? Evening classes?
Funeral services? Restaurants?

Are there any other services?

7 In groups, act the four ways door-to-door salesmen try to bamboozle you. Show how you would deal with them!

Questions

1 'I want to feel my money in my hand each pay day.' Discuss this statement.

2 'Rainy days' can't happen in a Welfare State. How far is this true today?

3 Would you be prepared to buy any items on hire purchase? Do you consider this a good way of getting:

(i) holidays;
(ii) clothes;
(iii) durable household articles, e.g. washing machines;
(iv) a car;
(v) luxuries, e.g. a record player;
(vi) food, e.g. the Christmas turkey?

4 How would you help your child to save. Think of ways of encouraging him? How would you persuade your teenage daughter to save?

5 Your new employer wants to pay your salary by cheque. Do you welcome this? How exactly will you set about opening your bank account?

6 Do you collect Co-op stamps? Would you become a member? What improvements would you suggest?

SECTION II · HOMES AND PEOPLE

CHAPTER 4 · LIVING ACCOMMODATION: TO SHARE, TO RENT, TO BUY

'Home is where the heart is'—where we should be able to relax and be happy. What does our happiness come from? Rarely I believe from solitude—which is next door to loneliness—though sometimes it can make a refreshing change. We need companionship, people to enjoy our pleasures with, to laugh at our jokes and to sympathise with our worries—to halve our troubles by sharing them.

A home is made of people, not of bricks. The building is merely the place in which the family lives, though, of course, if the building is pleasant it will help to bring happiness to the family. But it is no good living in luxury with people you dislike, greater happiness will come from sharing a bedsitter with those you are fond of, and who in return are fond of you. There is an awful feeling of emptiness when you rush home—perhaps with good news—to find that the people you expected to be there are not in. It is unimportant whether you are rushing home to a semi-detached house, a terraced cottage or a caravan. It is the person who opens the door and welcomes you who matters, not the building.

So a home is made of people, and because when living with them we are bound to want to be happy, we must be very careful to see that we bring happiness to the people we live with, and that we give them a chance, in return, to make us happy. Later on in life you will have the opportunity to choose the person, or people with whom you want to live, and this, of course, has to be done with great care.

Choosing your first independent home

Let us suppose you have reached this stage—you have left school and the job you want to do, or the training you want to take, is some way from the home in which you have grown up. You must look for a new home. Probably your grant or allowance or first wage packet is far too small to allow you to live on your own, so you realise you need to share a home. You will have a choice of several ways of sharing, the main difference being that you can either pay for and prepare your own food, or you can pay extra for someone else to do this for you, in other words you can pay extra for 'board and lodging'. This is more commonly called 'digs'.

'Digs'

How do you find 'digs' suitable for your special needs, that you can begin to think of as a new home? If you know anyone in the town to which you are moving, they can probably help you. If not you can seek similar help from the nearest Women's Voluntary Service or Citizens' Advice Bureau. Later on we shall find out exactly what these two very useful organisations do, but one thing you can usually rely on them for is a list of local residents who are willing to provide board and lodging.

The local paper Here is another source of help. When you go for your interview for a job, it is always a good idea to buy a copy. Under the column appropriately headed you will find either the addresses or box numbers of people offering 'digs'. Some advertisers prefer not to have their names and addresses published; instead they give this information to the newspaper office, and in return for a small fee—about 10p—the office staff will send them replies addressed to the box number allocated to them in the advertisement. This sort of thing appears:

> BOARD AND LODGING. ROOM FOR YOUNG LADY. FULL BOARD. CENTRALLY SITUATED. BOX NUMBER 606 NEWTOWN NEWS.

If you reply to Box No. 606 you will get an answer from the people who inserted the advertisement. If none of the advertisements interest you, you can, of course, insert your own advert. in the BOARD AND LODGINGS WANTED column. Then you can choose whether to use your name and address, or to ask for a box number. Usually you will pay about 4p a word for the advertisement. Finally you will probably collect several addresses and off you will go to inspect your prospective 'digs'.

What to look for

It is never wise to accept digs without visiting them first, no matter who has recommended them. It is especially important to meet the person who will be giving you board. There are many questions to be asked besides the obvious one of 'How much do you charge?' First of all you must find out what your prospective landlady means by 'board and lodging'. Here are some questions you may find it useful to ask.

1 How many meals per day will you get?

2 How many of these will be cooked? Can you choose to have a cooked breakfast or not?

3 If you need a packed lunch, either to take to work or for a Sunday picnic, will she provide this?

4 If given plenty of warning will she charge you less for being away for a whole day, or weekend or even a two-week holiday? Most landladies expect a retaining fee—about a third to a quarter of the board and lodging charge—during holidays.

5 Can you invite a friend to your digs to a meal? Will this cost you any extra?

6 Will your special tastes, if you have any, be catered for? You may be a vegetarian or not wish to eat meat on a Friday.

Restaurant and Snack Bar meals can be very expensive. They are a treat, but make a huge hole in your small income if you have to rely on them to bridge that gap. It is most important to be sure that you are not going to be hungry. You can't raid the larder in someone else's house, and after just a quick snack lunch you may be badly in need of a substantial high tea after a long day's work.

Now for the accommodation

Always ask to see your room, that is, the room you will actually be sleeping in. Do not assume it will be furnished in the same way as the room you have been shown into downstairs! Notice if the bed looks comfy—the 'old hand' at digs seeking will probably feel it, or sit on it! If too shy to do this, but in doubt, ask about the type of mattress. Is there ample room for your clothes? Can you hang some of them away from the dust? What sort of outlook have you got from your window? If you want to study, find out if there are facilities downstairs for this. If not you will want a comfy chair in the bedroom for reading, heating of some kind and a table and chair. You will also need a good light—I have known some landladies who only allowed a 60-watt bulb in the bedroom—to save electricity! This meant either bad eye-strain, or no reading. Have you got a mirror, drawers, a bedside lamp, and something besides lino on the floor? Perhaps you have a favourite chair or bookcase at home; you could ask for permission to bring them with you. You will not be going out every evening, and it is so important to feel at home, and not an intruder in someone else's house.

One of the family? The big difference is really whether you are going to be treated as one of the landlady's family, or just as a lodger. Both have advantages and disadvantages. Will you be sharing the family's living room? If so it will probably be warm and comfortable, and you will have to watch the television programmes the family wishes to see—not necessarily the ones you would choose. If you have a room downstairs to yourself or to share with other lodgers (or paying guests as many landladies like to call them!) the standard of comfort may be lower than you have been used to. On the other hand it will be quieter, and you will have more privacy providing there are not too many other lodgers! It will be easier to entertain your friends in such a room, but on the other hand it is not much fun always eating and sitting on your own—or even with a comparative stranger.

What price privacy? As part of the family, where are you going to have that private natter to your friends, so dear to the teenager's heart? Will you be allowed to take a friend up to your bedroom—any friend? Can you in fact treat it as a bed-sitting room and play your transistor, or record player up there? When you decide to go out for the evening, this new family will probably be very interested to know where you are going. They will be happier if you decide to tell them—that is always provided you are sure they will approve of your choice of entertainment. If your landlady is a vegetarian it is perhaps not wise to rush off to a bull-fight!

Shades of Cinderella One thing she will always be interested in is the time of your return from your evening out. If your mother has helped you to choose your digs, she has probably had a chat to the landlady about this. Perhaps you will be given complete freedom to come and go—in other words a door key of your own. But this depends largely on your age. If you have no key, the time factor must be discussed. Your landlady may say, 'In by 10 p.m. on weekdays and 11 p.m. on Saturdays.' You know where you stand, and you must decide if these times are reasonable. Once you have agreed to such an arrangement you must stick to it. If you have not been given a door key you know that she will have to sit up for you if you are late—remember too that you will have to face her at breakfast.

Board

Board should also include some laundry, certainly your sheets and pillow slips. Ask about this. Who provides towels, and who washes

16 Some *landladies will allow you to use the kitchen sink* . . .

them? What about your personal laundry? Some landladies will wash and iron for you, but this often costs you a little extra. They find this preferable to having blouses soaking in wash basins, and nylons dripping on to bedroom carpets. Some will allow you to wash at the kitchen sink one evening a week, and iron on another. They must then find you room to dry your clothes, and this is not always easy with drip-dry garments in winter. A landlady who has no experience of teenage daughters may simply not understand your needs at all. Talking to her should give you some idea of her knowledge of your age group.

Value for money

Ideally you should have a wash basin in your bedroom and frequent use of the bath. Ask about bathing and hair-washing facilities. Obviously you must keep your bedroom tidy and probably make your bed each morning, but are you also expected to clean your room? How is your room heated? Is there a meter in your room? If there is a telephone, can you receive and make telephone calls? How far away is the nearest bus which will take you to work? Finally the cost—this may have been mentioned in the advertisement, or be the first thing you asked about. Be careful to think of the amount in terms of *exactly* what you are getting for it. It should not take up more than half your rather small initial income. If it does, how are you going to manage for fares, a midday meal, clothes, toilet accessories and entertainments? If you are lucky enough to find digs where a good packed lunch is provided, where your washing is done for you, and central enough to cut bus fares out, then, of course, it may be worth paying extra to live there.

'*Give and take*' Can you really ask all these questions—have you the nerve? Would it be better to take an older friend, or your mother with you to help with the awkward questions? You will not have to ask them all of course—the answers to many will be obvious, and the landlady—if she has taken a fancy to you—will be anxious to tell you all the good points about her accommodation. Finally, you can judge a little on the sort of person she is. Do you think you could get on with her? Do you think she has a sense of humour? You certainly will not get on with her, or any landlady, unless you treat her with the consideration with which you are hoping she will treat you. Be punctual, polite, as tidy as possible, and pay your rent on the day she is expecting you to. Be reasonable about noise, about the number of friends who visit you, about lateness and about the number of hours you spend in the bathroom. Remember that other people like hot water, and a good place near the fire—and if any meal is especially nice *say so*! If you can remember some of these things most of the time, you'll deserve the sort of consideration in your new home that will make you happy—and make you begin to regard it as your new home—it's mainly up to you!

Hostels

If you cannot bear the thought of being in digs on your own, and yet have no close friend to share with, you may find you enjoy hostel life. Here I am talking of residential hostels, not the holiday ones.

Associations such as the Young Women's Christian Association, or the Salvation Army run hostels to provide accommodation for young people who are working or learning away from home. In them you still need comfort, warmth, good food and washing facilities, so all the things to look for in digs apply here as well. But they are easier to find because the hostel will have printed rules. You will know at a glance when meals are served, at what time you have to be in, where you can do your washing, and who you can entertain in various rooms. In exchange for these rules and regulations you will have the company of many girls of your own age, considerable comfort, good food and lots of fun. There will always be someone to lend you nylons, to go out with or to set your hair.

Few and far between

Unfortunately, only large towns and cities possess such hostels, and if you are lucky enough to have one near your place of work, you will probably find they have a long waiting list. This, of course, proves what very good value they give, and how happy the girls are who live there. The charges are sometimes as low as £4 a week including everything except a fire in the bedroom. For this there are slot meters, but a warm lounge, television, laundry facilities, telephone and as many baths as are required are provided. The food is plain but well cooked and sustaining, without being too fattening! Local authorities, for example the Greater London Council, also run hostels. Enquiries to:

> The Secretary,
> Central Information Bureau,
> 7–9 Baker Street,
> London, W.1.

Hostels are available in three areas:

Craven Hill, W.2
St. Georges, S.W.10
Susan Lawrence, W.C.1

Furnished rooms and flats

One day you will wish to cater and cook for yourself, to look after yourself, and to have more personal freedom. This means you must find a place to rent, either furnished or unfurnished. You can either look for rooms or a small flat of your own, or you may have a friend in a similar position, who will share with you. Perhaps you will be willing to take a chance of sharing with a group of girls who meet through this sort of advertisement in the paper:

> THIRD GIRL WANTED. EARLY 20S SHARE HAMP-
> STEAD FLAT. OWN BEDROOM. £5·50.

This does involve a risk of course, not about the flat—by now you should know what to look for—but you may find the other two girls very difficult to live with. Strangely enough this is sometimes true of your own friends.

It takes all sorts!

You may find new friends very good fun at work or sharing a snack in a coffee bar, but sharing a kitchen or bathroom with them may be a very different matter. The lively, beautifully dressed ones may play the record player full on all night because they cannot stop being lively! Or the high standards of grooming they achieve may cost you hours of waiting outside the bathroom door. On the other hand the girl who sacrifices *all* to improve her mind may not be able to tear herself away from her encyclopaedia to do her share of the chores—let alone have a break from Wagner for a spot of 'Pick of the Pops'.

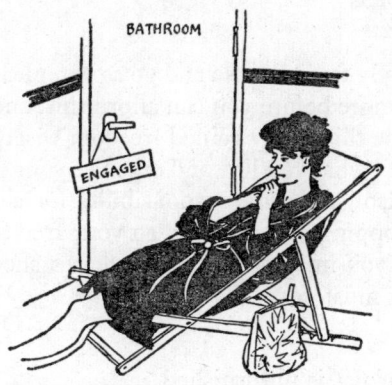

17 *Sharing a bathroom with your friends may not be good fun*

Choose carefully, try to get to know your fellow sharers first, and if you decide to risk it with them, make certain of important points before you move in. Exactly what is your share of the rent? (if you have the tiniest bedroom, you should have the tiniest share). How are heating, food and other bills going to be shared? How are you going to share the chores? If you write down a scheme and stick to it, you will save endless squabbles later.

JOB 1	JOB 2	JOB 3
Does all shopping	Does all cooking	Does all cleaning
Washes up	Tidies kitchen	Wipes up
Pays food bills	Pays gas bill (5p in the slot)	Pays milk/drink bill
	Fair shares rent and electricity bill	
WEEK 1 Pam: Job 1	Tina: Job 2	Sally: Job 3
WEEK 2 Pam: Job 2	Tina: Job 3	Sally: Job 1
WEEK 3 Pam: Job 3	Tina: Job 1	Sally: Job 2

This needs careful planning—the girl using the gas cooker should put the money in the meter! The girl doing the shopping should pay the food bill, then she will be careful! She and the cook will have to think ahead and plan the week's meals. This avoids impulse buying, repetitive meals and last-minute panics. But if you make it work, this sort of pulling together can be tremendous fun.

A flat of your own

Now you are really free to come and go as you please. Usually you will be earning more before you can afford this, and will be a little older and can use this newly gained freedom wisely. You can now do as you like, eat what you like and organise your own little home. But you have also gained the responsibility for cleaning, tidying, washing up, shopping and cooking, so your free time will not be quite as free as you imagined! Your expenses shoot up too; now your pay packet must cover:

1 rent
2 rates if your flat is unfurnished
3 food
4 fuel
5 lighting
6 replacements (crockery, light bulbs, linen, etc.)
7 cleaning materials
8 furniture repayments; TV rentals
9 insurance (see Chapter 3)
10 personal expenses (clothes, entertainments, etc.)

Fortunately not many girls face this lot alone for long, either along comes a husband or she finds a girl she really wishes to share with on a long-term basis. Either way you will not be owning the property you are living in so you are a tenant and you will have a landlord.

Landlords

Before occupying any rented premises there are certain things you ought to know and have written down as confirmation, in an agreement or contract, and both you and your landlord should have a copy. It is wise to agree upon the following points:

1 The rent, how much it is, how and when it must be paid. Cash, a cheque in advance, weekly, monthly? A rent book is a good idea, you then have a record of what you have paid and when—and what you owe.

FURNISHED ROOMS AND FLATS

2 Is it *inclusive*, that is, does the figure quoted represent all you have to pay? Or is it *exclusive*, are such payments as rates excluded, and must you pay them as well as the rent?

3 Are there any extra facilities you could obtain for an extra payment such as use of a garage, garden shed or shared telephone?

4 How will you be assessed for the amount of gas and electricity you use? Meters installed by the boards supplying these services are the most satisfactory, but you might find that there are meters which have been installed by the landlord. Be careful in this case, you might be paying more than you need.

5 Where can you store coal, should you need it? Where can you put your dustbin? Have you easy access to these places or have you to go through someone else's kitchen?

6 Which parts of the building do you share with either your landlord or other tenants? Perhaps the front door, hall, stairs and a landing. Possibly even a bathroom, toilet or kitchen. Who is responsible for furnishing these places, cleaning and maintaining them? If a cleaner is employed by the landlord—or a caretaker in a large block of flats—do you contribute towards these wages?

7 Can you, in any circumstances, sub-let your flat?

8 Does any part of the garden become your responsibility? If not where can you hang your washing, or put a bicycle or a pram?

9 If you live upstairs can you leave the bike or pram in the hall?

10 Are your apartments furnished, semi-furnished or unfurnished? If any of your landlord's furniture or furnishings are left for your use are you allowed fair wear and tear on them? Is there an inventory? Will the landlord expect worn furniture to be renewed when you leave, and how will you know just what belongs to whom without a check list of some kind?

11 Will you be responsible for repairs to any equipment in the flat, such as a cooker or refrigerator?

12 If you have central heating, how do you pay for this? Who pays for maintenance and repair?

13 What fittings will be in the apartment for your use? Curtains, mats, kitchen utensils—have you to pay extra for these?

14   Are you responsible for repairs and redecorations in your part of the building? If so is this just internal maintenance or will you be responsible for the condition of the roof, the drainpipes, the gutters and so on? What about the attic and cellar?

15   Finally, under what conditions must you, or can you, 'vacate the premises'? You can either enter into a long-term (1–3 years perhaps) agreement, or be subject to 2–4 weeks' notice to quit, on either side.

Security of tenure

The long-term agreement gives you security, but if you are unhappy in the flat or if you marry and want to move away, your agreement or lease could bind you to continue to pay rent for several months or years after you have moved. Usually the landlord will transfer your lease if you find him a new tenant. Frequently he has a waiting list of people longing for you to move out —so all is well. If you have only the security of several weeks' notice, you may find that having paid the expenses of moving in, perhaps having redecorated the flat, you are then required to move. The landlord may be justified in asking you to do so—perhaps you are not paying your rent regularly, or the neighbours have complained about the noise you make! Or you may simply be unlucky, perhaps the landlord's mother is suddenly widowed, and he needs a home for her, near his own. He may really need your flat.

Supply and demand

The problem today is that there are usually far more flat-hunters than flats—especially in large towns—even more so in London. That is, of course, they are looking for reasonably priced, comfortable flats, not poky, ill-lit converted cellars, or slope-ceilinged attics, cold and leaky at £7·50 a week! Even such flats as these are eagerly sought for in some cities. Some of the better flats have unreasonable clauses in their agreements—'no children' or 'no pets'.

Because demand exceeds supply many rents are still high, and some landlords unfair. Sometimes very high prices are asked for rubbishy fittings, or a little furniture; for example, £250 for curtain rails and a stair carpet. If you pay such a price, it is really a bribe for the landlord, to persuade him to rent you his flat. Such payments were known as key money during the last war. Fortunately now they have been exposed and are less common. There are, however, landlords who will try to turn out a tenant who has no agreement, simply because he can find one willing to pay more, or who will tell a young couple to move just because a baby is due. Often such landlords remain anonymous and send agents to collect the rent, so avoiding the complaints of the tenants. In November 1964 the Protection from Eviction Act received its second reading in Parliament. The aim of this Act is to protect tenants from such landlords. It has strengthened the power of the Rent Tribunals which were originally set up to protect tenants, in two ways:

(*a*) It is now a crime for a landlord to evict a tenant without first obtaining a court order to do so. This crime is punishable by a 6-months' imprisonment, or £100 fine.

(*b*) County courts have the power to put off, or 'stay' the carrying out of an eviction for 12 months. So even if a landlord wins his appeal to have his tenants evicted, the tenants can still be given a fair amount of time to find a new home, if the court feels that they will otherwise suffer hardship.

Once again it is most important that both tenants and landlord know their rights.

Home—not so sweet home?

Why should you be unhappy, and want to leave your flat? If you have checked carefully upon all the details of the flat, the following sources of annoyance should have been noticed before you moved in, but this is often very difficult, especially if you are flat hunting from a distance.

1 *The neighbours* These may be just the other side of a thin partition. They may become firm friends and make your life—especially if you are out all day—much easier to manage. They could take in the milk, bring in the washing, sign for the coke, answer the telephone, etc., etc. On the other hand they may sing, play the cornet, or imitate pop singers for hours on end. Or worse still they may argue and shout at one another. Their chief food may seem to be garlic, the smell of which fills your flat. They may have a motor bike, large dog or a squalling baby. They may ignore you totally, or intrude upon your privacy at the slightest excuse, often beginning 'Can I borrow . . .?'

18 *Choose your flat carefully*

2 *Noises off* A recent television series was concerned with a charming country cottage, handed over by a rogue agent, late at night, at what seemed a bargain price. The early hours revealed that this cottage was on the end of a main runway, and each departing plane shook the little building to its very foundations. Of course only a comedian could fail to notice the presence of an entire aerodrome. But how busy and noisy is the road your intended flat is in—have you noticed? What sort of noise (and smell) does that factory next door make? Is it a bakery or printing works—hard at it all night—or does it make glue? If you are situated over a fish and chip shop are you ever going to be able to open your front windows in comfort? Do you overlook the backyard and 'gents' of the nearest public house? How near is the railway?

The final plunge

When, eventually, you consider buying a house or flat or maisonette of your own, all these considerations are even more important, and there are several others too you must think about. Because of the permanence of a bought home, and of the considerable expense

involved in selling a property, moving house and buying another—
as we shall see—you must be absolutely certain that the house you
are going to invest in is not only a sound investment but will be
somewhere where you are going to be really happy.

Buying a house

Girls are seldom, if ever, faced with the question of buying a house
on their own; it is nearly always with a husband. This purchase
will probably be the most important and the most expensive in
your lives. Take care and take time before you reach a decision.
Few people have enough money to buy a house outright, you
would need between £5,000 and £20,000 in cash to do this. The
cost of a house depends not only on its size, its design and its age
but also where it is situated. Those in London, or its commuter
districts, are usually the most expensive. Those at a popular holiday
resort are also expensive. On the whole the further you travel
north the less expensive property becomes. Age can also put value
on houses. Your tiny genuine Elizabethan cottage could well fetch
the same very high price as an ultra-modern architect-designed
house; or the same sort of price could be paid for a 3-4-storey
Georgian terraced house. Whereas the same sized house in
Victorian style could well be much cheaper, and the post-1918
terraced house would be cheaper still. Fashions in houses change.
The Mews cottages in London were once servants' quarters. Now
you have to be in the super-tax bracket to afford one! Recently
£8,500 was paid for a 3-bedroomed house in Enfield (10 miles from
London) and an almost identical one was priced at £5,500 in a
Nottingham suburb. Popular though Nottingham is, more people
wish to live near London, so up go the prices.

Buying outright

Sometimes middle-aged couples who have been paying off the
mortgage on a house for about 25 years find that they make the
final payment at about the time when their own family has grown
up and left home. Consequently, the house that has taken them so
long to pay for is now too large. In their position they can, if they
choose, sell their house and buy a smaller one outright. Sometimes
this is done by an elderly couple on retirement, who are no longer
tied to an area because of work commitments. Obviously, buying
a house outright is a very good thing. If you decide to rent a house,

say at £6 a week (and at that price it would not be a very big house), at the end of 25 years you will have paid your landlord £7,800. This is probably twice the value of the house, and at the end of all that time he still owns the property. So, if you can afford to, buy it. If you cannot afford to buy it outright you will have to pay interest on a loan for years and years. This interest, over such a long period, often costs the house purchaser double the original price of the house. For example—on a house costing £5,000, a 20% deposit of £1,000 was paid. The remainder, £4,000, was borrowed at an interest of 11% to be repaid monthly over a period of 25 years. The monthly repayments were about £39·21. The total cost could therefore be worked out like this:

$$£39·21 \times 12 \text{ (months)} \times 25 \text{ years}$$

So the total cost was in fact more than double the original price paid for the house. Loans repaid over 15 or 20 years would cost less of course. You can borrow a sum this size from several places, among them:

a building society,
a local authority,
an insurance company.

The payments are usually worked out in this way—if your weekly wage is £20 then it is considered that you will not be able to afford more than £8 a week as a mortgage repayment. Your husband's annual income must be two and a half times as great as the necessary repayments for you to be allowed a loan or a mortgage. If you and your husband are both working your joint salaries, or pay, may well be more than this, but very few societies will consider your joint income to be a *steady* income. They know by experience that most young wives soon give up their jobs as motherhood approaches. They also know that you will have rates to pay (see Chapter 11) and furniture to buy. All three will grant you a loan or mortgage in slightly different ways, but usually they make similar conditions before they grant the loan. Some societies take a quarter of a wife's income into consideration, when assessing an application for a loan.

Conditions of a mortgage

1 The title deeds (or deeds of ownership) of the property are held by the lenders until the debt is paid in full.

2 You sign a mortgage deed promising to pay off the debt. This deed lays down how much the repayment instalments are and when they are to be paid. It also states the amount of interest you will be paying on the loan. This can be between 10–15% per year.

3 You pay for the company's or authority's surveyor to carry out a survey and valuation of the property, to ascertain for them what the house is worth. It depends on his report how much the company will be prepared to lend you. If the house is over 40 years old, or if it is more modern, but in poor condition, you might only have a loan of 70% of the selling price. This survey will cost you £5–£10, and has no connection with the survey you should have had carried out on your own behalf. (See page 79.)

4 You must insure the house from the date of transfer against *all* accidents—that is, comprehensively.

5 You declare how much you earn and provide a reference from your employer to confirm the figure you have given. This is most important because the lender of the money must be sure that you are able to pay regular and substantial repayments on your house. This is usually required on a monthly basis.

How to set about home-finding

There are several ways of finding a suitable house:

1 Looking in the local or daily paper, or in weeklies such as *Dalton's Weekly* for privately advertised 'Houses for Sale'. The advertisements may have been inserted by the house owner, or by an agent.

2 Going to the area where you wish to live and looking for 'For Sale' notices. These may be stuck in the window by the house owner, or on boards outside—usually professional ones, put there by an estate agent who has been commissioned to sell the house.

3 Visiting the offices of an estate agent and instructing him to seek a suitable house for you. This will not cost *you* anything—the person who is selling the house pays the agent for this service. The usual charges are £25 for the first £500 of the selling price, £2·50 for each £100 of the next £4,500 and £1·50 per £100 for the

rest—that works out at a cost of £137·50 for selling a £5,000 house (+8% V.A.T.).

4 Buying a house at an auction. This is complicated. Always enquire first about the local conditions, and then go to a solicitor for advice.

Estate agents

Although I have called the notice put up by estate agents 'professional' this refers to the notice, and does not mean that the agents are necessarily qualified to buy or sell houses. At present anyone may set up in business and call himself an 'Estate Agent'. We hope this position will be changed before long, as do the many qualified surveyors and auctioneers who practise as estate agents. All qualified practitioners are members of one of the professional bodies—Chartered Auctioneers' and Estate Agents' Institute, R.I.C.S. or Royal Institution of Chartered Surveyors, the Land Agents' Society or the Incorporated Society of Auctioneers and Landed Property Agents. It is wiser to go to a qualified estate agent because he will have gained this status at the end of a period of training and he must observe the codes of behaviour laid down by the professional bodies. If he fails to do this you can appeal to them as they guarantee that their members will adhere to a strict code of conduct.

When you go to your estate agent he will want to know several facts:

1 How much can you afford to pay for the house?

2 In which area do you want to live? How many rooms do you need? Do you want a dining room *and* sitting room, or can this be a large combination room? How many bedrooms do you need, remembering that the average new house has 3 bedrooms? One more can put up the price by as much as £1,500.

3 What special features do you require—a garage, central heating, a downstairs toilet, a dining area in the kitchen? What sized garden do you hope for?

4 Do you mind if the house is in a row or terrace? Do you prefer it semi-detached with one adjoining neighbour, or completely detached and standing alone? The last type is usually the dearest.

Viewing

Examine the house that you have chosen to view very carefully. Besides all the things you looked for and asked about in a flat you must consider its structure, its aspect and its amenities. You will be wise to call in a surveyor. He may charge you about £35 for examining and valuing the house. If you ask for a brief examination you will get just this and a small bill. But it is probably better to ask for a really thorough one, mentioning different things you wish him to check, and you will be charged more. The examination will be very carefully carried out, for, should he make a mistake and miss a structural fault, especially one which you have particularly asked him to check, the surveyor knows you are legally entitled to claim damages against him.

Structure

In a new house the structure, that is the way it has been built, should be faultless. Many builders give a guarantee and if any faults appear during the first 6–24 months they will be repaired free of charge. In an old house there will probably be some faults. Some of these can easily be put right, others, however, mean that the house is just not worth buying. For example woodworm, woodrot or rising damp may be present. Such problems must be carefully identified and treated. A firm such as Rentokil Ltd., with offices throughout the country, has a team of advisers who will inspect any house, make a full report and give an estimate for any treatment needed. There is no charge for this and you are not obliged to take the advice given. But professional guidance may save you money because there is a form of woodworm that needs no treatment; damp walls are not always caused by rising damp; and wet rot and dry rot require different degrees of treatment. The charge for curing a small infestation of woodworm could be £50, a severe dry rot attack could cost several hundreds. So a free estimate is well worth having especially from a firm like Rentokil's who give a twenty-year guarantee on completion of their work.

However, problems such as cracks may mean ground subsidence. They may be only minor surface cracks or they could indicate that the house is built over a disused coal mine. You can check this by a visit to the local Land Registry Office.

The solicitor

Once you have chosen the house and had it surveyed and valued, you then offer the seller a price. This may be slightly lower than the one he has quoted. This may either be done directly, or through an estate agent, or a solicitor whom you have asked or instructed to act for you. If you are borrowing money from a large organisation, they will send a solicitor who can act on your behalf and theirs. This will save you a little in solicitor's fees, but you may prefer to have your own in any case. If your price is accepted you are then usually expected to pay a 10–20% deposit on it. Often there is room for some haggling. You may agree to the price asked if the house is first redecorated. Or you may offer £150 less, and end up by paying £75 less. Remember two things: you must immediately find at least a 10% deposit, say £500 for a £5,000 house; you must also find someone to lend you the balance, £4,500. No one will lend you this if the house has only been valued at £4,000. It must be worth the price you have agreed to pay.

Next a contract is drawn up between you and the seller. These contracts are complicated and both sides are wise to ask separate solicitors to act for them. This business often takes 6–8 weeks, but they are doing a job which should not be hurried. Your solicitor will want to ensure that the house is legally the property of the person who is selling it and will make him prove his ownership. He will also check, among many other things, whether the property is freehold or leasehold, whether there are road charges to pay, development plans for the area, who has the mineral rights and where the exact property boundaries lie. Neighbours have been known—when the owner of a house moves out and leaves it empty—to move the fence to give themselves a bit more land!

The seller's solicitor will want to know if you can raise the sum—let us say the £4,500—you have agreed to pay. You will have paid the 10% deposit of £500, so he is anxious about the £4,500 balance. When all the details have been thrashed out by the two solicitors the contract is drawn up and signed, and the house is said to be 'conveyed' from the one person to the other. Your solicitor then hands over the money to the seller's solicitor, who on a prearranged date hands over the keys and title deeds of the property to the new owner.

The new owner This is not really you, but the people from whom you have borrowed the balance of the purchase price—the £4,500. You get the keys and they get the title deeds.

How shall I ever afford it?

Just how much then do you need before you can take the first steps towards buying a property? These are very approximate figures for a house costing about £5,000:

	£
Your surveyor's fee	35·00
The mortgagor's surveyor's fee	7·50
The initial insurance premium	7·00
Your 10% deposit on £2,250	500·00
Your solicitor's fees (approximately)	67·50
	617·00

Extras

If to this you add nearly £300 for basic furniture you will see that you need about £1,000 to start a new home of your own. It is a great help if you come from a flat and already have some of your own furniture but there will probably still be curtains and stair carpets to buy. £300 is the *very* minimum you could start with if you have no furniture, even with wedding presents. The bill for one double bed and bedding, one wardrobe and dressing table, one bedroom rug and stair carpet, and curtains could easily come to £150. If you work out what you have and what you can save, you may well find that the outlook is not as depressing as it seems. I know several young people who very determinedly banked £3 each a week and in less than 2 years started to buy their new home. It was a struggle but it was worth while.

Further reading

Homes for Today and Tomorrow is available from Her Majesty's Stationery Office, Cornwall House, Stamford St., S.E.1, at 20p

The Law for Consumers, published by the Consumers' Association, 14 Buckingham St., W.C.2, at 40p

Your Own Home, by M. J. Joyce, published by Harrap and Co. Ltd., at 42½p

Value for Money, by Burman and Macnab, published by the National Savings Committee, is free on application to Alexandria House, W.C.2

Practical work

1 Look in the local paper under BOARD RESIDENCE or in a shop window which has a display notice board. Copy out any advertisements offering 'digs'. Compare those you have collected and see who offers the best value.

2 Rehearse a scene with a friend, one of you as 'landlady', the other as a prospective lodger. Inspect new 'digs' and ask appropriate questions. The class can criticise your efforts and another couple repeat the inspection with improvements.

3 Find out where you can obtain a list of vacant digs in your area. Ask how often these organisations are asked to help in this way.

4 Collect 'To Let' advertisements for rooms, houses and flats. Compare prices in various areas. Make a list of the abbreviations used and find out their meanings. For example: b/sit,—Kit./Bth. — Nov–Dec. — O.N.O. — S.A.E. (f) — p.w. — c.h.w. — Pt.Furn. —Sep W.C.—c.h. (70)—mod. cons. This will be useful. Here is an actual advertisement.

> 'Attrac. bed-sit, rm. priv. hse. ckg. facs. g & c.w. ch. no linen—.'

5 Take a look round your neighbourhood. Which streets would you avoid living in and why? Which factories or shops would you rather be well away from? What else have you locally that you would rather avoid—a sewage farm, a gasometer? Let each girl in the class find something in the area that she would avoid—if possible go there and ask the local residents how they feel about it. Then report to the class.

6 Now look for the 'desirable areas'. Where would you buy a house in your own locality? Now check in the paper for the cost of houses in that area, compared with those in other areas. Try to account for the different prices in areas you know. What is the difference in price and meaning between freehold and leasehold?

7 Take a 'For Sale' advertisement. Try to guess the location of the house. Who seems to have the best bargain? Which adverts would make you go and look at the house—and why?

8   Several types of architecture have been mentioned. Find out what is meant by a Georgian house. How can it be recognised? Have you any in your neighbourhood? Repeat this hunt and observation for:

A Regency house
An early Victorian house
A late Victorian house
A 'Post-War' house (which war?)
A contemporary house (what *does* this mean?)
A 'Pre-Fab'
A terraced house

9   Go to an estate agent's office (pick a time when they are not busy). Ask for a leaflet for the class to see showing mortgage repayment figures. If they cannot spare you one write to a building society for one. See how many building societies the class can name.

10   Find out what is meant by the 'aspect' of a house? What are 'amenities'? Think of a family, jot down its members, and consider which amentities each would need. Find out if your locality is in a 'smokeless zone'. What exactly does this mean?

Questions

1   Prepare an advertisement to send to a local paper for digs. Write the covering letter explaining that you require a box number at 9p and work out the cost at 4p a word.

2   You have lived away from home for a year. Write to your mother explaining why you have left your digs and moved into a hostel. Tell her all about the hostel.

3   You have just seen this advert:

> 'Regent's Park/Camden Town: girl to share s/c
> flat with 4 others and 2 cats. Rent less than £5 p.w.
> incl. Phone: 123 8749'

You are interested. How would you set about making sure you would be happy in this rather crowded flat?

4   You have been offered an unfurnished flat and must make a quick decision without viewing it because it is so far away. Write to

the landlord asking about the points it is essential to know. Your husband dislikes gardening and you have a baby and a toddler.

5 Your husband has died recently and you have decided to take in two girl lodgers. Your income is £15 a week and your house repayments and rates are £9 a week. How much would you charge them for separate bedrooms and a room (with fire) of their own downstairs. Draw up a list of rules you would want them to observe while living in your very much loved home.

6 You, your husband and two small boys, plus 1 dog and 2 goldfish, are driving round looking for a house to buy. Exactly what sort of house would you look for, how big, what extras, and near which amenities?

7 Having stated the area the house is in, suggest a price for the one you would like. How much extra money would you need to buy it, as well as the purchase price? What is this extra money needed for—you already have all the furniture you require?

8 Look at the job plan on page 71. Is this entirely satisfactory? Suggest ways of altering it.

CHAPTER 5 · GETTING ON WITH PEOPLE

Friends and neighbours

These are the people whose companionship brings you happiness. If you are lucky, and if you give as much as you take, you will find friends within your family. If you are very lucky, and deserve such luck, you will find friends outside as well as inside your home—and not just the neighbours either!

The family

It is easier, of course, to find friends at home because they are always there—mother, father, sisters and brothers at your own doorstep. But it is sometimes hard to appreciate just what good friends your family can be to you. We either take them for granted, or we are so busy resenting their interference with our hopes and schemes that we forget it is possible that they may sometimes be right and we may be wrong! Your family is the last to desert you in times of real trouble—and this surely is one of the first tests of friendship.

All families have some common interest, even if it is only sharing the same meal table. Many families enjoy the ideal link of affection and mutual respect. A few, unfortunately, interpret the idea of a family tie as a family bond. Such families stick together through a sense of duty rather than through love, and duty is a very poor adhesive! For one thing, people seldom agree about what such a duty actually means, let alone how it should be acted upon.

Communication

When we are small we tell our parents everything. We usually tell our mothers because they are there most of the time. Each finger that is squashed is kissed better, and each snub received by a family member is explained away if possible, or else looked into! As we grow up we confide less and less—and this is good because it shows we are growing up and becoming independent. But we must not forget the good common sense of seeking advice and consolation. We must not be too proud to admit that others often know

19 *Television—the hostile intruder*

more about solving our problems than we do. And we, too, must be ready to help sometimes if we are turned to in this way, and we should listen patiently and act generously. This two-way exchange of advice and opinion, helpfulness and affection, is the basis for security within the family. Each member knows where to turn, and what to expect. This is also important when there is owning up to do. It is easier if you know you will get a fair hearing, and a just punishment or rebuke. It helps you to be honest, and so be respected, loved and secure. Unfortunately this sort of family communication sometimes breaks down, and conversations become trivial and superficial. Often there are long uncomfortable silences because the family members sheer away from discussing important things. Then the silences become accepted and usual, and often television hides just how long and empty they are. Things that must be said—'Where have you been?' or 'Who with?' or 'Do you know what time it is?' when you come in late—cut like a knife if they are the only things that have been said to you all day. This sort of feeling in a family causes great unhappiness, so before you start to think about a family of your own, you must try to remember what causes such unhappiness and how it can be avoided.

When things go wrong

Usually there are faults on both sides, but the beginnings of lack of communication in a family often go back right into early childhood. The parents must ask themselves if they were ever too busy to answer their children's questions, too busy to listen to endless tales of woe, too occupied with other things to give comfort when it was needed. Was television ever put first, or talking to a neighbour, or going out for the evening? I have seen a toddler out shopping with his mother, and desperately trying to attract attention. But she had just met a neighbour who had a bit of gossip to relate. By the time what Mrs. X had said to Mr. Y about Miss Z had been gasped over, a small puddle had appeared between the shoes of a little damp and dejected scrap who never got the chance to say 'Toilet'. It is obvious to children that there is no point in trying to talk when you are not listened to. It becomes equally obvious that if the only answer you get is, 'Not now—perhaps later!' or 'Tell me about it tomorrow', it's useless unless parents *mean* what they say. It is equally useless to try to communicate troubles, if promises of help are made and the help never materialises. How many children are fobbed off with 'I'll get your Dad to see to it when he comes home!' or 'I'll give them such a piece of my mind, one of these days!'

20   *Too occupied to listen*

Always two sides

I am sure that most of these parents mean what they say when they say it—but they forget. They forget two other things as well: that they are not being strictly honest with their children, and that little things, though trivial to them, may be very important to you. You, on the other hand, must, as you grow older, make sure that your complaints are important. Do not make your parents look foolish by making a fuss over something which turns out to have been your fault. They may not back you up next time. Try to attract their attention at a sensible time, *not* in the middle of the football results, the news or a favourite TV serial. Try not to ruin their evening out by raising an issue then and there, which could have been left until the next day. Finally, do not ask the impossible of them—remember, they are human too.

Your friends

It is easier to entertain your friends if you feel free to bring them home, to introduce them to your family, and to gain your parents' interest in them and approval of them. Your first childhood friends are usually the nearest toddlers in the neighbourhood—the children of your mother's friends or your neighbours. Until the age of five it is important to a small child to have *somebody* to play with, *who* that is does not matter.

At school you have more of an opportunity to choose your friends. Usually you find a group with whom you have something in common—shared hobbies, similar tastes, mutual interests. Out of this group you may find one or two who seem special in one way or other. You may travel on the same bus with them, sit next to them in school, or be in the same team. This gives you the chance of really getting to know them and to like them.

Try to make friends slowly. Our first impressions of people are often wrong. Do not pledge eternal friendship to someone you cannot stand the sight of a week later! But remember your new friend will also be trying to get to know you. Many young people are plagued with shyness, and the best way to get over this is to ask yourself honestly what shyness is. You become shy because you imagine that all eyes are on you, and all ears are waiting for you to speak. Now why should you imagine this, unless you also imagine that there is something so special about you that you will automatically command all this attention?

Shyness

In other words shyness is often a form of conceit. Recognise it as such—remember you are not all that important. Very few people will stare at you, so there is really nothing to be shy about. I know it is not easy to overcome shyness, but it helps to be honest about it. Once you have made friends life is easier. They are your escape valve. You can let off steam, tell them your troubles. Your plans and schemes will not seem nearly as hair-brained to your friends as they often seem to your parents, because your friends are as inexperienced as you are. Remember that Marie Curie's decision to become a scientist was regarded as a hair-brained scheme by her parents. What a blessing for the world that she received encouragement from other people, most of all from her friend Pierre, who was later to be her husband!

Again, give and take

Friendships must never be one-sided; the two-way exchange is just as important here. You must be as good a listener as you are a talker. Remember your friend's troubles are as important to her as yours are to you. It is strange how often we are better mannered to strangers than we are to our friends or to our family. This is sad if we really value their friendship. Try to be:

1 Loyal—do not tell, or listen to tales.

2 Sympathetic—really try to put yourself in their place when they are in trouble, and act accordingly.

3 Honest—if your friends cannot rely on your words and behaviour, they will not value and respect you for long.

4 Good fun—you will never again be as free of responsibilities—make the most of it!

5 Considerate—do not have your fun at the expense of your friends, or anybody else.

6 Punctual—are you often late? This is a form of conceit—why should you expect others to wait for you?

The older generation

For a time you and your friends have to live in a world where adults have the last word. As you get nearer and nearer the almost grown-up stage yourself, this gets harder and harder to bear. Adults nearly always think they know best—and what is so really infuriating is that some of the time they are right. But times and fashions change, and the outlooks of two generations are bound to differ.

Often we are prepared to accept the opinions of teachers, youth leaders, politicians and clergymen, and yet reject those of our parents. This is partly because we know of the proper qualifications of these outsiders; we probably see only the sides of their characters that they choose to show us, and we do not see enough of them to know them well. But because we see our parents making mistakes we know that in many ways they are fallible. We tend to forget all the mistakes they avoid. We may have learnt a foreign language or a mathematical subject they know nothing about, and this makes us feel vastly superior. But just you try tackling your father's job, or organising the home for a week while your mother is ill, and you'll soon get a fairer picture of their abilities. Try to respect your parents' opinions in the same way you hope they will respect yours. *Talk* out differences, try not to *shout* them out. You will find some common ground somewhere if you look hard and carefully enough. Later, when we are discussing marriage and children, you will see what a difficult job it is to be a successful parent. For now —listen, sift many ideas and learn from them.

Sharing the home

If it is possible to bring your friends home, your parents will have the reassurance of knowing who you are with, and what they are like. But they will not want their home taken over by a bunch of noisy youngsters. Be considerate—is there anywhere but the living room where you can play your records and gossip? You will get along far better if you are not under their feet, or on their nerves the whole time. If there is only one living room, perhaps you could have your friends in on a regular planned-for evening. On such an evening show that you can be trusted. Do not show off, or treat your home as a café, leaving dirty dishes and a mess in every corner. If you prove you can be trusted your parents may leave you to yourselves occasionally, but such arrangements do not just happen, they must be planned for.

Planned routines

This sounds dull—fears of rules and regulations arise—but nothing could be further from the truth. If you plan, you get things done in a more orderly way, and this nearly always means you are quicker and more efficient. This will leave you with more—not less —freedom for leisure, for doing the things you want to do once the chores are over.

The role of the host or hostess

This will be, inevitably, your role from time to time: how will you cope? How ought you to approach the entertaining of your friends in your own home either for the first time or on a more formal occasion? Basically the fundamental need is for consideration, but who are you considering? Although, it may sound selfish, you will put yourself first, for we all need companionship, then your guests and those who share your home. To enhance your friendships, you will want to make your guests happy so that they will want to visit you again and perhaps to share their home with you. Perhaps some of the following points will help you to achieve this.

1 Make your invitation definite, stating the time, day and place and making it clear which meals you intend to provide. Be sure that they know how to find your home and which 'bus or tube station is near by. 'Drop in any time' is all very well if you really mean it, but new friends will probably be far too unsure of themselves ever to do this.

2 Be on hand ready to receive your friends and make sure the part of the house or garden you are taking them to will give them the sort of impression you had hoped for. This may be one of casualness and informality or of impeccable tidyness and precision. It should honestly reflect the sort of person you are and at the same time have something in common with what they are used to.

3 Think of the seemingly trivial necessities that help your guests to relax. Where will they hang their coats, tidy their hair, visit the 'loo' and wash their hands? Try to indicate these details without making a thing about it.

4 Make sure that the entertainment you provide, or the food and drink you have prepared isn't too 'way out'. You could cause great embarrassment to a Jewish friend if you served pork chops or to most Hindus if there was no alternative to meat. In fact most very highly seasoned or spiced foods are better left until you are sure of your guests' tastes. Some folk can't bear card games or would be really afraid of your large dog. Some are allergic to cats or caged birds and would be bored to death with your holiday slides! When entertaining a group who know one another very well, your problems are few, but if several are strangers be sure you introduce them to friends with whom they have something in common. For a group who only know one another slightly, it may be a good idea to have some sort of entertainment 'up your sleeve'—competitions, dancing, treasure hunts, etc. As you mature, drinks, eats, background music, somewhere to relax, and lots and lots of interesting talk usually more than fill an evening.

5 If the home you invite them to is yours and your parents', a few extra considerations are worth a thought. You may be putting

your mother to special expense, shopping and cooking, so perhaps there is some gesture you can make in return. Certainly don't forget to say 'thank you' and let's hope your guests will too if it's sincere.

6 Far more formal occasions, a birthday or engagement party, a written invitation is a help. If some guests arrive with presents while others were unaware of the occasion, this can cause embarrassment.

7 If several presents arrive together make a quick note of who gave what. Then you can say or write a special thank you later.

8 Your very close friends in the group will usually be happy to stay behind to help to clear and wash up—provided you cheerfully join in with the chores at their homes. Students are usually marvellous about this.

9 Finally, 'be yourself'. Airs and graces, the sudden appearance of silver and linen and pastry forks, when you are more at home with beakers and buns, causes awful tensions. It's you and your welcome that counts.

Leisure

The teenager, young wife or mother who has no routine often ends up with last-minute rushes, jobs left undone and little time left for pleasure. Shorter working hours have increased the leisure of those who go out to work. Labour-saving equipment has increased the leisure of those who run the home. This leisure must not be frittered away, it is far too important for that. It is the time in which to have fun. Let us make the most of it. Planning can help even here.

Leisure, let us make the most of it

The job which occupies most of our time may be going to school, going out to work or running a home. The time we have free from these duties is our leisure time. There are several uses we can make of it:

1 We can use it for sheer enjoyment, visiting a cinema or theatre, dancing, walking, reading or having a party.

2 We can use it to earn pocket money. Many girls work on

Saturdays, or baby-sit in the evenings. Both boys and girls deliver the nation's newspapers morning and evening.

3 Some jobs which have to be done can either be skimped through or made more of and enjoyed. The shampoo and set evening, or home perm occasion can also be a make, do and mend evening shared with a friend.

4 *Hobbies*, such as knitting, dressmaking, gardening or painting, are enjoyed, for the pleasure of doing something creative.

5 *Further education.* This is the extension of a hobby. Under skilled instruction you might learn a language ready for a holiday abroad, take up pottery or have a go at 'keeping fit'. 'F.E.' classes are really intended for people who have left full-time education. But, as the classes are often held in the schools and by the teachers you know well anyway, many pupils approaching school-leaving age are allowed to attend. In some cases they are encouraged to do this to help them bridge the difficult gap between school and work, the F.E. classes being a mainstay of continuity, and to help maintain the habit of learning.

Uses of F.E. The classes can be regarded either in the nature of a hobby or they can be used as a stepping stone towards some form of higher education such as G.C.E., Technical Diplomas or City and Guilds' examinations, which can, in turn, be used as a stepping stone to a more rewarding career.

How can you find out what classes are available to you in your area? Go or write to your Local Education Authority or your Youth Employment Officer. If you are still at school your careers teacher will probably be able to advise you.

6 You could take part in *social services*, and do something for the community. This use of leisure often brings more satisfaction than seeking pleasure for its own sake. A list of suggestions for serving the community appears at the end of this chapter.

Probably the best plan is to divide your leisure time between some of these suggestions. Of course, you must put your homework and your share of keeping the home running smoothly before your leisure activities.

The money you can earn on an early morning paper round is useful, but not if it leaves you too tired to enjoy your leisure in the evenings and at weekends. It is even worse if your 6 a.m. rise

LEISURE

21 *A blind and deaf shopper gets a special market report tapped out on her hand by her cadet escort*

makes you sleepy until dinner time, when you revive again. Your failure to concentrate during those early lessons will reduce your interest in each subject because you will always be a bit behind and struggling to catch up. This could make such a difference to examination results that you lose your chance to *choose* a job; instead you are pushed into one, and for the rest of your life your earning power may be lessened through lack of qualifications. You will have gained pennies in your teens but lost pounds and pleasure in your job for later years.

Many firms are glad to have a girl to serve as an extra counter-hand on Saturday. The money you earn may be needed by your family, or it may be the only pocket money you would otherwise get, but be sure that you are really making the most of your Saturdays. Are you missing school outings, hockey or netball matches, weekends away with the Youth Hostel Association? You may be working on Saturdays for the rest of your life—is it essential for you to do so now?

When you baby-sit for a neighbour at 25p an hour do you still get your homework done, and what about your bedtime? I hope in any case your parents get first choice—remember how many years they baby-sat for you! You do not owe them anything just because they are your parents, but you owe them for every spontaneous loving thing they have ever done for you. If they are going out, do something extra to make their outing pleasurable. Press your sister's blouse if she has got a special date, and polish your brother's buttons if he is late to cadets. Then when it is your big occasion they will rally round you. What we get out of life depends very much on what we put into it.

Club activities

It is always more fun if you have friends to share your leisure with. Should you just have moved to a new district you may be a little lost and lonely. You will find there are organisations which will not only help you to meet friends but which will have a variety of leisure activities laid on for you. There are Scouts and Guides, Youth Clubs, Junior Red Cross, Boys' Brigade, Clubs of all kinds —Camping, Cycling, Youth Hostelling, Rambling Associations, Evening Institutes, etc. The address of the headquarters of some of these is at the end of the chapter. Write to the headquarters for the address of your nearest branch, if you are interested.

Later on you may find yourself forming a new group in a club to follow a pursuit you are specially interested in. I remember once asking a club leader, 'Are you interested in debates?' He said, 'No, are you?' When I said 'Yes', he replied—'Right, form a debating group, 7 p.m. Thursday nights in the small hall. I'll be along next week—start them with "Men are the weaker sex!"—that'll get them arguing'—and it did! Gradually you become a helper and a leader and you get twice as much fun because you're giving as well as getting.

Serving the community

So it is with social service, it sounds dull, but it is a real challenge. We are always sorry for old people, alone and on a small income. But sorrow is no help. How can we help? Dig pensioners' gardens, clear snow, bring in coal, chop wood, read the paper, do the errands

—just for a start. How can we help the overworked young mother with several infants under 5? Take the youngsters for walks, read to them, clean windows, knit, baby-sit, do the shopping.

What about your town park, market-place, local beauty spot or war memorial? Young people will always be blamed first, usually quite unfairly, if these places look untidy. Why not turn the tables, form a little squad and ask the local authority if you can clear them up? Thirty minutes once a week should do it if there are enough of you! If you *really* want to help, you have only to look round. There are jobs to be done by the hundred, and each one quietly and efficiently completed makes you just that little bit warmer and happier inside—makes life just that much more worth living.

Addresses

Boy Scouts } Imperial Headquarters, Buckingham Palace
Girl Guides } Road, London, S.W.1

National Association of Boys' Clubs, 17 Bedford Square, London, W.C.1

National Association of Youth Clubs, 32 Devonshire St., London, W.C.2

Youth Hostels Association, 29 John Adam St., London, W.C.2

Cyclists Touring Club, 3 Craven Hill, London, W.2

The Camping Club of Great Britain and Ireland, 35 Old Kent Road, London, S.E.1

Evening Institutes, c/o your Local Education Authority

Further reading

Your Holidays, by Pamela Carmichael, and *Your Friends*, by Gilda Lund, are published in the 'Modern Living' series by Longmans, Green and Co. Ltd. in paperback at 37½p

Y.H.A. Literature is obtainable from Trevelyan House, St. Albans, Hertfordshire

Practical work

1 Draw up a list of all the friends you can remember making since childhood. Notice how they form a pattern. Try to account

for the reasons why the friendship was formed and why it was either long- or short-lived. Learn from your conclusions!

2 Decide which girl or boy in your class you would like to form a lasting friendship with. Apart from looks (not grooming which you can do something about!) list the qualities which make you want this friendship. Without naming your 'hoped-for' friend (call them X) compare lists with your class-mates. How do *you* measure up to these desirable qualities?

3 Analyse the way you use your leisure time and compare it with your friends.

(*a*) How many hours per week of leisure time do you get?

(*b*) How do you use it? How much is spent on doing something positive and how much is frittered away? (Never consider such activities as reading, just thinking, looking at pictures or the countryside, or watching TV programmes you have *chosen*, a waste of time.)

(*c*) How much of your positively used time is spent on something unselfish?

4 Repeat the last analysis with your mother's leisure time—does she get as much as she deserves?

5 Go to your Town Hall, local clergyman, Police Station or Citizens' Advice Bureau and seek their help with suggestions for community service. If you want to tidy up the town park, see the superintendent first. Ask if, by doing this work, you will not be depriving someone who needs money of a paid job.

6 Go to your Department of Health and Social Security *or* local branch of the Women's Voluntary Service *or* the social worker at your local hospital *or* the Home Help Service organiser and find out where there are people in need, and how you can help them. If you have none of these organisations, see your local clergyman or policeman. They will help.

Questions

1 Make a list now—before you forget—of all the small things that have irritated you as a small child, and of the things which annoy you now in home routine (e.g. inflexible meal times, failure to see

eye to eye on various topics, receiving 'No' for an answer before you have had time to explain, etc.).

2 Study your list a week later and cross out anything that now looks exaggerated. Now try to account for the irritations. Are you partly to blame? For example, are you always late for meals no matter what time they have been carefully prepared for? When you have finally drawn up a list of fair complaints, should the opportunity to air them arise, do so *tactfully*. More important, keep the list carefully until you have a family of your own. Then study it—are you making the same mistakes? Or is what you once thought to be a mistake, just common sense?

3 Make a list of *what is going on* in your locality to help you to make enjoyable use of your leisure time. Study your local paper and consult any other places where such information is given, e.g. the Public Library. Now make a list of what will be available when you have left school.

4 Write an essay on 'Leisure—how I use it'. Remember to say why you enjoy the various activities you have chosen.

5 Make notes on 'Hobbies from 5–15'. See how your hobbies have changed and try to explain why.

6 *Community service* To Serve or Not To Serve? What is there in it for *you*, or is there another way of looking at this? Collect your thoughts and write an essay on this subject.

7 You are inviting two old school friends and one new college friend to supper. Your mother has a full-time job and she and your father will be out on the evening in question. Show fully how you would plan your evening.

CHAPTER 6 · THE HOUSE (1)

This section is largely concerned with you as a housewife with a home of your own. What a horrible word 'housewife' is—the inference being that you are married to the house, tied and committed to it. Many women still are, very many used to be. But nowadays if the work and running of the house dominates our lives it is probably for one of two reasons: (1) we are not organised; or (2) we choose to be dominated by housework.

There was a time when women spent most of their lives in the kitchen or wash-house because they had to. Their coal fires continually needed stoking, every drop of hot water they used had to be boiled, every speck of dust was removed by hand, washing, boiling, starching and ironing was carried out under the most difficult circumstances. It is obvious why and how all this has changed.

Today, although we still spend much of our working day in the kitchen, it is now a comparatively short working day.

Strangely enough this release from chores has left some women with a sense of loss. They feel guilty if the work takes 2 hours instead of 4. The doorstep no longer needs scrubbing, stainless steel has saved hours of cleaning and polishing. Often they deliberately *choose* a floor covering which will commit them to hours of polishing. If this brings them happiness and satisfaction, all is well, providing the rest of the family are not made to suffer by their self indulgence. It can be heartbreaking when, after you've spent hours polishing the hall, the children dash in with muddy boots, or your husband forgets to wipe his feet. But are your priorities right? They've come rushing home to see you, not the shine on your tiles!

Don't feel guilty; never mind if your older relatives or neighbours say, 'In my day . . .' If you've finished and are out by 10.30 a.m. enjoying the sunshine, well done, you're a credit to *your* day and age!

The fact remains that 75% of your working day is spent in the kitchen. It's largely up to you how long that working day turns out to be. Get your attitude to housework clear, right from the start. If you hate housework, finish it as soon as possible. It can even be fun competing with yourself to complete it. Then you'll have time to spare for flower decorations, gay arrangements and potted plants. Gradually the housework becomes less of a chore. You can even come to like it, because a clean, fresh, sweet-smelling house is the best background for your children to develop in, and your husband to come home to. You'll open the door proudly to greet your callers, you'll be happy and your life will be the richer. Your success in getting the housework done largely depends on the time you get up! It's no good my trying to make a timetable out for anyone. Doing the fires may mean 10–15 minutes coping with ashes, firelighters, wood and coal, or just a few seconds to turn on a switch. Let us consider which jobs have to be done daily and which less often.

Looking after the family, checking on their health, sparing time for play, reading with them, listening to them, feeding them and yourself are *hourly chores*.

Daily chores

These consist of cleaning any rooms used *daily*. This means:

1. living room
2. kitchen
3. occupied bedrooms
4. hall (up and down)
5. stairs
6. bathroom
7. lavatory
8. dining alcove or room, or playroom, etc.

How much you do to each depends on your own standards, how much the rooms have been used, and special priorities such as hygiene and sanitation.

The daily cleaning of the kitchen, especially the sink, the bathroom and the lavatory is most important.

Weekly chores

We usually either think of doing a job daily or weekly. There is no reason to be bound by this. In fact, I am not at all sure that cleaning the main rooms thoroughly once or more a week is a good idea. Often we set ourselves a routine: washing—Mondays,

22 *Don't let routine dominate your life*

ironing—Tuesdays, upstairs—Wednesdays, downstairs—Thursdays, Big Bake and Shopping—Fridays. But it may rain on Monday and so you will not be ready to iron on Tuesday and various other incidents may upset the routine. Do not follow a routine merely out of habit. Also while you have all the cleaning tackle out for the thorough cleaning session, it may well be more sensible to vacuum the whole house while you are on the job, do the polishing or paint wiping throughout while those cloths, cleaners, etc., are out. Clean *all* the windows while that equipment is in use and not just those of the room you are cleaning. Experiment, see what suits you best and get on with it. Remember though that the cleaning of the house is only one part of half a dozen such essential jobs. Here are some more:

Shopping

Mending

Constructive work: dressmaking, knitting, gardening, decorating

Odd jobs: disinfecting drains, turning out cupboards, putting up hooks

Repairs: mending fuses, tightening screws

The right equipment

This is not necessarily the most expensive equipment but that which, if chosen carefully, can save time and energy. When choosing it remember that your feet, legs and back take most of the strain of running a house. Anything you can do, or any equipment you can buy to lessen the causes of such strain, is worth having. Don't stand to do any job you can do adequately while sitting. For example, have a kitchen stool the right height for sitting at a sink, at a working surface or an ironing board. Without this, it is not surprising that many housewives suffer from varicose veins and back ache. They also get tired and depressed through steaminess and stuffiness in their kitchens. Put in a ventilator, or draught-proof window, and have good heating. You can buy new equipment but not a new back, lungs or pair of legs! Be selfish for once and think of yourself, and the whole family will benefit from your cheerfulness on their return.

The three main nuisances to a housewife are dust, dirt and grease.

(a) *Dust* This fine powder is brought in by fresh air and draughts. Sometimes it is lighter than air and settles readily on high ledges, tops of doors and light shades. Because it is merely a light powder it can be easily removed, provided the surface it comes to rest on is clean, and not sticky or greasy. What is this powder? It contains tiny particles of many substances, including soot, fibres, ashes, hair, garden soil, spores of yeast, moulds and bacteria.

To collect dust The most effective way is by suction, using a vacuum cleaner with a dusting brush on the end. If you merely use a duster, especially if it is made of feathers, you often simply disperse the dust by spreading it around more thinly so that it hardly shows! A slightly damp duster will be more effective especially if you are careful to gather up what you have collected. Always start from floor level and work *up* because as you disturb dust it flies *up* (dirt is just the opposite). A suction cleaner will suck in and trap the dust as it is disturbed, so you can work from whichever level you like. Originally vacuum cleaners were made just to clean the floor, today in home after home they are just used to do this. Tucked under the stairs and never used is a box of tools which would cut down the housewife's labour if only she would familiarise herself with them. The dusting appliance is particularly useful because it is so efficient. It takes less time to flick round the house with the duster, but you'll need to do this every day (or twice on some days) because you are disturbing, not collecting, dust. A thorough trip round all your surfaces and ledges with the suction cleaner will really *remove* the dust. Wrap up the collected dust and put it in the dustbin. Don't ever shake your dusters, mops, brooms and brushes out of the window; the dust will either fly straight back into your window, or a neighbour's.

(b) *Dirt* Don't confuse this with garden soil, though some soil may become entangled with it. Dirt is dust combined with grease. The combination is a fine breeding ground for bacteria. To get rid of dirt effectively you must get rid of the grease which makes it cling. A simple illustration is the washing of dirty hands. The best method is to use warm water to melt the grease, then a soap which emulsifies the grease, holding it in suspension in the water and trapping each particle in a tiny soap envelope. Finally a warm rinse to get rid of it altogether. Away with the grease goes the dirt. Unfortunately it doesn't all go down the drain. Grease floats and as the water level goes down it coats the sides of the wash basin. You see this clearly in the bath. When the emulsified grease and its clinging dirt floats on top of your water, you splash it to the sides and a ring of dirt settles round your bath. But when you have a bubble bath you introduce a *detergent* into the water. This dissolves the grease, it doesn't just emulsify it or hold it in suspension. So down the drain goes the grease and dirt with the detergent and water—you'll find no ring round your bath. However, this doesn't mean that detergents are necessarily better than soap powders for doing the week's washing. You must consider the effect of the powder on the material. When the magazine *Which?* (see Ch. 1) conducted a washing-powder test it was a soap powder, *Persil*, which emerged as top of its class!

For household cleaning purposes, paint cleaning and washing up, etc., detergents are very effective.

(c) *Grease* This must be washed away in very hot water. Once washed away, the sink too must be thoroughly flushed with hot soda, or sudsy water, so that the grease will not reform and solidify, blocking the U-bend in the drainage pipe.

The purpose of starching clothes and polishing surfaces is to form hard shiny finishes on which dust, dirt and grease cannot easily settle. Remember this when you study floor, wall and working-surface finishes.

Equipment for the removal of dust, dirt and grease

1 *Dusters* The best materials for dusters are those which do not leave fluff on uneven surfaces, as, for example, knitted wool does, or have a hard and shiny surface like nylon or rayon which does not pick up dust.

2 *Polishing cloths* Soft, clean remnants will do for this. Some can be bought impregnated with polish. These are quick and useful but dear, and they run out of polish.

3 *'Spongy' cloths* Spongy cloths make good dusters, house cloths and dishcloths. They are usually made of cellulose or foamy plastic. Their big advantage is that all the bits can be quickly rinsed out and they remain fresh. The old net and knitted dishcloths often trap the bits in. A quick rinse in bleach disinfects cellulose and keeps it a good colour, whereas cloth dishcloths need frequent boiling.

4 *Brushes* In addition to personal brushes such as shoe, hair, tooth, nail, bath and clothes brushes others are needed:

(*a*) a scrubbing brush
(*b*) a lavatory brush
(*c*) a yard broom

THE REMOVAL OF DUST, DIRT AND GREASE

(*d*) a soft sweeping brush (if you haven't the appropriate attachments on your suction cleaner)

(*e*) a soft hand brush if possible to clip on to your dustpan so that the two stay together

(*f*) a stiff hand brush for brushing the door mats

(*g*) a long handled, very soft dusting and cob-web brush (if your suction cleaner is not fitted appropriately) for ceilings and the tops of walls

(*h*) a hearth brush (if you have fires)

(*i*) a flue brush (if you have fires)

(*j*) blackleading brushes

(*k*) a washing-up brush

(*l*) a vegetable brush for celery and potatoes

5 *A dustpan* The plastic ones are cheap, bright, light and gay. Be sure they have a firm edge absolutely flush with the floor. Never put hot ashes in them.

6 *Mops*

(i) *Dusting*—not very efficient, but saves undue bending.

(ii) *Washing-up*—most effective are the spongy ones in a plastic or a rustless metal ring holder.

(iii) *Floor cleaning*—the old cotton-headed mops are dying out as they are difficult to wash and dry. Those made of self-wringing cellulose sponge are now popular, effective and labour saving. Be sure always to wash, rinse and wring them out before putting them away.

7 *Vacuum cleaners* These save labour rather than time. A fan creates a draught which sucks in air, and with it the dirt and dust. Some machines beat the carpets as they clean, though this is useful only if it loosens dirt. The dirt is collected in a bag which can be emptied or thrown away and replaced. Vacuum cleaners can also be used for a variety of jobs. They help you to shampoo carpets and blow warm air under to help with the drying, to spray paint and to clean high or low, upholstery or curtains. You can also buy polishing attachments, or separate electric polishers. There are also small hand suction cleaners.

8 *Carpet sweepers* These are non-electric. They will actually pick up *bits* more efficiently than most vacuum cleaners, but they are not nearly as efficient at collecting dust and dirt and they will only clean carpets.

Doing the washing

This used to be a weekly chore, traditionally carried out each Monday. However, the advent of washing machines, launderettes and the full-time working wife has changed all this. Often the washing is done at weekends either at home or in the launderette, or even through the night in an automatic washing machine. But for the mother with small or growing children, several washes per week will be necessary. Often this is made more difficult because not many women understand the washing process, or are aware of the short cuts which can be taken.

Choice of machine

The two main types are twin-tubs and automatic machines.

Twin-tub machines are a combination of washer and spin-drier. They load from the top and have to be constantly supervised and controlled. Some will heat the water and boil garments if necessary. The washing action is by an agitator or a pulsator. They cost from about £60 to £100.

Automatic washing machines These can be loaded from the front or the top and, once loaded, a programme chosen to suit the type of garment, fabric and degree of soilage is selected. Once programmed the machine will carry out the whole washing, rinsing and spinning process. Some will also tumble-dry the clothes. They cost from £90 to £200. They should be plumbed in if at all possible.

Choice of washing powders

1 *The washing water* Before choosing you should have some idea of how hard the water is in your area. Some areas such as Suffolk, Norfolk and Essex have very hard water. Others such as Devon, Wales and Cornwall have soft water. What does this mean? Temporary hardness disappears if the water is boiled and the soluble chemicals in it are deposited. Notice the inside of a kettle. The 'fur' is a deposit of calcium or magnesium bicarbonate. Permanent hardness is more difficult to deal with, it is caused by soluble salts, and can cause an unpleasant grey scum which hinders the washing and discolours whites. Washing soda or extra soap or detergent can counteract this.

2 *The type of machine* Special powders are made for automatic machines which are low on suds.

3 *The types and colours of fabrics to be washed* Most clothes have a care label sewn in to advise on the appropriate washing method (see Chapter 1) and may have colour-fast dyes but there are always exceptions. Any doubtful colour should be tested between two pieces of wet cotton (an old white hankie will do) with a warm iron. Care should also be taken to identify the fabric and then the appropriate washing process followed.

Main groups of washing powders

1 Soap products such as flakes or powders, e.g. Persil or Fairy Snow.

2 Detergents of varying strengths such as Surf, Tide and Daz (strong), Stergene or Dreft (gentle).

3 Mixtures of soap and detergents with biological action, Radiant, Omo.

4 Low suds powders for automatic machines such as Persil Automatic or Bold.

Pre-washing action

1 Sort out the garments, note the instructions on the care labels, test for colour running, identify unlabelled fabrics and put in piles with similar degrees of dirtiness and similar processes.

2 Empty pockets, do up zips and mend first if necessary.

3 Remove stains (see removal chart).

4 Set aside the garments which must be washed by hand.

5 Soak or steep heavily stained articles. If articles are soaked they must be completely covered by the water. Read the instructions on the packets of any powder used to aid soaking, e.g. the enzymes in powders with biological action do not work at a temperature of over 60°. They work best at around 40° (hand hot). Some fabrics should never be soaked, such as:

(*a*) wools,

(*b*) fabrics treated specially, e.g. with flame-proofing,

(*c*) fabrics where the dye is not stable.

The washing action

Check the washing instructions, the washing powder instructions and set the correct programme on the automatic washer. Fill the twin-tub to the correct line and with the appropriate temperature of water. Dissolve the powder first and then add the washing gradually, allowing the correct time for the process.

Rinsing

In a twin-tub the soapy water is spun off first before several rinses are carried out. Cottons, rayons, linens and woollens should be rinsed in the same temperature as they were washed in. Synthetic fibres must be cool or cold rinsed and only briefly.

Hand washing

Pure wool garments, glass fibres, synthetic fabrics which are heavily pleated should only be washed by hand. Wool can then be rinsed and spun but the others should be drip-dried after rinsing. Warm, *not hot*, water should be used throughout (see table).

Drying

Make sure the lines or racks are smooth and clean. Dry woollen knit and synthetic garments flat. If a tumble-drier is used, select a low temperature for synthetic fabrics or for minimum iron garments.

Ironing

Look at the care label for ironing instructions (see Chapter 1). Set the iron at the correct thermostat. If a steam iron is being used this should be filled before switching on and the steam indicator selected. If not, damp and roll up very dry articles. Make sure that the iron and ironing board are spotlessly clean before starting. Remember that wool and synthetic fibres can be harmed by too hot an iron. If unsure, always begin ironing on an inconspicuous place, and then continue to iron until the garment is dry.

Airing

This is wise to prevent mildew.

DOING THE WASHING

General fabric guidelines as taken from the care labels shown in Chapter 1, with additional finishing instructions.

Care label 1

White cotton and white linen with no special finishes

Machine wash: Very hot, maximum wash 95° C to boil. Spin or wring

Hand wash: Hand hot or boil

Finish: Damp, right side, hot iron

Care label 2

Cotton, linen or rayon articles without special finishes where colours are fast at 60° C

Machine wash: Hot, maximum wash 60° C. Spin or wring

Hand wash: Hand hot

Finish: Damp, right side. Rayon medium iron, cotton and linen hot iron

Care label 3

White nylon
White polyester/cotton mixtures

Machine wash: Hot, medium wash 60° C. Cold rinse. Short spin or drip dry

Hand wash: Hand hot

Finish: Nearly dry, either side, cool iron

Care label 4

Coloured nylon, polyester, cotton and rayon, articles with special finishes, acrylic/cotton mixtures

Machine wash: Hand hot medium wash 50° C. Cold rinse. Short spin or drip dry

Hand wash: Hand hot

Finish: If needed iron on the wrong side, cool iron

Care label 5

Cotton, linen or rayon articles where colours are fast at 40° C but not at 60° C

Machine wash: Warm, medium wash 40° C. Spin or wring

Hand wash: Warm 40° C

Finish: Damp, either side. Rayon medium iron, cotton and linen hot iron

Care label 6

Acrylics, acetate and triacetate, including mixtures with wool, polyester/wool blends

Machine wash: Warm, minimum wash 40° C. Cold rinse. Short spin, do not wring

Hand wash: Warm 40° C

Finish: Iron dry on wrong side if necessary. Do not use steam. Cool or warm iron

Care label 7	Machine wash	Hand wash	Finish
Wool, including blankets and wool mixtures with cotton or rayon. Silk	Warm, minimum wash 40°C	Warm 40°C Do not rub	Slightly damp, right or wrong side, warm iron
	Spin. Do not hand wring		
Care label 8			
Silk and printed acetate fabrics with colours not fast at 40°C	Cool Minimum wash 30°C	Cool 30°C	Minimum iron only if necessary cool iron
	Cold rinse. Short spin. Do not wring		
Care label 9			
Cotton articles with special finishes capable of being boiled but requiring drip drying	Very hot to boil maximum wash	Hand hot or boil	Drip dry
	Drip dry		
Care label 10			
Articles which must not be machine washed		Hand wash only	See garment label
	See garment label		

How to use launderettes Behind the shop front you will find a small counter, one to two dozen fully automatic washing machines, hot air spinners and rows of chairs to relax in. Sometimes a tea-bar, orange drink and milk dispenser or magazine collection is provided to make the customers' wait more pleasant. Sometimes there is a manageress in charge to help you. For every 7 lb. (dry weight) of washing you pay between 20p to 30p depending on the charge where you live. Your 7 lb. will fill one machine. If you have more, you will have to hire an extra machine and so pay double.

You can buy a small packet of soap powder or detergent, or you can provide your own if you wish. You are given a machine into which you put your washing. You then switch on. A red light comes on which tells you when to add the first lot of detergent. After a thorough wash, several rinses and a spin, the light again tells you to add detergent and the whole process is repeated. The entire double wash takes about 20 minutes. When the machine stops altogether, you can, if you wish, transfer the clothes to a high-speed hot air spinner for about 5p. Finally you take home your clean, nearly dry washing with most of the hard work done for you, cheaply and speedily. You have only the final stages of drying, the ironing and the airing to see to. You can leave your washing at some launderettes and, for an extra 20p or so as well as the normal charge, the manageress will do the washing for you.

Warnings 1 Be sure no garment has a dye which runs.
2 Empty all pockets, do up zips, remove brooches and mend holes.
3 It is risky to wash very fine fabrics and woollies in this way. They may get torn or shrink.

N.B. You must remember that you still have your fine fabrics and woollens to wash should you have used the launderette. Nevertheless, using it is time- and labour-saving, although it may be a little rough on your clothes. Less rough, but less thorough, are the machines which carry out a single, not a double, wash. Both types are in common use.

Dry-cleaning Either laundries or special dry-cleaning firms will take care of this for you. Some also repair garments. The cost varies according to the material, how complicated the cleaning process is and the type of garment. A straight skirt can cost as little as 26p, a lined suede coat as much as £4·60. Here are a few points to remember if you decide to have your clothes dry-cleaned:

1 Go to a well-known firm, but take the trouble to see that you will be compensated should a garment be lost or spoilt.

2 Ask the cost first, find out when your garment will be ready and keep your receipt ticket carefully.

3 Remove such things as leather belts, but be sure to include matching belts with the garments they belong to.

4 Ask about the removal of buttons or buckles.

5 Empty pockets and carry out repairs before sending.

If you live in a large town you will probably have the opportunity to use a coin-operated dry-cleaner. If you choose to do so, follow the instructions very carefully.

Stain removal and dry-cleaning

As many stains as possible should be removed before clothes are washed. If they cannot be washed then dry-cleaning will be necessary. Some are unsuitable for washing because of their material, such as gold lamé, Angora or suede, or because of their styling—padded shoulders, stiffened lapels or sequins. Such clothes need cleaning in dirt and grease solvents such as white spirit or trichlorethylene. On a small scale such cleaning can be done at home. We call it *Home Valeting* and this involves three processes:

1 stain removal
2 sponging
3 pressing

Types of stains and how to treat them

1	Fats of all kinds including lipstick, oil, face cream, cod liver oil, shoe and metal polish	Scrape off any visible surface layer very gently. Either wash in hot, soapy water and rinse thoroughly or if this is not possible use a grease solvent such as carbon tetrachloride. This is the main ingredient of such cleaners as Thawpit or Dabitoff. N.B. Do not inhale.
2	Blood, egg, milk, cream, ice cream, cocoa, chocolate, meat juices, gravy, soup	Wash at once using an enzyme detergent. If dried in, soak in a 1–4 solution of hydrogen peroxide first, then wash.
3	Creosote or tar—look out for this on the beach	Scrape off surplus. Then treat with carbon tetrachloride, and if possible wash in hot soapy water.
4	Nail polish, hair lacquer, waterproof glue	Apply amyl acetate (inflammable) on a cotton wool pad unless the fabric is an acetate rayon. Then wash in the normal way.
5	Ink—washable	Soak in cold water for about an hour. For stubborn stains soak in milk, then wash in warm suds. Treat any remaining brown marks as for rust.
6	Ink—ball point, indelible marking, felt tipped pen and carbon paper	Treat with methylated spirits (inflammable) on a pad. Then wash in warm/hot soapy water.
7	Rust (iron mould)	Sponge with a solution of salts of lemon or oxalic acid (1 level plastic teaspoonful to 1 gill of warm water). For persistent stains, cover them with oxalic acid crystals and pour boiling water through them, then steep in the solution. Wash and rinse thoroughly. These salts are very poisonous.
8	Grass and dandelion stains	Sponge with methylated spirits on a pad (inflammable). Then wash in the usual way.

9	Mildew	Bleach according to the fabric using hydrogen peroxide (1–4) for silks, rayons and wools. Use a hypochlorite bleach for cottons and linens such as Domestos, Parazone or Durazone diluting according to the instructions. Wash and rinse thoroughly.
10	Urine	Soak in cold water or a warm enzyme detergent immediately. Wash as usual.
11	Fruit juice, tea, coffee, jam, wine, beer, ice lollies	Wash at once. If stains are persistent, soak in a warm borax solution (1 level teaspoon to 1 gill) but not for babies' nappies or clothes. A diluted solution of hydrogen peroxide (1–4) can be used for soaking. This and borax must then be washed out and rinsed carefully.
12	Perspiration	Wash in warm suds using an enzyme detergent. Persistent stains can be treated with diluted vinegar or ammonia (1–3). Do not inhale. This must then be washed out.
13	Paint (oil and cellulose)	Scrape off surplus. Treat with turpentine or a 'turps' substitute (inflammable) on a pad. Then wash in warm/hot suds and rinse.
14	Paint (emulsion)	Dab off with cold water as soon as possible. Then wash according to fabric.
15	Ointment, suntan oil	Treat with carbon tetrachloride on a pad (do not inhale). If discoloration remains, treat with diluted (1–4) hydrogen peroxide. Then wash.
16	Chewing gum	Scrape off all you can. Chill or use an ice cube. Treat stains with carbon tetrachloride on a pad (do not inhale).
17	Scorch marks	Sponge with borax solution (1–4) or glycerine or both. Leave to soak for persistent marks. Then wash thoroughly.

Stain removal

1 Identify the cause of the stain if possible and treat according to type.

2 Always remove stains as soon as possible. The newer the stain, the easier to remove.

3 Use a mild remover first before resorting to a more drastic one.

4 Remember that sometimes stain removers, such as methylated spirits, are inflammable. Others such as salts of lemon or oxalic acid are very poisonous. Keep them out of reach and reserve special spoons, basins and measures to use just for this purpose. Wash the garment after treating.

Reminders Never use bleaches which smell of chlorine (hypochlorite bleaches) on silk, wool or leather. These three materials are also damaged by salts of lemon and oxalic acid. Never pour boiling water on wool or garments with wool fibres in them, and never allow such things to soak.

Sponging

When sponging away a stain, place an absorbent pad—cotton wool or a doubled-over tissue will do—under the mark. Start from the outside of the stain and work into the middle. Keep the outer sponging limit an inch or two from the stain and work round in an irregular line always working inwards. This avoids spreading the stained area and lessens the chance of a ring showing at the end.

Sponge grubby patches—on lapels and collars for instance—with a little warm diluted detergent. Then sponge again with warm water to remove detergent and allow almost to dry before pressing. This can freshen up the drabbest-looking garment.

Pressing

If possible press on the wrong side of the material and through a single layer only, unless pleats or creases are deliberately being pressed in. If you have no steam iron, press through a damp cloth, then remove the cloth and press until dry. Do not rub the iron over the material as you do when ironing; place it on, press firmly, lift, replace and press again. This avoids marks and shiny patches.

Washing at home

There is a wide range of new laundering equipment and care must be taken to make the best choice.

1 Read an independent assessment of any apparatus, e.g., a washing machine, which you want to buy.

2 See it in operation, either at a neighbour's, or ask for a demonstration at the show room.

3 Make sure you (*a*) really need it; (*b*) can afford it; (*c*) can keep up the repayments; (*d*) have room for it.

4 When choosing soaps, soap powders and detergents, remember that nearly half of them are made by one firm. Choose the one that suits you, your water, your fabrics, your hands—never mind what it says on TV. Always rinse it out thoroughly after washing.

TYPES OF STAINS AND HOW TO TREAT THEM

5 Before washing with a powder, read the instructions.

6 Before washing a new garment, read the washing instructions on its label.

7 Never wear damp or un-aired clothes.

8 Don't let ironing be agony. Sit on your kitchen stool to do it, and buy a board which will permit you to do this. Once you are competent, you can do the ironing while chatting or listening to a radio play.

Detergents

This term simply means 'cleaning materials'. For laundry work we usually use one or more of the four main types. The first three, all of which can be used with one another, are made from *soap*, which is a form of animal or vegetable fat combined with caustic soda.

Soap

We buy this in bars or cakes. For laundry work it is usually inexpensive and unscented. Fairy and Sunlight are two of the many makes on the market.

Soap powders Soap with certain additives in a fine-powdered form. Rinso, Fairy Snow and Persil are examples.

Soap flakes Soap in a fairly pure form is finely divided to give flakes. Lux and Crysella are examples. Each packet explains what its contents are especially good for, and how they should be used.

Synthetic detergents have the general advantage of their washing-action's being unhampered by hard water. In hard water there are chemicals which combine with soap to form an unpleasant scum which reduces the soap's effectiveness. This cannot happen with synthetic detergents. Dreft, Omo and Tide are examples.

N.B. Put everything away as soon as you have finished with it. This is one of the main secrets of the good housewife. Give everything a place and train the whole family to keep to this arrangement. Remember the saying, 'a stitch in time saves nine'. Do your simple repairs as you go along. Here are a few hints to help you:

Simple repairs

Many of these can be carried out by using the appropriate *adhesive*.

Before you start extensive patching or darning—which you will learn about in your needlework course—make sure that there is not an adhesive which will do the job less visibly, and more quickly and easily. It may not save you money, but will prevent sore thumbs and fingertips, especially if you have to mend something like a frayed carpet.

Prices for tubes of adhesive range from about 4½p to 26p. When you have used all you want, put the top back on the tube and the adhesive will last almost for ever. What can you repair with an adhesive? Here are just a few examples:

China, earthenware or glass

There are several transparent plastic cements which will repair these almost invisibly. Such repairs are probably more suitable for ornaments and vases than for cups, saucers or plates which, after a while, might come apart in hot water, or give germs a chance to breed in their joins.

Metals

Some glues and plastic metal solders will repair metals—but you must not expect them to withstand too much strain afterwards.

Wood

Many glues repair wood. Tubes of plastic wood come in different shades and can be used to fill in blemishes or cracks.

Walls

Polyfilla will fill crevices in cement or plaster. Plastic Padding, a new slightly dearer adhesive, will do all the jobs mentioned above and many more. It has exceptionally strong adhesive qualities.

Fabrics, carpets, etc.

Hems of curtains, frayed carpet edges, torn upholstery and loose covers can be mended by ironing strips of tape on to the back of the material. Such tape is bought with the adhesive already on one side and this is fixed by the iron's heat. Alternatively, an adhesive especially designed for this purpose, such as Copydex, can be spread on tapes or hessian to secure such a repair.

Wallpaper

Copydex or Polycell glue is equally good for making invisible patches on wallpaper. The secret of this 'invisible mending' is to find a section of wallpaper which will match the design on your wall and then tear round it irregularly before sticking it in place.

Plastic articles

Plastic glue securely mends those precious toys that, left on the floor, were trodden on. This glue is sometimes inflammable, so read the label carefully.

N.B. After repairing toys, cots or prams, if you decide to paint over the repaired section, be sure never to use a paint containing lead (see Chapter 10).

Electrical repairs

Apart from renewing fuses, do not attempt electrical repairs unless you have been taught exactly what to do. Do it under supervision until you are really experienced. Inspect flexes and cover kinks or worn outer coverings with insulating tape.

Fuses

Most fuses today are of the cartridge type. This is what they look like:

23 *A cartridge fuse*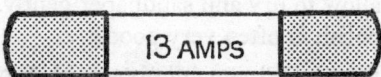

You find the smaller ones inside electric plugs and the slightly larger ones in the main fuse boxes. Each is clearly labelled with the measure of current it carries. This is counted in *Amperes*. We are familiar with the two-amp. fuses used in a radio or bedside plug, with the thirteen-amp. ones for a washing machine or electric fire and the powerful thirty-amp. fuses which are used for electric cookers. When changing a fuse in a fuse box, there are only three things to remember:

1   Switch the power off at the mains before opening the fuse box.

2   Identify the one that has burnt out by looking for slightly blackened marks at the ends.

3   Replace the faulty one by one of the *same* amperage. Close the box and switch on the current.

Plug fuses

If only one piece of apparatus is out of action, it is likely that the fuse inside its own plug has blown. You have to disconnect the individual plug from the circuit by pulling it out of its socket before you can get at its fuse, so there is no need to switch off at the mains as well. Once the plug is disconnected, remove the large brass screw from its back and it will fall open. Gently lever out the fuse and replace it with one of the same amperage. Replace the screw and the plug should be in good order again.

Repairs—a warning

Often furniture and furnishings are damaged through carelessness, through our failure to see what damage could occur. Cigarette burns, rings on table tops or scorches in fitted carpets are examples of such carelessness. Learn by such mistakes and take stock of the rest of the house to see how further need for repair can be avoided. Let us examine three examples:

1   A cigarette burn on a dressing table. Rub the blackened part away with a fragment of wire wool held in tweezers, or fine sandpaper round the end of a pencil. Fill the dent with plastic wood, allow to dry and sandpaper gently. Colour with dark polish—shoe polish is often very good.

Note   Did you supply an ash tray? Have you enough of these in the house?

2   A ring from a hot teapot on a polished table. Again rub gently with wire wool, or a trace of abrasive on a cloth. Rub linseed oil into the ring over and over again until it disappears.

Note   Where was the mat or teapot stand? If you have small children, might not a formica-topped table be more practical all round?

3   A scorch in a fitted carpet. This cannot be turned round and the burn hidden, so it must be patched. With a fitted carpet you

are sure to have odd pieces over. Cut one a little larger than the area of the burn plus its immediate surround. Be sure to protect the underfelt by slipping a tin plate or something similar beneath the burn. Place the patch over the burned area, and, with a razor or sharp knife, cut down through the carpet round the edge of the patch. Stick the patch to the middle of a stout piece of hessian with a glue such as Copydex, leaving a border of two to three inches all the way round. Cover this border also with glue on its upper side and slip the patch into position from underneath the carpet. The glued hessian border holds it firmly in position and the patch should be almost invisible.

Note Would either a cheaper fireside rug or a mesh fire-guard have saved you this trouble? What about your insurance? Will it cover you for the damage?

Aids to the housewife

Probably the three most important of these are clean warmth, constant hot water and ventilation. These are dealt with fully in the next chapter which is mainly concerned with the kitchen. So far in this chapter we have been dealing with the removal and collecting of dirt from your house and your clothes. Now, in connection with this, we will discuss another important aid-to-the-housewife, easy-to-clean surfaces. Obviously it is easier to collect dirt from surfaces to which it will not cling, so cut down your work by making the surfaces in your house as easy to clean as possible. This is something which we all can do gradually. We can't often re-plan kitchens from scratch, very rarely can we knock down walls, put in windows and so let the sun in where we'd like it, but we can brighten and transform our homes by skilful redecoration.

Easy-to-clean walls and ceilings In a new house wallpaper should not be used, for your new house needs to dry out. You may like to put it on just one wall—a Scandinavian idea—knowing it may have to be replaced. After one or two years you can choose how to cover your walls. Examine them carefully before deciding. If they are rough and uneven, if the ceiling is badly cracked, then probably a good thick wallpaper will cover some of this, unless you are prepared to replaster and rub down under the paint.

Paint

There are two main types of paint: *gloss paint* which has to be used on wood work and *emulsion paint* which can be used on walls and ceilings. Both are washable. If your walls are damp use a waterproof primer; if they are very damp use two coats. Most priming paints contain red and white lead oxide and are poisonous. Half a litre covers about 8 square metres and costs about 42½p. If walls are absorbent you will need more.

Undercoat Undercoating is very opaque and has no shine. You will need it under gloss or emulsion paint, and over a primer. It is not usually the same colour as the main coat, near it and like it but paler. Your paint dealer will advise you. For instance Magnolia should have Off White underneath, Columbine over Pale Lilac, Black over Dark Grey. Be careful about colour names, the shades differ with each make. Contrary to popular belief, it does not go further than the top coat, covering about 8 square metres at 58½p for half a litre.

Gloss paint

This sometimes contains lead—be careful—lead is poisonous. It is essential for all exterior wood and metal work and is the best finish for interior wood and metal work. It has a hard lustrous finish and washes well. Half a litre covers about 8 square metres at around 51½p.

Emulsion paint

This does not contain lead. You can get it in a matt or lustre finish, that is with a dull or shiny appearance. Both are easily washable. Avoid using abrasives on this and gloss paint, a little detergent should remove stubborn marks. It goes further than gloss paint—one litre should cover 15 square metres, depending on how absorbent the surface is of course, and it costs about 70p–£1. Unless you choose a very cheap wallpaper this is the cheapest way to decorate a room.

Thixotropic paints

These give a finish like gloss or emulsion paints and cost very slightly more. They are very useful because of their jelly-like texture which is non-drip and easy to use.

Polyurethane paints

These are again a little dearer but dry with an extremely hard finish. They will withstand heat, scratches and knocks.

Painting

You will need:

1   Two brushes. A wide one of about 2 inches' width and a small one of about ½ inch in width for the edges.

2   A paint tray and roller if you have large surfaces to cover.

3   Paint remover—Polyclens or turpentine.

4   Clean cloths.

5   A large overall.

6   Something sturdy to stand on.

Prepare the walls or woodwork. Rub down uneven surfaces or dark paint with glass paper, or use Polystrippa to remove it. Fill up cracks with a material such as Polyfilla and allow to dry. Rub down until smooth. Remove all traces of dust and cobwebs. Keep out draughts—they bring dust in on to the wet paint.

If necessary use a primer and let it dry. Then apply an undercoat and let that dry.

Always read the directions on the paint pot. Does it need stirring or diluting? Do not get too much paint on your brush. Dip it in so that only half the bristles are submerged. Then drain it against the side of the tin before using.

If you are using a roller pour plenty of paint into the tray (a cheap baking tin will do, lined with tin foil. Be sure it is a little wider than the roller).

Roll the roller in the paint, then apply to the surface. Start at the top and work quickly, re-rolling the roller in the paint when necessary.

Finish off corners or edges with your small brush, whether you have been using a roller or a brush.

If necessary put on a second coat, but always allow the first to dry thoroughly beforehand.

If you find painting difficult, try one of the non-drip jelly paints (thixotropic). They are a little dearer because they don't go so far, but it is far easier to paint with them.

When you have finished, wash your brushes or rollers thoroughly with warm, soapy water. Emulsion paint will wash off this way if still fresh. When using gloss paint you will need Polyclens or turpentine to leave the equipment really clean.

Wallpaper

This is not such a suitable finish if you have toddlers with sticky fingers or boys with muddy boots. You can get 'washable' papers, but they are dearer at 46p–£3 a roll. Only the dearer ones of that range can really be washed thoroughly. The others are only 'wipeable'. A child's bedroom looks charming with emulsion paint on the three walls at the sides and head of his bed, and space-ships or teddy bears or nursery rhymes on the paper at the foot of his bed—so that he lies and looks at it, but is less inclined to fiddle with it. A toddler can undo in 5 minutes what it took you and your husband 5 hours to do and may have taken you 5 months to save up for!

Cost One roll of paper contains 11 yards, $20\frac{1}{2}$ inches wide. Measure the wall space, allow for the windows and doors. Then add a little, as sometimes you may be forced to discard some when matching the pattern strip to strip. The price per roll can range from about 40p upwards. Look at the cheapest first but, obviously, the dearer the paper, the better the quality and the longer it will last.

At first avoid very cheap paper—it is so thin that it sometimes tears. Very expensive paper, on the other hand, is so thick that it is equally difficult to manage. If embossed heavily, it sometimes

24 *What a toddler can do in 5 minutes*

wrinkles. Vinyl paper is expensive but as it washes easily and is grease- and steamproof, it is excellent for kitchens and bathrooms. Its rolls are 11 yards 21 inches long. Wallpaper is not yet measured in metric lengths. Avoid complicated patterns; every strip has to be matched. Stripes cause endless complications. As a beginner, choose a moderately priced, fairly plain paper.

Wallpapering

You will need these:

1 A large soft brush—a distempering-brush will do.
2 A large pair of scissors.
3 A bucket for the glue.
4 Several clean cloths.
5 A firm chair or pair of steps.
6 An old, enveloping overall.
7 A plank or table.

Prepare the wall first. If the ceiling is to be papered, start with this. Old paper or flaky distemper must be stripped off. Sometimes it needs soaking off first. If the wall is very porous—it will be dry and knobbly in appearance—give it a coat of size to stop the glue from sinking in. Then prepare the glue—the cellulose ones are best, because they leave no marks. The wallpaper edgings should have been cut off for you by the shop, but, if not, trim them carefully. Cut the paper into strips of the length you require, plus an extra 4–6 inches. Lay the paper face down on the plank or table, paste it down the middle (do not have too much paste on your brush) then work your brush well out to the sides. Place the top of the strip carefully in position with several inches overlapping at each end and smooth down the centre first. Then smooth the sides. Mark through the paper where the picture rail is, pull the strip gently off the wall and cut along the mark. Press back to fit exactly. Repeat at the lower edge against the skirting board, round fireplaces, etc. When the next strip is in position press the seam gently with a clean cloth or, better still, a seam roller.

Panels

If any walls are very bad, uneven, cracked and damp, it may be best to panel them. Not with the wooden panels we see in old buildings, since they are now a prohibitive price, but with sheeting of the Formica type mounted and battened to the wall. This also looks effective in small areas in the kitchen, such as between the back of a working surface and the wall cupboard above it. It is very difficult to do it yourself.

Tiles

There are various different types of tiles. You can buy linoleum tiles for the floors (3p for a tile 9 inches square), polystyrene tiles for the ceiling (3p for a tile 12 inches square—they go up in size), as well as ceramic tiles. These are hygienic, hardwearing and can be most attractive. They are most useful round the sink, the washbasin and the bath and in the larder and toilet. You can fix and replace them yourself, but this is not easy. They range in price from 95p–£1·10 for 4½ square feet for plain black or white ones, £2–£3 for coloured ones, £5–£6 for ones with hedgehogs, flowers and nursery figures on them. One or two of the decorated tiles can be attractively set among the plain ones. Self-adhesive Vinyl wall tiles measuring 9 square inches cost about 5½p each. They are hardwearing, attractive and easy to fix.

Damp

None of these finishes will be a permanent success if the wall or ceiling is damp. Finding the cause of the damp is the first essential.

Causes of damp 1 *Simple leaks:* blocked gutters, tile breakages or displacements, and cracked flashing (the lead edgings of tiles) all cause leaks. Sometimes the rain beats down a chimney in such a way as to cause walls to become damp. A new cowling will put this right.

2 *Rising damp:* curing this is not a simple matter. It is caused by moisture rising through floors and up walls from the ground underneath, either because there is no damp course, or because this has been damaged. To test for this dampness, take a piece of glass a few inches square and seal its edges to the floor with a mastic sealing compound. Make sure it is in a place where it will

not be stepped on and loosened, otherwise moisture could get underneath it from other sources. After 48 hours, any signs of damp under the glass will show that rising damp is present. One very good cure is to take up the floor and to replace it with one containing a waterproof membrane, usually two layers of concrete sandwiching, a layer of bitumen or sheet of polythene. As this is so drastic a cure, it is, of course, most important to diagnose rising damp correctly. So, if you think you may have it in your house, get a builder or a firm like Rentokil to check it carefully.

3 *Condensation:* lack of air vents often causes this. Steam which cannot escape condenses in cool places, the moisture often causes mildew. Simple ventilation is often the answer.

Floor surfaces

1 *Carpets*

Always tell the salesman which room you plan to carpet. He wil then advise you about the quality you need. Little-used bedroom floors can be covered with a much cheaper form of carpeting than the living room or hall floors.

Probably the easiest to keep clean, the nicest and the most luxurious is the fitted carpet—but it is expensive. The cheaper ones, at £1·50–£2·77½ per square yard, are only suitable for bedrooms. For a living room or hall they will cost £2·75 to £3·75 a square yard. Some manufactured from a man-made fibre, Bri-Nylon, are now coming on to the market carrying a 7-year guarantee.

The heavy wool carpets, such as Wilton and Axminster, have been unparalleled for wearing qualities. It will be interesting to see if man-made fibres can compete with them. Cotton carpets are fairly hard wearing, they can be bright and attractive and are quite cheap.

All carpets need a good underlay. This will cost from 35p to 70p a square yard. It increases the life of a carpet considerably. The disadvantage of a fitted carpet is that it cannot be turned round to spread the wear evenly, whereas square or oblong carpets can be moved.

Cord carpets These are fairly cheap and very hard wearing. Their price varies according to width and quality. For example, a carpet 27 inches wide will cost between £1·05 and £2·25 a yard. For one 36 inches wide, the cost will be between £1·55 and £3·25 a yard. You can get one as wide as 12 feet. These carpets come in a very wide range of colours. They are suitable for all rooms, but are not as soft and comfortable as wool, cotton or nylon carpets.

Rugs and mats All types of carpeting can be used for mats or rugs. By mats, we usually mean small, cheaper floor coverings. By rugs, something bigger and perhaps more luxurious. The Scandinavian rugs are an example, with their long strands of fairly coarse wool firmly woven into a jute and cotton backing. They are made in a range of lovely colours and patterns which can bring a vivid contrast into a room. A large one, perhaps for a bedroom floor (6 feet 6 inches × 4 feet 6 inches) costs between £16 and £20. This type of rug is not supposed to be used by the fireside.

Rugs designed to protect the carpet from sparks from the fire get very dirty and often wear out quickly. You can either buy a very cheap rug—£1–£2 from Woolworths—which can be renewed every year, or a more expensive nylon rug (about £7) which will not burn. In heat, nylon merely melts, and it does not spread the flames. When a spark touches a nylon rug, it just melts the spot where it lands. Such rugs can be washed and dried easily and often.

For the kitchen and bathroom plastic mats with rubber foam backs are available. A small one (26 × 18 inches) costs about £1. These are warm and comfortable to stand on, but are about twice the price of the popular sheet rubber mats found in most bathrooms and toilets.

Cleaning

(a) *Preventing unnecessary dirt* Obviously anything which is under the family's feet all day will get very dirty. To insist on shoes being changed *every* time people come in is unreasonable. On very wet days, or after sessions in the garden or sandpit, it is rather different. The provision of scrapers outside and a doormat of coir matting just inside the back and front doors will lessen the dirt brought into your house, and so on to the carpets. Dirt does not do any serious damage if removed thoroughly and regularly. Stiletto heels, on the other hand, damage floors permanently, whether carpeted or not. Remember this when you buy shoes and when you visit your friends' houses.

(b) *Removing the dirt* These rules apply to all carpets and mats:

1 When a carpet is new, avoid the use of a vacuum cleaner until the pile has had time to settle.

2 Clean regularly with a carpet sweeper or dustpan and stiffish brush, then later on with a vacuum cleaner, if you have one.

3 Wipe off and sponge up stains at once. This is easy to do on man-made fibres—they resist stains—they spring back into position and dry rapidly. Wool fibres can be damaged by heavy rubbing or sponging, too much detergent or moisture which dries out very slowly. Be very gentle when sponging and use as little soap and water as possible.

4 As soon as the carpet begins to look grubby, clean it thoroughly with the vacuum or carpet sweeper, and then shampoo it, using a well-known detergent.

5 Read the instructions for use of the shampoo very carefully and follow them exactly. It is most important to have the correct dilution of the detergent.

6 Apply evenly, making sure that the minimum amount of moisture sinks into the carpet. Sprays, or vacuum cleaner spray attachments or special shampooing appliances can be used for this.

7 Rub gently into the fibres. (The brushes and rollers on shampooing appliances will do this.) Then remove all traces of the shampoo.

8 Remove as much moisture as possible with a clean absorbent cloth. Then dry thoroughly. Draughts of warm air from the window on a hot day, from a fan heater (turned low), or blown from a vacuum cleaner or even a hair drier will help to do this.

9 Dry the carpet as quickly as possible. Do not walk on it while it is still damp.

10 As soon as it shows signs of wear, alter its position, or that of the furniture.

Remember, carpets are expensive items. If you take care of yours, you have the right to expect it to last. These points will help you to choose wisely:

1 See that your carpet measures up to the British Standard. If it does, it will bear the Kitemark—see Chapter 1.

2 Send to the British Standards Institution, 2 Park St., London, W.1, for their leaflet on carpets and fabrics.

3 Refer to the excellent advice in the *Which?* issues of March and April 1963 on carpets. You will find them in your library.

4 Ask advice from the carpet salesman at a reputable shop.

5 Avoid buying carpets at the door or at a sale of a mobile firm.

6 Only order carpet bargains through the post if they carry a money-refund guarantee.

7 Buy a good underlay—see *Which?*, November 1964.

2 *Linoleum*

There are two main types:

(a) *Printed linoleum* where the pattern is on the surface and will wear off. This is cheap, from 30p to 70p a square yard, and does admirably for a surround, or edging, to a carpet.

(b) *Inlaid linoleum*. Here the pattern goes right through and the quality is better. It ranges from 55p to £1·35 a square yard. Really good lino should be over 3 mm. thick and have an underlay of felt paper. Properly treated it can last a lifetime.

3 *Wooden floors*

The actual floorboards can be rubbed-down or sanded to make them smooth, and then stained. This is another cheap and effective way of edging a carpet or rugs.

Wood block floors are quite different. A mosaic of wood blocks is laid carefully in a pattern. Often families save to have their halls inlaid in this way. It is very expensive—about £4–£5 a square yard laid for you—very hardwearing, and needs regular polishing.

4 *Cork block flooring*

This is new and attractive, quiet and warm and *needs no polishing*. Unlike wood block flooring you can lay it yourself. It costs about £1·30 a square yard.

5 *'Vinyl' tiles* (and similar types)

These can also be laid by you. They are colourful and can be laid in attractive patterns. They need washing with the minimum of hot water containing detergent and re-polishing with a seal or plastic floor dressing every one or two weeks—less in a room—more in a hall. Wire wool removes ingrained marks. They cost from £1·05 to £2·25 a square yard. Keep paraffin well away.

6 *Quarry tiles*

Hardwearing, attractive but cold and not easy to keep clean. You cannot lay them yourself. They need frequent washing or scrubbing if in a kitchen, but an occasional wipe and polish in the hall. They cost about £2 per square yard, laid for you.

Working surfaces

1 *Plastic laminates*, e.g. Formica, Warerite

These are today's most popular working surfaces and with very good reason. They are made in attractive colours and patterns, are readily available and have merely to be stuck on to existing surfaces—provided they are flat—and then edged. You can have them cut to exactly the size you require. They resist heat, stains and water; only really excessive heat or strong acids will affect them. Don't use too sharp a knife to cut on to them with, and after using a lemon on the surface keep the extra hot base of the chip pan away. The double effect of the heat and acid may cause a blister. Cost about 20p a square foot.

2 *Pseudo plastic laminates*, e.g. Fablon

This is really *plastic sheeting*. It is easy to fix. You merely cut to size and then strip off the adhesive back and press on to the former surface. It looks just like a laminate, colourful and decorative. It gives you a smooth, easily worked and cleaned surface, but it is easily stained and damaged. It is excellent for lining shelves. Cost $42\frac{1}{2}$p–$47\frac{1}{2}$p a square yard.

3 *Stainless steel*

This is so expensive that apart from its use in draining boards and sinks it is little used in the house. It costs around £9 a square yard. It is indestructible but prone to scratches.

4 *Vitreous enamel*

This is made in attractive colours and used for draining boards. It chips and cracks. Sinks made from this are about one-third of the price of stainless steel.

5 *Marble*

Wonderful for sweet making and rolling pastry. Go to your auction rooms—you may pick up an old wash-hand stand for 25p. I did!

6 *Wood*

Wooden-topped kitchen tables are increasing in popularity. This is partly because white wood can now be permanently sealed. For pastry and chopping boards teak and beech are the best.

Furniture and furnishings

We have so far dealt with the three basic essentials: wall-coverings, floor coverings and working surfaces. Furnishing the rest of the house is mainly a matter of taste in relation to what you can afford. Here are just a few hints to guide you in your choice.

Furniture

Look for these things, no matter what furniture you are buying:

1 Is it really suitable for the purpose you have in mind?

2 Is it made from a suitable material?

3 Is it attractive?

4 On testing—opening doors or drawers, sitting on a chair, lying on a bed—does it seem to be well and solidly made?

5 Is it unblemished and is the finish likely to remain so?

6 Will it go well with your other furniture?

7 Is the delivery date far ahead?

8 Does it carry a British Standards Kitemark (see Chapter 1) and, perhaps, a Design Centre Award label?

9 Has it a good guarantee?

10 Have you the right to examine it on arrival and to return it at once if damaged or not identical with the item you have selected?

What is furniture made from?

Because of its variety and adaptability, *wood* is still the first favourite for nearly all furniture.

The soft woods, such as pinewood, are used to make white wood furniture. This can be bought painted, or you can paint it at home. They also form the framework for veneered furniture.

The hard woods, such as teak, oak, walnut and mahogany, are used for making solid and very expensive furniture. They are used far more often to make veneers for more reasonably priced items.

Veneers These are thin strips of naturally well-coloured and well-grained wood, which are glued to cheaper, less attractive wood surfaces. If the veneers have been touched-up and are over-pronounced in grain or lurid in colour, ask yourself why this has been done. The answer is probably that the veneer is cheap and thin and the piece of furniture shoddy. The touching-up may have been an attempt to hide this. Ornate carvings and gimmicky effects are sometimes stuck on to furniture to hide poor workmanship. Avoid them, you will probably tire of them quickly and they usually become a dust trap. Extreme fashions date very quickly; the plain, good line of a piece of unadorned furniture rarely goes out of fashion. Compare a teak Scandinavian sideboard with a Victorian what-not. Veneers chip and crack unless treated with care. They need a 'finish'. I will deal with this point later.

Laminated wood There are two kinds of laminated wood used in making unit furniture—chipboard and plywood. Chipboard is made by treating wood with resins. Plywood is built up from thin layers, the grain of each being reversed, which are glued together under very great pressure. These are both very strong and light and make practical kitchen furniture.

Treatment of wood Because wood is porous it must be 'finished' in some way to protect it. It is then treated according to its finish rather according to its type. Ideally, it should be finished in such a way as to completely protect it from dirt, moisture and scratches.

These finishes consist of oiling, waxing, French Polishing and varnishing. The first two must be repeated regularly to provide complete protection. French Polish is beautifully smooth and has a high, even gloss—but it scratches and shows heat marks. Though normally hard wearing and needing no regular attention, once damaged the surface has to be re-treated professionally. Varnishing is a cheap and unsuitable finish. Painted surfaces are satisfactory, particularly if two coats are applied. If light in colour they must be washed, but the paint is easy to renew.

Plastic finishes There are two types: (*a*) Synthetic resin polish is steamproof, almost scratchproof and by far the best natural wood finish. (*b*) Laminated layers, such as Formica, need to be firmly glued in place.

New materials Both plastics and metals can be used with wood, with one another, or by themselves to make modern furniture. Metal is often used for bed frames, table or chair legs, but it can also be processed and shaped into chair frames. Plastics, too, can be moulded to make such frames, with often a precision not possible when using wood.

Notes on a few essential items of furniture:

1 TABLES The finish of a table is of great importance. Make sure it is hard wearing. Do not let the table take up too much space in the room. Perhaps a smaller one which could be expanded might be a good idea. Try to avoid putting it in the middle of the room.

2 CHAIRS (*a*) for dining. Do they go well with your table? Are they the right height? Allow 12 inches' clearance for knees;
(*b*) for relaxing. Avoid a heavy, expensive suite unless every member of the family likes the same sort of seat at the same angle. It is probably better to buy chairs to suit single tastes. Remember that children will grow, so get them chairs a little bigger than their first requirement. Make sure, too, that all the chairs go well together. Would a studio couch which would give you an extra guest bed be a better idea than a settee? If upholstered, see that the cushions and base are well sprung and ask what the stuffing is made from. Foam rubber is very resilient and popular. Can you remove the covers for washing? Remember you have got to move the furniture when you clean. Is this possible, or can you sweep underneath?

3 BEDS A bed should have a firm base beneath the mattress. You will spend roughly one-third of your life on this piece of furniture, so buy the best you can afford. Do not be afraid to

remove your shoes and lie down on it in the showroom (most shopkeepers will provide you with a piece of plastic on which to lie). Sitting on a bed will tell you very little about it. Whether you choose a soft, medium or hard one is a matter of taste. The Council of Industrial Design leaflet, *How to buy Beds*, is well worth reading. Get it from the Design Centre, 28 Haymarket, London, S.W.1.

Many young couples who live in a small flat make the mistake of buying a 3-feet double bed which is cheaper than the standard 3-feet 6-inch size. Remember that 3 feet only give you 18 inches on which to sleep. Do not economise here, your sleep is far too important.

4 WARDROBES A built-in wardrobe is by far the most practical. It takes up very little room and remains inconspicuous. If you do have to buy a free-standing wardrobe, make sure that it stands firmly and is not likely to topple forwards. Do the doors fit easily? They often have a tendency to stick. Do you really need a high shelf for hats? How many hats have you anyway? If you have not too much money to spare, wardrobes can often be bought fairly cheaply at an auction sale. Go along the day before the sale, when you can examine anything you like the look of. Look out for woodworm. On the day of the sale, be sure not to bid any more than the limit you have set yourself. You can get a good wardrobe at anything from £1 to £5.

5 DRESSING TABLES These should have four main features:

(*a*) A good mirror or mirrors.
(*b*) A moisture- and stain-resistant surface.
(*c*) Small drawers for odds and ends.
(*d*) Room to sit down comfortably.

Drawers Test the drawers carefully, whether they are part of your dressing table, sideboard, chest or kitchen unit. They must have firmly fixed handles which are easy to grip and should slide easily. They should also have a safety device to prevent them from sliding straight out. Make sure they are not too deep.

General advice

If the furniture carries the Kitemark it has been tested and conforms to a laid-down British Standard. Copies of leaflets giving further details about the standards for individual pieces of furniture are available from the British Standards Institution (address p. 141).

The Council of Industrial Design selects articles of really good design—that is they are of pleasing appearance, a practical shape, good proportions, a suitable finish and of materials to fit them for their intended purpose. The articles which are submitted to the Council vary from toilet-roll fittings to Hi-Fi record players and cover nearly all types of furniture and furnishings. Those selected for exhibition in one of the five design centres in the British Isles are allowed to display this sign, yet another mark of quality.

25   *The Design Centre sign*

The five centres are in London, Manchester, Bristol, Nottingham and Glasgow. The Council arranges exhibitions in towns all over the country, so look out—the Design Centre may visit you soon.

Furnishings

This term usually covers curtains, carpets, linen, blankets and towels. Often when you are setting up home you are lucky enough to get some of these last few as presents.

1   Bed linen

This is not so frequently made of linen as it used to be, partly because cotton sheets can be of excellent quality and are obtainable in sets or pairs in many dainty colours and attractive designs. If you can afford real linen, it will outlast even the very best cotton sheets. Nylon is now being used to make sheets, but it is rather expensive. You can, however, save money in the long run by buying nylon sheets, since they are very hard wearing. They also have the advantage of being easily washed and dried and need little or no ironing. Allow two pairs of sheets per bed and at least two spare pairs. They should measure 70 × 100 inches for single bed sheets and 90 × 100 inches for those for double beds. The narrower widths do not allow for a good tuck in. The extra inches are well worth the money. Sheet sets will include two pillow cases. As many people like to have two pillows, you will need quite a few extra. Allow two cases per pillow. The 'Bedding—standard sizes' article in *Which?*, June 1967, is well worth reading.

2 Blankets

It is most important for warmth and comfort to put a blanket under the bottom sheet. An old one will do, but allow for this, plus two more per bed, or three if you have a thin bedspread. Blankets can be made from man-made fibres, such as Acrilan and Courtelle. Cellular wool is expensive, but some of the blankets made from it carry a 10-year guarantee. No blankets are cheap so, before you buy, it would be wise to study the *Which?* survey on blankets (January 1965).

Flannelette Flannelette serves either for sheets or blankets. It is cotton fluffed up to look and feel like wool. This process traps in air so that sheets made of flannelette are considerably warmer than those made of ordinary cotton. They are also very cheap. This fluffiness washes and wears out quickly. Flannelette is often popular with young children and old people, but both groups are very vulnerable and flannelette burns easily and rapidly.

3 Bedcovers

Eiderdowns are probably as warm as two blankets. The nylon or terylene ones are very good because they dry so easily. They are often filled with tricel. Make sure the surfaces are not too slippery—bedspreads can so easily slip off the bed. Candlewick bedspreads are popular because they are gay, quite warm and need little ironing. Woollen and cotton folk weaves and tartan rugs are also popular. Be sure your bedspread does not clash with your curtains or carpet.

4 Table linen

Though seersucker cloths are good and gay for everyday use (and they need little ironing), nothing flatters a table of good food so well as a starched white one. Keep one for special occasions. Table mats on wood or on formica surfaces look most attractive.

5 Towels

Allow two bath and two hand towels per person. In the kitchen paper towels are more hygienic; you will also need tea towels. Linen ones are cheap and well worth the extra money spent on them. *Which?* examined Terry towels in the August 1964 issue. This article is worth reading.

6 Curtains

Measure your window carefully and calculate how much material you will need before you go shopping. Remember these points:

1 Most curtain material is 48 inches wide off the roll.

2 To allow your curtains to drape or hang well you need not just enough material to cover the width of the window, but at least half as much again to allow for fullness. If your window is 5 feet wide (60 inches) you will need at least 90 inches of material to cover it in width alone. So two curtains, each 48 inches wide, will just do the job, allowing a little for turnings.

3 The length of your curtains will depend upon whether you want them merely to cover the window alone or whether you want them to reach the floor. Measure the length required and then add 4–6 inches for a hem at the bottom, plus at least 2–4 inches for the top edge.

4 Curtain material is available in colourfast and fadeless fabrics. It is rarely shrinkproof and will probably shrink between 3–4 inches when first washed. You will be wise to add at least 12 inches to allow for this shrinkage, for the top edging and for the hem.

5 Remember, you add this on to *each* curtain.

6 If your curtain has a pattern it must match exactly the curtain hanging next to it or the section to which it is joined. Allow $\frac{1}{4}$–$\frac{1}{2}$ a yard per curtain—depending on the size of the pattern—to make this matching possible.

7 Curtains last longer and hang better if they are lined.

8 Always check the measurements with the salesman. Tell him the size of your window and let him advise you.

General advice

Subtle colours and simple designs give a room a restful atmosphere. Blatant, contrasting colours and bold stripes and patterns give a startling effect. Make sure you get the right effect in the right room. Your bedroom and sitting room should encourage you to relax, but a playroom or kitchen is a busy room where you can be gay. Do not overdo it, though, one definite pattern in a room is quite sufficient. From this you can pick out colours to repeat in other finishes or furnishings. For guidance why not try *Fibres and Fabrics*, published by the Consumers' Association, 14 Buckingham St., London, W.C.2, *British Standard* No. 2747 (textiles for laundering purposes), and *British Standard* No. 3257 (guide to fabric descriptions)? Also obtainable from The British Standards Institution, Orchard House, Orchard St., Oxford St., London, W.1.

Further reading

Your Own Home, by M. J. Joyce, published by Harrap and Co. Ltd., at 42½p

Running Your Home, by Anne Allison, published by Mills and Boon Ltd., at 30p

Fabrics and Laundrywork, by L. M. Gawthorpe, published by Hulton Press at 85p

Washing Wisdom, by K. J. Mills, published by Forbes at 91p

A Home of Your Own, by Margaret Kirby, published by Routledge and Kegan Paul at £1·40

Home Lighting and *Home Electricity*, both by Antony Byers, published by Pelham at 40p

A Place of Your Own, by Pamela Westland and Avril Rodway, published by Elm Tree Books at £2·10

Practical work

1 'A woman's work is never done'—debate this.

2 Find out from someone who runs her own home and who won't mind your questions how she plans her week's work. Is she contented with her lot as a housewife?

3 Do you dislike the word 'housewife'? If you do, can you suggest an alternative? Discuss in class whether you are looking forward to being called one?

4 Plan the redecoration of your bedroom, measure it and work out the cost of: (*a*) emulsion-painting it, and (*b*) papering it. Remember you'll need gloss paint as well, and undercoating. Allow yourself 40p per roll of paper.

5 Go to your nearest Home Decorating Shop. Choose a time when it's empty and ask if they can spare, or lend you, an out-of-date wallpaper sample book, and some paint colour charts. The wallpaper will be priced (on the back of each sheet) but ask for the price of the paint. Now plan the imaginative redecoration of your living room either at home or in the school flat.

6 I haven't put in the prices of all the cleaning equipment mentioned. Find them out and list them in the back of your book. Illustrate where possible from leaflets, magazines, etc.

7 See if you can visit a laundry in your area. Notice the methods used. Compare prices, conditions and compensation given at different laundries.

8 As a project, make an illustrated folder on one of the following:

(*a*) Laundry, yesterday and today.
(*b*) Wall, floor and working-top surfaces.
(*c*) Kitchen equipment.

9 Each choose an important piece of furniture such as a wardrobe, sideboard, dining room table and chairs, and collect pictures, articles and advice about that one item. After careful selection of a really good example, give a one minute's talk to the class justifying your choice.

Questions

1 Look at the list on pages 105-6 of the jobs a housewife must tackle. List them in your idea of their priority. Explain why you have chosen that special order, and give the approximate portion of a five-day week you would devote to each.

2 How much do outside appearances matter to you? Do you care *now* what the 'Jones' think? Are you going to care what the neighbours think? Consider carefully before you answer and explain your decisions.

3 Would you rather live in a brand new house in a town, suburb or estate, with everything as up to date as possible, or would you rather tackle the conversion of an old rural property. List *all* the aspects (amenities, schools, friends, shopping, health, view, etc., etc.) and then explain your answer.

4
(a) What are 3 mm?
(b) Why do you keep paraffin away from Vinyl tiles?
(c) What are goffering and crimping irons?
(d) What is a Dolly tub?
(e) What was a Steam Laundry?

5 Compare the advantages and disadvantages of doing your washing: (a) at home; (b) at a launderette; or (c) at a laundry.

6 Compare a twin tub washing machine with a fully automatic one. Which do you prefer and why?

7 Of all the household chores which one do you like *least*? Why? Think out and list ways you can find it more bearable—remember you may have hours of it ahead.

CHAPTER 7 · THE HOUSE (2)

The kitchen

A great deal of nonsense is talked about kitchen planning. How many of us will ever be in a position to plan our kitchen from scratch? Seeing good kitchens, talking about them, thinking about them, going to the 'Ideal Home' or similar exhibitions, to Design Centres or to the big shops does us the world of good. Back we come, full of inspiration, and if we haven't spent too much while we were there, we see what we can do to brighten up our own little corner!

Hours spent laboriously with squared paper, pencil and rubber might well be better spent giving the rubbish bin a coat of scarlet paint! Nevertheless there are a few fundamental bits of kitchen planning to look for when you are house hunting, or to remember when the man calls to say, 'Where shall I put the electric control panel?' or 'Where shall I run the gas pipe?' Because once those are *in*, the position of your gas stoves, electric cooker and equipment is partly determined.

Let us think first of kitchen equipment in order of importance.

The sink

This is a first consideration because once it is plumbed in you cannot move it. It is usually installed by the builder who places it by an outside wall, partly for drainage and inlet reasons, and partly so that you will have the advantage of a window over it. You can have one or two draining boards beside it.

The cooker

The main purpose of the kitchen (which comes from an old English word meaning 'to cook') is for cooking. Apart from the safety aspect clearly dealt with in Chapter 10, there is very little to say here. The relative merits of a gas and electric cooker must depend on the cost of gas and electricity in your area. The modern 'solid fuel' cooker has many advantages. It can be fired by gas or oil as well as by solid fuel.

Working surfaces

A food store

Orders of work 1

This probably happens 1–3 times daily: you enter the kitchen, get out the food, wash it, prepare it, cook it. Remembering the number of times you will do this (shall we say twice a day for 50 years? 36,500 times?) in order to preserve your feet, your back and your temper, look for an arrangement of your first four essentials as far as possible in this order.

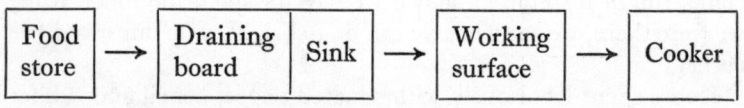

26 *Order of kitchen equipment*

Don't take one single step further than you need. If these four pieces of equipment extend 3 yards and you have walked once there and back you will eventually have walked almost *65 miles* there and *65 miles* back. So squash them up at once—

| Food store | Draining board | Sink | Working surface | Cooker |

27 *Positioning of equipment*

or if you are left handed reverse the order. Incidentally you do not have to clean in between each piece of equipment now. You will most probably find, however, that most units are already fixed in place when you move into your house, but, if you bear these points in mind, you will find that useful alterations are often feasible.

Orders of work 2

You have been shopping, you enter by the back door, unpack the food and put it away. Now you need

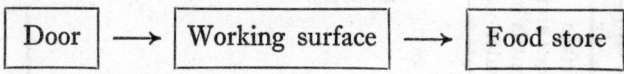

28 *Positioning of equipment*

Can we link this to our essential four?

It is important not to put the back door in line with the sink or cooker otherwise you'll have draughts round your ankles. Draught-proof your back door in any case.

Food store	Draining board	Sink	Working surface	Cooker
Working surface				

Back Door

29 *Positioning of equipment*

Orders of work 3

You cook, you strain your vegetables and put your saucepans to soak, you serve your meal.

Our scheme still holds good, but we now need either a table (and stools or chairs) in the kitchen, or a dining annexe fairly near the cooker, or a hatch through to an adjacent room.

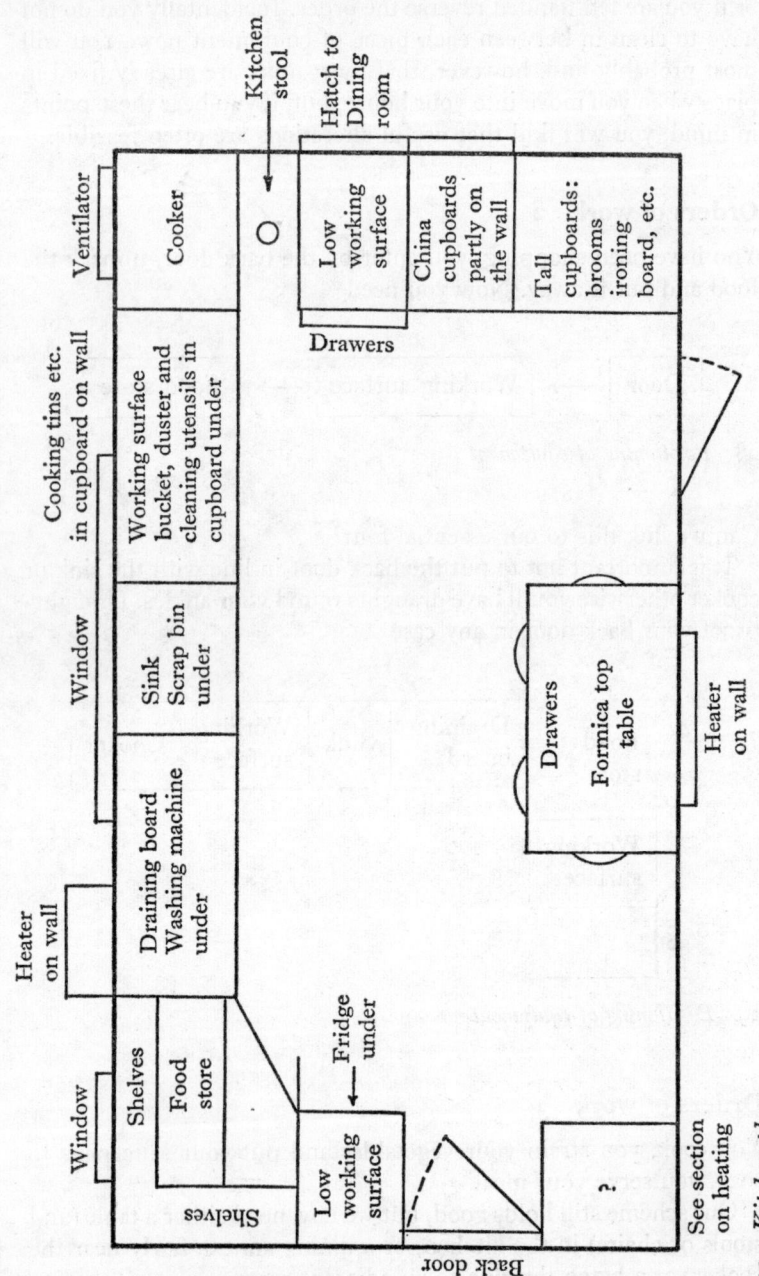

30 *Kitchen plan*

Orders of work 4

You clear the table, dispose of the scraps, wash up, drain the plates, put away the china, knives, forks, spoons and saucepans.

We need cupboards near the cooker for the saucepans, cupboards for dishes, drawers for cutlery, etc., places for detergents, bit tin, tea towel, plate rack, colanders and so on. You may prefer to have your pans and dishes on show. In this case choose open shelves or, for saucepans, hooks on the wall, instead of cupboards.

Cupboards are vitally important, and so is shelf space. Bearing in mind that continual bending will put a strain on your back, have your cupboards fitted at eye-level.

Orders of work 5

You place the washing machine near the sink, keeping the sink one half clear so that you can do hand washing at the same time, you rinse, spin or carry drip-dry clothes straight out to the line. Now you need space for the washer, buckets and pegs, both near the sink and working surfaces. Later you will need an ironing board, iron, clothes airer, all preferably kept in a cupboard.

Our final scheme begins to look like the diagram on page 140. You have tried to arrange the equipment thoughtfully, cutting down wasted effort and time. Having looked at the reason *behind* planning (the measurements are far less important) it may be possible to do a little time-and-motion study—for that is just what we have been doing on your own kitchen.

Heights are important too

So we have now saved your feet and legs a few miles—notice the stool! Now what about your back? It not only looks neater to have most of your surfaces at the same level but it is far easier to clean this way—providing that everything is at the ideal level for you. The average height for *working surfaces* is 36 inches above the floor and they should go back for at least 21 inches. A *sink* should be about 8 inches deep with the draining boards sloping very slightly. The height of 36 inches is normally ideal for the cooker, sink and draining board, but it is rather high for every working surface. One of them, especially if it is on its own, should be lower, about

32–3 inches. This is a much better height for creaming or rolling pastry. Notice we have two low working surfaces in the scheme. At the base of all these there should be toe hole space of at least 2 inches, on cookers 1–2 inches to enable you to stand right up to them. *The table* should be even lower, at 30 inches, and the chair

31 *Heights are important, too*

seats 18 inches from the floor. The *kitchen stool* should accommodate you at exactly the same height as if you were standing and should be fitted with a bar about 6–8 inches from the floor for you to rest your feet on.

Wall cupboards These are excellent both for saving precious space in the kitchen and for reducing the distance you will have to cover during the day. Place them conveniently, about 15 inches above a working surface. Have baking tins near the cooker. Put china near the table. Shelves should be narrow, getting even narrower towards the top shelf so that you can see its contents.

Drawers too should be shallow. Deep drawers and wide shelves in a kitchen mean you are always looking behind or underneath for things. Work surfaces should always extend beyond drawers, so that spilt liquids can be easily mopped from the floor, and not from cluttered drawers. *Shelves and store cupboards* above your arm's length are for rarely used articles. You could keep the first-aid box and medicines there, out of toddlers' reach.

32 *Drawers should be shallow*

All this applies to a person of *average* height, that is 5 feet 3 inches to 5 feet 6 inches. If you are shorter, ask for 1–4 inches to be put on or taken off work surfaces, cooker heights, etc. If this cannot be done, either stand on something when necessary, or put an upturned plastic tray in the sink under your bowl or a board on your working surface. It's better to save up for a large formica working board on battens, than have constant backache.

Ideally, ovens and refrigerators should be at eye-level height, 3–4 feet. Grills are frequently at this height and it is hoped that it will soon be possible to have the others in this position also—and at a reasonable price, not at the high extra cost that is being asked at present.

Kitchen equipment

Of the pieces in the scheme, only the refrigerator could nowadays be called a luxury, and to many who have tested and tried them they are no longer in this category. They will pay for themselves if properly used, but the fact remains that, with the British climate, we can do without them.

Now for the *Essential Items* and the not so essential.

ESSENTIAL	NICE TO HAVE (as extras)	LUXURIES
Pans		
1 milk pan (silicone)	1 large saucepan	1 set silicone-finished saucepans
1 small saucepan	1 double saucepan	
1 medium saucepan	1 omelette pan	1 Pyrosil (covered) pan
1 frying pan	1 deep fryer	
1 large saucepan	1 electric kettle	1 coffee percolator, electric
1 kettle	1 coffee percolator (non-electric)	
1 fireproof coffee jug		1 3-tiered steamer
1 teapot	1 pressure cooker	1 colourful cast iron enamelled casserole/pan
	1 graduated steamer to fit large saucepan	
	1 preserving pan	
Tins		
2 baking tins	1 Swiss-roll tin	1 ring-mould tin
1 large cake tin	1 gingerbread tin	1 heart (or similar fancy shaped tin)
1 small cake tin	1 loaf tin	
2 sandwich tins	1 flan tin (sponge)	1 sweet-mould tin
1 roasting tin	Any of the essential ones siliconed	1 Charlotte Russe tin
1 cooling tray		
1 set cutters	1 set enamel plates	
1 enamel plate	1 sponge finger tin	

Pie dishes, casseroles, and basins of oven glass, enamel, brown earthenware, Denby or cast iron enamelled

Casseroles		
1 2-pint, both parts of which can be used separately	1 set 1½-pint, 3-pint and 4-pint	Any of them in Denby special ware or cast iron enamelled

KITCHEN EQUIPMENT

ESSENTIAL	NICE TO HAVE (as extras)	LUXURIES
Pie dishes		
1 1-pint	1 set 3 different sizes	Soufflé dishes
1 2-pint		Chafing-dishes
Basins		
1 mixing bowl	1 set mixing bowls	
1 ½-pint basin	1 set basins	
1 1½-pint basin	1 oven-glass flan dish	
	1 oven-glass pie plate	
Jugs		
1 graduated jug	1 set of jugs	
1 1-pint jug		
1 ½-pint jug		
Storage equipment		
1 bread bin	several sets	sets decorated
1 biscuit tin	storage tins	china and earthenware
1 cake tin	or airtight plastic	jars, or coloured
1 coffee tin	containers	stone with wooden
1 tea caddy	spice rack	tops
	flour bin	
Utensils		
1 colander	1 rotary whisk	1 electric mixer
1 egg whisk	1 stainless-steel	attachment for
1 grater	square grater	shredding
1 basket sieve	1 Mouligrater	1 juicer attachment
or strainer	1 hair-mesh strainer	
1 lemon squeezer	1 rolling pin, glass,	
1 chopping board	to contain ice chips	
1 mincer		1 mincing attachment
1 potato peeler		
1 vegetable knife	1 set Prestige knives	1 set French knives
1 round-edged knife		
1 cook's knife	1 egg slicer	1 electric carver
1 bread knife (serrated)	1 parsley cutter	
1 carving knife		
1 sharpener		
1 wooden spoon	1 set wooden spoons	

ESSENTIAL	NICE TO HAVE (as extras)	LUXURIES
Utensils (*contd.*)		
1 flour dredger	1 Skyline set kitchen tools	1 Prestige set kitchen tools
1 pastry brush		
1 fish slice	1 potato masher	1 sugar thermometer
1 strainer spoon	1 kitchen paper-roll holder	1 set nylon forcing bags
2 tablespoons		
2 forks	1 flan ring, fluted	1 set meringue nozzles
1 tin opener (hand)	1 wall tin-opener	
1 bottle opener	1 United Yeast Co. set icing tubes	
1 corkscrew		
1 pr. kitchen scissors	1 set cream horn tins	
2 teaspoons	1 set Dariol moulds	
Miscellaneous		
1 jelly mould	1 set moulds	1 set aspic moulds
1 graduated dry measure	1 set kitchen scales	
1 plastic bucket		
1 wash-up bowl	1 detergent dispenser	1 washing-up machine
1 plastic draining rack		
4 tea towels	1 egg timer	
2 sponge cloths		1 waste-disposal unit
1 sink tidy		
1 pedal bit bin	1 swing-top refuse bin	
1 washing-up mop		
1 pan scrubber		

The list is formidable. It is intended for the average housewife at home all day with perhaps two children. To start with you will need far less, but this 'essentials' list is probably the one you will work and collect for. As many pieces of equipment are powered by electricity, make sure you have sufficient power points in the kitchen for all the things you might want in the future.

Each item you choose must be selected with care; make sure you are getting value for your money. Ask what materials the item is made from. Examine the finish. Will it rust, stain or warp? Learn something about the basic materials to help you to choose sensibly.

Metals, for pots and pans and ovenware

1 *Cast iron* This is strong and heavy, it conducts heat swiftly and evenly. It must be covered to prevent rusting. New processes for doing this have brought cast iron back into popularity. No longer is the iron pot just black and clumsy. Instead it is smoothly and subtly coloured with pale enamel inside and brilliantly finished outside with jewel colours, which cover the lid as well. Sometimes the inside is of a non-stick finish and, with the more expensive models, the vitreous enamel on the outside is gaily patterned. Iron pans are not cheap, but, since they last so long, they are very good value for money.

2 *Sheet steel* This also rusts and must be protected inside and out. The coating can be of tin or enamel, the latter's being more usual today. The price varies according to quality. The cheaper pans are usually thin and chip easily.

3 *Copper* This is now only in general use as a base covering for pans of other metals. It is too expensive and needs too much scouring and polishing to be a practical proposition for the housewife today. Therefore its modern use is to ensure evenly spread heat in pans of all varieties.

4 *Stainless steel* This is expensive, but long lasting. It is worth spending extra for a copper base coating, for it not only supplies the steel's deficiency for spreading heat evenly, but it also will prevent slight warping which may occur. And this really is stainless.

5 *Aluminium* This is the most frequently used metal for the manufacture of pans today. The cost of aluminium ovenware is high in comparison with cheap tinned sheet metal bun tins and baking trays. But because this metal does not rust, an aluminium baking tin will outlast all others. It is very easy to clean, but does stain if brought into contact with alkaline substances. It is very expensive to buy aluminium pans, but cheaper ones are available, although they tend to dent easily and sometimes become wobbly.

6 *Teflon coated* This is the trade name for one of the best silicone finishes. It is very tough and saves lots of time and energy. Teflon pans are reasonably priced.

Final points on pots and pans
Whichever you choose, remember these considerations apply to all types:

1 Only buy a set of pans if you really need a saucepan in every size.

2 If you have an electric cooker you will waste heat if the diameter of the base of any pan is less than that of the hot-plate. If you have solid hot-plates the base of your pans must be absolutely flat and as heavy as possible. Remember, too, that small pans on gas stoves sometimes wobble and tilt.

3 You have got to clean your pans and tins regularly. Make sure their shapes are simple, without difficult corners or crevices, and that they are rounded wherever possible.

4 Lids must fit exactly, yet be easy to remove. Have they wooden handles so that they will not burn you when you try lifting them from a hot pan?

5 The handle must also remain cool when the pan is hot. Is it fixed securely to the pan, and is its angle and length satisfactory?

6 Put your pans to soak at once after using them. The less you scour them, the longer they will last.

7 Do not touch your non-stick surfaces with anything metal—spoons, fish slices, knives, forks or wire wool—you'll spoil them if you do.

Ovenware

Apart from the baking trays already mentioned, there is probably little to choose between the five main types of ovenware used for pie dishes and plates, casseroles and deep roasters. Personal preference and what you can afford are the main criteria.

1 *Enamelled steel* This is inexpensive. It heats through quickly and spreads the heat evenly. Enamel pie dishes have good, wide rims and make attractive pies. But you cannot see the contents as they cook. These dishes will stand up well to oven heat and they do not break, but, eventually, the enamel chips or wears through.

2 *Ovenglass* This is attractive and fairly cheap. It is available in a wide range of colours and designs, but the clear glass has the advantage of transparency. Sometimes highly decorated dishes detract from the appearance of the food baked or served in them. Ovenglass stands up well to the heat, but is, of course, breakable.

3 *Earthenware* This is inexpensive, but breakable. English

earthenware is usually of a red-brown colour glazed in fawn. French earthenware is also available. It comes in a range of colours and is a little more expensive.

4 *Stoneware* The popular Denby ware is an example of this. Plain coloured and simple in design, this ware need not be too expensive. It is also available in highly decorative shapes, colours and designs, but for this you pay far more. It is never really cheap and it is breakable, but it is reliable, easily replaced and long lasting—if you take care of it.

5 *Porcelain* (fireproof) This is in the luxury class. It is delicate and beautiful, yet tough and reliable and will withstand severe oven temperatures. It often has a lustre or coloured decoration. Though it breaks if roughly handled it only does so through carelessness, and not from being overheated. The same applies to the last three types of ovenware.

General advice

(*a*) Ovenware needs to be handled with a cloth—make sure you can grip it easily. Handles or projecting knobs are necessary to make it possible to lift a hot lid.

(*b*) Avoid placing hot dishes on cold surfaces such as marble because, if made from any of the last four materials, they will crack.

(*c*) A lidded oven dish is very useful. It keeps in fat splashes (roasting tins). It retains most of the steam (casseroles). And it can also be used on the table as a second dish.

Kitchen implements

There are too many to be treated individually, but knives deserve a special mention, since they are probably a cook's most frequently used implement.

1 *Serrated-edged knives* Their cutting edge is at several angles and therefore remains sharper than those of other knives. When it does need sharpening, it is a specialist's job and you must return it to the manufacturer. These knives are very useful for cutting or sawing soft food such as tomatoes, grapefruit or bread. They are made from stainless steel.

2 *Plain-edged knives* Today most of these are made from stainless steel because the tinned and chromed ones wear out so quickly. If you cannot afford the better ones, it is a good idea to replace them gradually over the years. Only buy a set if you really need everything in that set. Do not let yourself be persuaded into buying gimmicky equipment—always ask yourself, 'Do I *really* need it?' 'If I buy it, how often will I use it?' If you then decide to buy, choose the best you can afford. This nearly always saves money in the end.

Refuse disposal

If you've a flat, three flights up, you are going to be very careful to keep your refuse disposal down to a minimum. *Waste-disposal units* fit into sinks with an opening about 3 inches wide. Into this you can scoop all your bits—no tins or bottle tops, but all your vegetable peelings, fruit cores and so on. You let the water run and press a button. In a few seconds (or minutes, depending on the amount of rubbish) electrically driven sharp knives revolving in the container under the sink will grind up all the waste and it becomes small enough to go down the drain. You must be careful to keep your fingers well away from the opening to the unit. You must also check with your Local Sanitary Engineer to make sure your drains can accommodate the pulp that this machine passes to them. It is very much a labour-saving device when you consider that all your greasy messes, left-overs and peelings can be dealt with and disappear from your sink. This is definitely a luxury and costs about £40 plus installation charges.

Where does the waste go? We dispose of three different types of waste from three different sources.

1 Waste from the toilet, bath and wash basin.
This is usually flushed away down one soil pipe situated between or near the bathroom and toilet, which leads into the main sewage system. This soil pipe is ventilated by means of a tall vent pipe which reaches above the guttering level and which is netted at the top to keep birds out. Every house or group of houses has an underground inspection chamber so that soil pipes can be easily examined before they join the main pipe which links all the houses in the road.

2 Waste water which often contains kitchen scraps, foam and grease from the kitchen sink.

REFUSE DISPOSAL

This is sometimes added to by the water from a plumbed-in washing machine, dish washer or waste-disposal unit. All this passes into the soil pipe to join the bathroom waste. Each of the pipes which joins the soil pipe has a two-way safety device, known as a U-bend. The soil pipe itself is usually fitted with one before it joins the wide bore main pipe on its way to the sewage works.

The U-bends are installed to provide permanent water traps in the pipes so that germs and smells from the sewage cannot get back up the pipe into the house. The shape of the bend also prevents foreign objects from passing from the house (down the sink or wash-basin) to become jammed in an inaccessible part of the pipe. Instead, these objects, such as hairpins or salt spoons, will usually stick in the U-bend and can be easily removed through the screw hole in the base—as shown in the diagram. All indoor U-bends should be fitted with a screw which can be removed to clear the pipe.

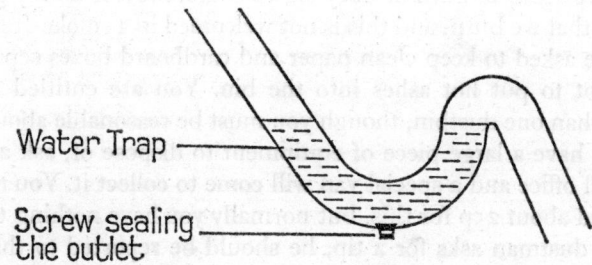

33 *The U-bend*

These two points are worth remembering:

(*a*) Make sure the U-bend has fresh or disinfected water in its trap, not the remains of the washing-up water. A few seconds' flush with fresh water, plus a drop or two of Dettol will ensure this.

(*b*) If you do remove the screw under the U-bend, you will let out not only the contents of the water trap, but also those of the pipe you are trying to unblock. So, be sure to have a bucket underneath to catch them all!

3 Solid waste. Any waste which goes into our scrap bins and dust bins which is not really solid, like a tin or packet, but which is damp, smelly or messy, must be carefully drained and then thickly wrapped. Now for the bins themselves.

Rules

Keep lids tightly on both bins. Wash the scrap bin out at *least* once a week and the dustbin once in 2–3 weeks in summer, 4–6 weeks in winter. Stand the dustbin slightly away from the house and up on bricks so that the air can circulate round it. Never let children play near it. Line both bins with paper, and wash thoroughly after you've touched either. If you are one of the unfortunate ones who has to take out the dustbin each week, don't forget it. From now on it is the responsibility of the local authority's sanitary department. They have two sections, one for dealing with dry-waste from dustbins, and one for dealing with sewage.

Our responsibility

In your dustbin only put household and not garden rubbish. Once we were asked to burn or bury all we could. Now it is only garden refuse that we burn, and this is not welcomed in a smoke-free area. We are asked to keep clean paper and cardboard boxes separately and not to put hot ashes into the bin. You are entitled to use more than one dustbin, though you must be reasonable about this. If you have a large piece of equipment to dispose of, ask at your council office and a special van will come to collect it. You may be charged about 25p for this, but normally you have nothing to pay. If the dustman asks for a tip, he should be reported to the local sanitary engineer.

Their responsibility

The dustman will empty your rubbish into the cart or skip. Some authorities provide local residents with good solid dustbins for 25p a year. The service is paid for out of the rates, subsidised by a government grant. The so-called 'dust cart' is usually a high-powered articulated lorry with an automatic tip-up and tip-out device. It closes completely when travelling, and the driver's cab is big enough to seat all the crew, usually 2–6 men. Some areas provide bins with quiet rubber or plastic lids and others are experimenting with disposable heavy paper bags. Many of us still have to supply our own bins though, and often these get badly dented. It will be cheaper in the long run to buy the sturdiest one you can afford. Get one that is really big enough with a well-fitting lid.

Final disposal

1 *Rubbish tips* Small towns in country areas use this method a great deal; it is the cheapest and simplest, but not the best. It is very unsightly, often smelly, dangerous to young children and the rubbish blows about. Rats and flies are frequent visitors. The rubbish is burnt in the pits, covered with a layer of soil until the pit is full.

2 *Rubbish barges* Towns on the coast can fill barges with rubbish, take it out to sea and dump it. It is taken out sufficiently far to prevent it from floating back to land.

3 *Sorting and salvaging the rubbish* This is done at a refuse disposal plant. The refuse is tipped on to moving belts which travel over sieves, under magnets, and past human sorters so that everything that has any value is salvaged and used, and the rest is burned in huge incinerators. These give off heat to work electric generators and the salvage is sold. This greatly reduces the cost of the operation, which is by far the best way to dispose of refuse.

In the last chapter we mentioned three of the most important 'aids to the housewife':

Warmth
Hot water
Ventilation

Also important are:

Lighting
Drainage

Heating

Heating to produce: (*a*) house warmth and (*b*) hot water. The mysterious ? in the kitchen scheme could be part of a heating system, or just a space to put up the clothes airer, so that the kitchen warmth would dry or air the washing on it.

Warmth—fires

We have three main types of fires:

1 Solid-fuel fire
2 Gas fire
3 Electric fire

1 OPEN SOLID-FUEL FIRE These are usually coal, partly because coal is easy to ignite, is comparatively cheap, looks cheerful and is almost always available. If you live in a so-called 'smokeless' zone, there are smokeless fuels such as coke or Gloco, Rexco, or Coalite. They are dearer but burn more slowly and more efficiently.

Advantages

1 Attractive appearance of the flames or glow.
2 It ensures ventilation by producing chimney draughts. Air circulates by being drawn in to replace heated air which rises up the chimney.
3 It is the cheapest fire to run over a long period.
4 It will heat a back boiler so producing hot water at the same time.
5 It heats by radiation so that the air is kept cool and sufficiently humid.

Disadvantages

1 50–60% of the heat goes up the chimney. Only half or less of the amount produced reaches you—slightly more with an enclosed fire.
2 Coal causes dirt, dust, ashes, grime *in* the house.
3 Coal also releases soot, sulphur dioxide, into the atmosphere in its smoke. This causes smog which affects hearts and lungs. It also causes buildings to decay.
4 It causes extra work.
5 It cannot warm immediately.
6 It has to be replenished frequently.
7 It involves the need for storage space, coal bins, buckets, shovels, tongs, pokers, etc.
8 There are by-products to dispose of—ashes regularly, cinders to be sifted, and soot occasionally.
9 If the latter is not removed, the chimney may catch fire.
10 It causes draughts.

ENCLOSED SOLID-FUEL FIRE Many modern fires may be closed in, with the glow showing through mica windows. They burn slowly, will stay alight all night and are more efficient than an open fire. This means they give *out* more of their heat. Recent models have been developed to provide full or partial central heating, as well as an attractive enclosed fire in the main living room, plus plenty of hot water. Such models as Parkrays, Redfyres or Everglows provide for up to eight radiators. These appliances have all the advantages of open fires and few of the disadvantages. They burn fuel which is permitted in a smokeless area, and some even consume the little smoke they do produce as well as their own soot. Such fuels as the coke-types 'Sunbrite', 'Gloco', 'Coalite' or 'Rexco', or others such as 'Anthracite' or 'Phurnacite' are suitable.

These fires are attractive to look at and safe to live with. They provide continuous warmth, day or night, and their convection currents spread this heat evenly throughout each room. They only need refuelling twice a day and the de-ashing is simple and clean. Perhaps the most important thing about them is that they provide one of the cheapest forms of central heating. The price, inclusive of installation, labour, a 'glass' fronted room heater, its back boiler, a 30-gallon cylinder and header tank, all the necessary piping and five radiators is about £260 or £1·23 a week for 5 years. The running costs are also comparatively low. Take for example the production of 600 therms of heat:

1 Glass fronted room heater—£52 a year
2 Gas fired boiler—£91 a year
3 Electric heating—£98 a year

Compare this with the other central heating installation and running costs later in the chapter!

2 GAS FIRES These must have outlets for fumes. The modern ones are attractive, self lighting and easily adjustable.

Advantages

1 Heat is instantly available.
2 Pleasant to look at.
3 Clean and labour saving.
4 Normal running costs are reasonable.
5 Heats by radiation.
6 Fume outlets assist ventilation.

Disadvantages

1 About 25% of the heat is lost up the chimney flue.

2 Does not heat water at the same time.
3 If used for long periods is rather costly.

3 ELECTRIC FIRES Today there are many kinds: radiant bar fires, fan heaters, infra-red heaters, turbo-fan heaters, oil-filled or water-filled radiators, heated by electricity, or electric storage heaters.

Advantages

1 Instant heat with all but electric storage heaters and filled radiators.
2 Almost 100% efficiency; the heat goes straight out into the room.
3 Some are portable.
4 They heat by radiation or by convection. Some by both methods.
5 They can incorporate fans to blow the heat out.
6 They can be fitted with thermostats so that they switch themselves on or off at set times, or when they reach set temperatures.
7 They are clean and labour saving.
8 They can be fitted on wall or ceiling—a good idea in the bathroom, with a cord attached to turn it safely on and off.

Disadvantages

1 They are expensive to run.
2 Some are very expensive to buy.
3 They do not assist with ventilation, they tend to dry the air.
4 They do not heat water for the domestic supply.

4 OIL HEATERS Not so frequently used because they can be very dangerous, if they flare in a draught or are knocked over. These can be drip-feed radiant heaters, or convector heaters. They are cheap to buy and cheap to run. They give off water vapour, making the air humid. They are portable. They need frequent replenishing which is messy. They also give off fumes and an occasional smell.

N.B. All these fires must be fitted with guards if you have children under 7 in the house.

HEATING

5 CENTRAL HEATING This is gradually gaining in popularity. You have four fuels to choose from:

1 Solid fuel
2 Gas
3 Oil
4 Electricity

This either gives background warmth to be supplemented by fires, or full heat. It always can give a hot water supply if you require it.

Costs

You have four things to pay for:

1 the installation of the central heating system;
2 the cost of the equipment used in the system;
3 the fuel for the system and its storage (oil and solid fuel);
4 the maintenance of the system.

The fuels

Starting at the cheapest and working up to the dearest, here are extra points worth considering over and above ones mentioned in the use of these fuels for fires.

1 SOLID FUEL Usually coke or anthracite is used. It must be ordered in good time and in bulk. If bought during the summer months it is cheaper. Storage space is needed. Not a fully automatic system because it has to be stoked—but with a good boiler only once a day or less.

2 GAS A wider bore pipe is needed than for normal gas consumption. Check to see that this will not mean a prohibitive cost increase. But bear in mind, however, that gas is the only fuel which is likely to get cheaper—a fairly substantial initial outlay might save you money later on.

3 OIL OR KEROSENE Must be stored in large tanks. It is cheaper if bought in bulk, i.e. a large amount at a time, but it can be paid for monthly and delivered perhaps twice a year. This fuel

is imported. Electricity switches the motor which pumps the oil on and off, so power cuts will put it out of action.

4 ELECTRICITY *Night storage heaters* 'pick up' heat during off-peak charge hours and give it out gently all day. Not too expensive. But often need boosting in the afternoon. *Oil-filled radiators* heated by electricity—costs far higher. Both systems subject to electricity cuts.

Comparative costs

Whatever fuel or type of system you are considering you measure your heating requirements in *British Thermal Units* (B.T.U.s). You assess how many you need, taking two factors into consideration:

1 the total floor area to be heated in square feet;

2 whether you want *background* heat and a hot water supply or *full heating* and a hot water supply.

Background heating

This should give you 60° in one room (living room or kitchen) and 55° elsewhere. Obviously you will need to boost this in cold weather with other types of heating.

Full heating

This should give you 65° in the living room, 60° elsewhere, 55° in the bedrooms.

Get an estimate from at least one heating engineer and make sure these are approved by the Gas or Electricity Board, The Coal Board or oil supplier, e.g. Shellmex, B.P. or Esso. He will tell you how many B.T.U.s you need for the number of square feet to be heated. Each house differs with respect to its flooring, insulation, window space, thickness of walls and to whether it is sheltered or exposed to cold winds. Now we must consider two points:

COMPARATIVE COSTS

1 the efficiency of the various fuel boilers, i.e. how much heat they lose and how much they give out;

2 the cost of the fuel per B.T.U.

FUEL	% of heat given out by boilers/ radiators	Cost for 1 Therm i.e. 100,000 B.T.U.s
Coke	60	4½p–6½p
Anthracite	75	5½p–7p
Gas	80	6p–10p
Kerosene	70	5½p–6p
Oil	80	5p–5½p
Electricity storage heaters	70–95	9p–13p*
Electricity, oil-filled radiators	100	17p–29p

* Off-peak tariff

Now let us look at the comparative costs in two typical houses:

1 a semi-detached 2-bedroomed house;
2 a detached 3-bedroomed bungalow.

EXAMPLE A

2-bedroomed semi-detached house consisting of:

1 living room with dining recess
2 bedrooms
Kitchen
Bathroom

Total floor area 725 square feet, insulation adequate.

Owners choose to have background heating with hot water supply (60° F in kitchen, 55° F elsewhere).

Heating engineer recommends 30,000 B.T.U.s plus a little to spare.

Price and running costs of a 31,000 B.T.U. installation.

TYPE OF BOILER	PURCHASE COSTS		ANNUAL RUNNING COSTS		7-year total including Purchase Costs
	Boiler, etc. £	Storage tank £	Fuel £	Service £	£
Diplomat 31 (Gas)*	99	—	46–72	4	450–630
Coke boiler	50	—	55–77	—	434–580
Anthracite boiler	99	—	57–60	—	452–522
Kerosene boiler*	83	28	50–55	6	495–525
Other heating					
Gas-fired warm air*	104	—	50–78	4	474–674
Electric night-storage*	Costs of equipment included in total purchase costs	—	77–113	—	539–793
Electric oil-fired radiators*		—	105–146	—	731–1,024

I would be inclined to add another £75–£125 on to the total cost. Manufacturers often tend to *under*estimate in an effort to sell their product.

EXAMPLE B

3-bedroomed detached bungalow consisting of:

Lounge and dining room
3 bedrooms
Kitchen and bathroom

Total floor area 1,000 square feet with more than adequate insulation.

Owners choose full heating and hot water supply (65° F in all rooms).

Heating engineer recommends 44,000 B.T.U.s.

COMPARATIVE COSTS

Price and running costs of a 44,000 B.T.U. installation.

TYPE OF BOILER	PURCHASE COSTS		ANNUAL RUNNING COSTS		7-year total including Purchase Costs
	Boiler, etc. £	Storage tank £	Fuel £	Service £	£
Diplomat 44 (Gas)*	108	—	66–105	4	592–870
Coke boiler	60	—	78–107	—	604–807
Anthracite boiler	126	—	72–87	—	627–734
Kerosene boiler*	132	28	70–75	6	680–721
Other heating					
Gas-fired warm air*	160	—	70–111	4	667–960
Electric night-storage*	Costs of equipment included in total purchase cost	—	110–160	—	770–1,102
Electric oil-fired radiator*		—	146–206	—	1,026–1,446

Even with payments spread out over several years the costs are still heavy. Nevertheless the systems marked with an asterisk * will give you heat and hot water at the press of a button; or by clockwork. You set the clock and the heat turns itself on when you choose and off when you choose, cutting in and out, as it reaches the temperature you have selected. Worth saving for?

Keeping in the heat

This is the result of the 'adequate insulation' mentioned several times in this chapter and, of course, it is bound to entail keeping out the cold. It can be done in several ways.

It is a sad fact that about one-third of the heat produced in a house escapes through the roof. Most of this heat loss (about $\frac{3}{4}$) can be avoided if the attic floor or the roof itself is efficiently insulated. This means that it must be completely covered with a material which does not easily conduct heat.

Glass fibre, mineral fibre or granulated cork are three suitable insulating materials. The cost of insulating the attic floor of an average-sized 3-bedroomed house is about £15 to £18. If you wish to use the attic as a bedroom and decide to insulate the roof, the cost will be higher—about £28 to £34. Tanks in the attic should always be insulated to prevent the household supply of water from freezing in winter. This is usually called lagging. Another method of insulation is using ceiling tiles which cut down heat loss, and if used on a ground floor, noise from above is also reduced. Yet another method is possible if you have cavity walls. Specialist firms offer a service which entails drilling holes in the walls and filling them with insulating material of a plastic foam type. Though this is initially expensive, it could cut your heating bills down by a quarter.

Draughts bring in cold and reduce temperatures. However, all rooms need fresh air for their occupants and for the fires, so try to have a small window open. The draught-proofing of doors and windows is an obvious need, but less obvious are the cracks between floor boards and between walls and skirting boards. There are sealing compounds and plastic foam strips to deal with this. Double glazing helps prevent the escape of heat through window panes. This form of insulation is dealt with later in the chapter.

Hot water

It would be nice to think that the ? in the corner of your kitchen stood for a neat streamlined central heating boiler so that your house would be warm, your cleaning cut to a minimum and your water always hot. But as we have seen the cost is considerable.

Other ways of ensuring plenty of hot water are:

1 Solid fuel boiler such as an Ideal Boiler. These can make a mess and cause more work, but they warm the kitchen, heat the water and the costs are reasonable.

2 A solid fuel cooker—Aga, Rayburn, Esse, etc.—on which you can cook and with which you can warm the kitchen and heat the water.

3 Instant gas water heater over sink and/or bath.

4 Storage gas water heater.

5 Instant electric water heater over sink.

6 Electric immersion heater in hot water tank upstairs, carefully insulated.

VENTILATION

7 See that all hot water pipes and tanks are carefully lagged to keep in heat and to help prevent bursts during the winter.

The remaining important 'aids to the housewife' are: (*a*) Ventilation and (*b*) Lighting.

Obviously these two are related. As we saw earlier one of the reasons for housewife fatigue has been proved to be lack of oxygen.

The last section, and our scheme, has provided her with heating in the kitchen so she should be able to open a window without feeling the cold too severely.

Ventilation

The ventilation of the house is an easy matter. Most of the rooms are empty all day so the windows can be opened to air the room thoroughly without causing discomfort.

Types of windows

Most modern windows are *pivot-hung windows*, or 'swing' windows. The catch in the centre base releases the base of the window to swing out-and-open on the two pivots half way up the sides. The top of the window swings in and usually the window is so constructed as to have a limited swing, unless the lock catch is released. This is only released if the whole window is swung over for cleaning like this—

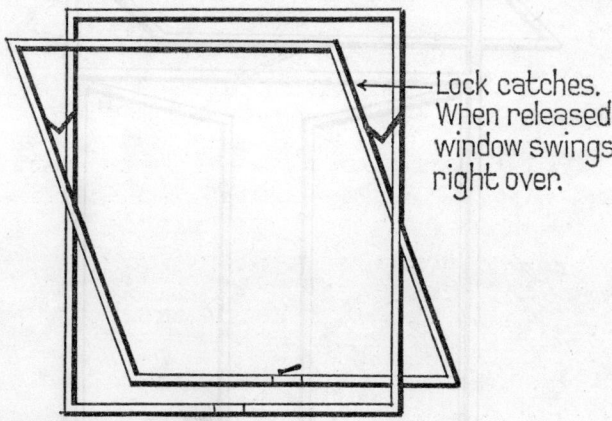

34 *A pivot-hung window*

These are good windows because automatically on opening you have a space at the bottom for fresh cold air to enter, to replace the hot stuffy air that escapes at the top—and the catch-release for easy cleaning saves you window-cleaners' bills!

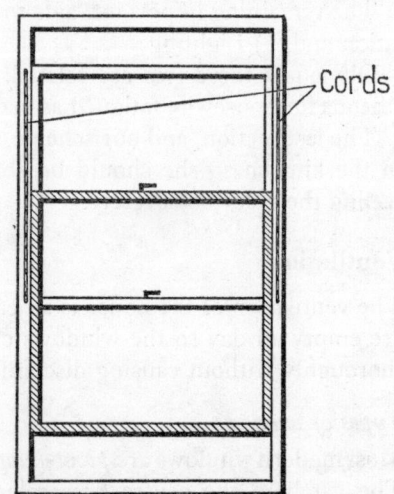

35 *A sash window*

Sash windows also open at the top and bottom, of course, but are cumbersome to push up or down, and the sash cords eventually break.

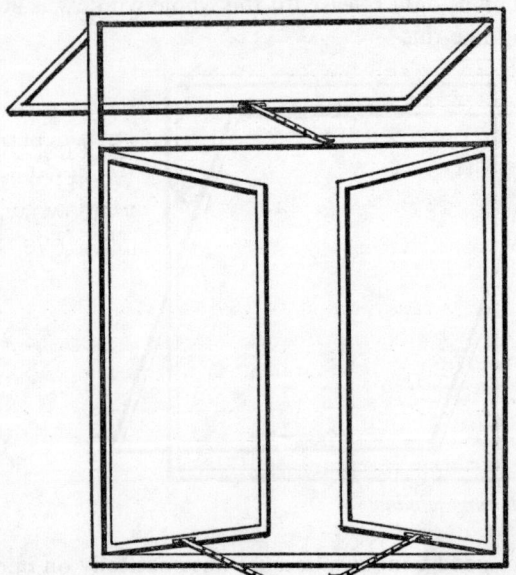

36 *Casement window with pivot upper window*

Casement windows are improved by having a small window at the top, as shown. However, in a kitchen it is desirable to have permanent ventilation of some sort which does not have to depend on opening a window. It has been recommended that the air in the kitchen should be changed 15–20 times each hour. A fan extractor easily does this and a small one installed costs about £18. Air bricks are essential in bathrooms and larders. Extra ventilation may also be necessary.

French windows have a very large expanse of glass. They let in plenty of light and they need a lot of cleaning. Children love them, they can always see through at some point and can rarely resist the temptation to touch the glass with sticky fingers. Care must be taken to see that their enthusiasm does not lead them to fall heavily against the glass, or to take aim at it. The main advantage of French windows is that they provide you with an extra door, an easy way out into the garden, and an easy way in for sunlight and fresh air. Their main disadvantage is that they provide an equally easy way in for draughts (and prowlers). Be sure they fit exactly and lock securely. Windows are large in modern houses. Consequently rooms are lighter and more airy, but there is one snag—the great loss of heat through glass. But with *double glazing*—two panes of glass with an air space between—you are provided with an excellent insulator, and the loss is much reduced. It is well worth looking for in a new house, or if you gradually re-fit each window in your own home, the cost of the glass and fittings will soon be offset by what you save by preserving heat. This is not a difficult job if you use the plastic fittings specially made for the purpose.

Lighting

It has been calculated that you need 100 watts of light for each 60 square feet of floor space. Light is especially important in the kitchen where you have many intricate things to do. Notice that most of the time you have your back to the centre of the room and face the wall. This is where the light should be, not in the middle of the ceiling throwing many shadows. Some equipment, such as the cooker, may have its own extra light above it, and there is often a light in the oven. Many refrigerators light up when opened. Big cupboards should have a 25-watt bulb in them, the larder a 40–60-watt bulb, depending on its size. This saves so much groping in the dark and helps prevent eye-strain.

Glare from naked bulbs blazing down is very tiring to the eyes. Enclose them in a translucent globe so that the light from them is softer and diffused.

Fluorescent or strip lights These are excellent in kitchens or passages, especially if these are dark and the light is frequently in use. Initially they are expensive but they are very cheap to run, and 'daylight' the area with a bright shadowless effect. Don't ever sacrifice light because you like a certain shade. Be sure if you are reading, writing or sewing that you have adequate light. If you want any advice, get in touch with the Electrical Association for Women.

Daylight This is the best light. Have as generous a window as you can in the kitchen, preferably at the back of the sink—provided the view is reasonable. Don't clutter up your windows with curtains, particularly net ones. They are dust traps and the only thing they seem to keep out effectively is the Vitamin D which should be reaching you in sun's rays. At the kitchen window they get particularly messy.

Blinds

Should there be considerable glare from a window, or should you be embarrassingly overlooked, blinds may provide you with the answer. The modern blind is of the Venetian or slatted type. These have the advantage of tilting slats—usually 2 inches wide—which can be adjusted easily to any angle. It is therefore possible to keep out the sunlight but let in the air, or to reflect the maximum light in dull conditions. Some manufacturers make these blinds in as many as twenty different colours, and you can get multicoloured blinds. Made of plastic, or better still, in stove-enamelled aluminium, they can be cleaned with a wipe and the aluminium ones do not warp or snag. An 18-inch-wide blind with a 2-feet drop costs £3·45; a 3-feet-wide blind with a 3 feet 9 inch drop costs £5·75. Plastic blinds are cheaper. Both kinds can also be used as room dividers—to screen off a kitchen, for example.

Remember that, however warm and bright your house, however efficiently run your kitchen, your home will lack something if you do not take care both of it and you. A dusty, untidy living room or a tired, irritable wife will have the effect of spoiling everything you have planned, worked and saved for.

Further reading

Hygiene in the Home, by Elizabeth Norton, published by Mills and Boon Ltd., at $47\frac{1}{2}$p

Science and Your Home, by J. Gostelow, published by Blond at 71p

Information from the National Heating Centre, 34 Mortimer Street, London, W.1

Practical work

1 Is there a Solid Fuel Advisory Bureau near you, or one you can write to? Look it up in the phone book. Find out:
(i) Which fuels you would use on a closed solid-fuel fire and how much they cost.
(ii) How solid-fuel cookers work and what they look like.
(iii) What is coke?

2 Carry out a Time and Motion Study programme for your own practical cookery at school. How many paces do you do to the yard (or 6 yards)? Now you'll know how many per mile.

Trace your journey in paces—then yards, then miles—from your table to the larder, to the ingredients table, back to your table, to the sink, then to the cooker—or whichever areas you normally visit when starting your practical lesson. Now, how many lessons do you get per week, and how many school weeks are there in a year?

N.B. Don't forget you don't do that journey only once per lesson, do you?

3 Carry out a lighting survey at home. Measure the area of one room and see if you have got the number of watts recommended. Is there anywhere at home in which you are in shadow as you sit to do close work? Notice the difference between pearl and clear bulbs. Which do you like best and why? What is the average 'life' of a bulb?

4 'You can't beat a coal fire!' Debate this.

5 As a project, make an illustrated folder of *either*:

(*a*) Kitchens—demonstrate recent improvements *or*
(*b*) Heating in Britain today.

6 Find out what the *Electrical Association for Women* exists for. Can it be of any use to you?

7 Is there a Design Centre in your town? If so, go and have a look at the things there. Discuss whether you think the designs are good or bad, and why.

Questions

1 Imagine you are moving into a bed-sitting room on your own, where there is a Baby Belling Cooker for your use (grill, oven, 2 hot plates). Adapt the kitchen equipment list to suit your requirements.

2 One year later you are getting married. Bring the list up to your new situation in which you have to provide for your husband, in a flat of your own, and with the use of a full-sized cooker. Imagine you have £25 to spend, and supplement this with a wedding present list.

3 Plan a baking day 'order of work' as we did for shopping, etc. How does it fit in with the scheme? See if it can be improved on.

4 'Central heating is a "must" in the home of today.' Write an essay discussing this.

5 You are trying to persuade your husband to buy you either:

(*a*) an electric food mixer or
(*b*) a refrigerator or
(*c*) a waste disposal unit

Choose which one you are aiming for, and write what arguments you could use to persuade him.

6 You are a dustman. Give your opinion of various housewives' 'dustbin habits', and end up by telling the local authority how it ought to dispose of its rubbish!

SECTION III · HEALTH AND SAFEGUARDS
FOR YOU AND YOUR FAMILY

CHAPTER 8 · HYGIENE FOR YOUNG PEOPLE

Health and happiness go together. If you are run down, get frequent headaches, are listless or bad tempered you will not be very good company. If your breath, or your person, is slightly unpleasant, if you suffer from spots, or if your flashing smile reveals gaps, this is even worse! Your indifferent health could be isolating you and causing you unhappiness. What can you do about it?

Firstly, it doesn't sound as if there is anything seriously wrong. It sounds rather as if you have been just a bit careless and thoughtless, and have been ill-treating the one and only body you are ever going to have. If any other vehicle were neglected in the way some people neglect themselves, our garages would be far more overworked! A car that is not maintained regularly, put away for the night, oiled, washed-down, re-charged and filled with suitable fuel is a car that will not last long.

How about you?

Sleep

Do you get at least 9 hours per night of regular, uninterrupted sleep? You need it (never mind about that novel under the bedclothes, or that late night TV show). If you start looking tired you will soon start looking worn! The amount of sleep you need depends not only on your age, but on your own physical requirements. Some of you will need as much as 10 hours sleep, others less.

Food

Are you just filling yourself with food, or are you nourishing yourself with it? As well as eating to stop feeling hungry we must eat to build, repair and protect our bodies. Especially in winter we need food for warmth, and at all times we need food for energy. Even if we are ill and in bed we still need this energy-food because four-fifths of the energy we use just maintains the regular working of our bodily functions—heart beats, digestion, breathing and perspiring. Only about one-fifth is used in physical exercise and doing the things we usually think about when using up energy is mentioned. You will learn in your Cookery lessons all about the value of food but let us look here at diet in relation to appearance as well as to health.

Body-building foods (or proteins) These have nothing to do with getting fat or thin. They alone provide the materials for building and repairing the body, for creating and replacing cell tissue. If too many proteins are eaten the excess will be burnt by the body to provide energy and heat. They cannot be stored by the body and this indicates two things:

1 that a fresh supply must be eaten every day;
2 that protein, even if eaten in excess, cannot make you fat. Be careful though—we think of meat and cheese as protein. But neither is all protein; a chop may be 25–50% fat and cheese will certainly be 30% fat.

Excess protein You are not likely to have too much protein-rich food in your diet, and if you did it would do you no harm. Unfortunately protein foods are, on the whole, the expensive ones, and often the ones we cut down on when funds are low. By Friday you may find yourself serving only a small portion of protein food —one egg, or two sausages, and a large portion of chips. If anyone gets two eggs or four sausages it will probably be Father—in fact he is not the one who needs it most, the growing children do. Try hard to make a good portion of a protein food form the core of each meal. When you do, see how many *bonus* vitality foods they give you. Let us look at the best protein-rich foods, all of which come from an animal source.

Protein:	*Milk*	*Eggs*	*Fish*
Bonus:	Vitamins A, D, C Calcium Phosphorus	Vitamins A, D, B Iron Phosphorus	Vitamins A, D Iodine Calcium Phosphorus
Protein:	*Cheese*	*Meat*	*Offal*
Bonus:	Vitamins A, D, B Calcium Sodium Phosphorus	Vitamin B Iron Phosphorus	Vitamins A, D, B Iron Phosphorus

Are these bonus items important? What can they do to help? We call them the *Vitality Foods*. These used to be called Protective Foods but the illnesses they protected us from are now very rare. They can be found in the protein foods and, to a lesser extent, in the groups of foods that supply us with warmth and energy.

Warmth and energy foods These are mainly the starchy, sugary and fatty foods. Obviously we need warmth (somehow, whether the weather is 'boiling' or icy our bodies stay at 98·4° F) and energy. These are the groups of foods that the body stores for emergencies. It packs them away round the internal organs or just under the skin, so if you indulge in too many of this group your weight will increase and your figure will suffer. These foods, called fats and carbohydrates, are often cheap, very tasty, and easy to prepare. Many need no preparation and so there is a great temptation to fill up with them instead of benefiting from a mixed, balanced diet. However it must be remembered that we get about 30% of the proteins in our diet from bread, flour and cereals. These are known as vegetable proteins and although useful, they are not as valuable to humans as are the animal proteins listed above.

Here are a few examples, with the tempting food items in brackets:

Potatoes	Bread	Cakes
(Chips and crisps)	(Rolls and cobs)	(Eclairs and doughnuts)
Sugars	*Flour*	*Fats*
(Sweets, ices)	(Puddings)	(Cream)
(Lollies and jam)	(Pastry)	(Butter)
	(Dumplings)	(Dripping)

Some give a vitality bonus too:

Potatoes	*Brown bread*	*Flour*	*Butter* (and some margarine)
Vitamin C	Vitamin B	2nd-class protein	Vitamins
	Calcium, iron	Calcium	A and D

You need some but not too much of all classes of foods. An over-fatty or too-rich diet in your teens can cause stomach upsets and a greasy or spotty skin (acne). If in your teens you are a 'podge' or a 'bean pole' this may just be that your glands have not yet settled down to stabilise your growth mechanism. Later, as an adult, you will have to be far more careful.

The vitality foods Vitamins and mineral salts. Small doses of these cannot work miracles, but if they are regularly included in the diet from the days before your birth they can help to keep you fit and strong. Healthy teeth, gleaming hair, strong nails and straight limbs moulded on to sturdy bones depend on vitamins and mineral salts, especially these three:

	Vitamin D	*Calcium*	*Phosphorus*
Rich sources	Milk	Milk	Milk, eggs,
	Dairy produce	Cheese	cheese, meat,
	Cod and halibut liver oils	Green vegetables	offal, fish
	Herrings, salmon, sardines		

Did you notice how often *milk* gave you a bonus? Are you drinking enough? It could come from an ice cold milk vending machine at 3p a glass. If this is not available ask your teacher to contact the Milk Marketing Board about the Milkpak system.

Clear healthy skins

Skin troubles normally come from within. Look carefully into your diet, instead of studying the skin food in the cosmetic windows.

37 Be 'with it' with milk

Vitamin B helps both with the health of the skin and the well-being of the nervous system. Remember that your skin is a mass of nerve endings (the nerve disease, shingles, appears as a rash on the skin). A 'Yeast Pac' on your face will do you far less good than yeast in your diet; try Marmite, a yeast extract, wholemeal bread instead of white, Bemax on your cereals, liver, kidney, bacon and nuts. Your skin is also a mass of sweat gland endings—don't let them get blocked. See that you have plenty of roughage in your diet so that you do not suffer constipation and the spottiness, listlessness, bad breath and depression that goes with it.

Roughage: fresh fruits and vegetables (skins and stalks where possible too), brown bread and cereals. *Drink lots of water.*

Eyes, gums and tongues, mucous membranes

When bacteria enter the body it is by way of the nostrils and mouth, lined as they are by delicate mucous membranes. If these are too delicate, the onset of infection is easier. The strengthening of the membranes is assisted by *Vitamin A*. This, with Vitamin D, is fat soluble and so both are found in the fat of milk, in cream, cheese, butter and in fish oils. As Vitamin A is stored in the liver, it is found there also. *Carotene*, another less rich source of it, is found in carrots, tomatoes and green vegetables. Not only is our resistance to infection lowered by lack of Vitamin A but our eyesight too can suffer. Finally, it affects growth, particularly of the bones and teeth.

Vitamin C is found in oranges, rosehip syrup, blackcurrants (and not in expensive over-publicised drinks!), all fresh fruits and vegetables—even potatoes. But if you peel your potato, cut it into chips, leave it to soak and then fry it, very little Vitamin C will be left in it. If you pull up your carrot, quickly wash or scrape it and crunch it up straight away, it will be very rich in Vitamin C. Why? These things kill it:

1 Heat
2 Cold
3 Exposure (being left about)
4 Sun rays
5 Soaking
6 Alkalis (bicarbonate of soda)

This last of the 'big four' protective vitamins also has an effect on growth. It protects the health of teeth and gums and prevents scurvy. This is not just a gum disease, but soreness. There is often the beginning of soreness in other joints and consequent pain. Such pains were until quite recently called 'growing pains' and were just accepted as something to be put up with, like the voice breaking. Now we know they are a sign of mild scurvy and can be cured. Better still they can be prevented, for Vitamin C is easy to obtain. But as it is the one vitamin which cannot be stored, so, like proteins, some must be eaten every day.

Energy

Your listlessness may be due to *anaemia*. This is not lack of blood but lack of the haemoglobin in the blood. Lack of this means that not enough oxygen is absorbed into the blood, for that is the job of haemoglobin. As one of the jobs of oxygen is to burn up your energy foods to produce energy, we get this pattern:

| Short of iron | means | Short of haemoglobin | means | Short of oxygen | means | Short of energy |

Gently pull down your lower lid and look—is it pink or white? It should be pink; if not see your doctor. You lose quite a quantity of blood each month, so your haemoglobin supply will decrease unless you regularly include in your diet such foods as: almonds, raisins, liver, egg yolks, kidneys, baked beans, curry powder, peas and cocoa. These are the iron-rich foods which will keep your haemoglobin healthy.

Exercise

Exercise your limbs—not only on the dance floor but out in the fresh air. Sunshine will give you a Vitamin D bonus straight from its rays. Then they will be trim and shapely and when the gang says, 'Let's go for a day's hike,' you'll be fit enough to go, strong enough to keep up with the others, and good company all the way.

Cleanliness

The best cosmetic of the lot! The skin of an average adult contains some two million sweat glands. These give out over two pints of perspiration per day—more on a hot or busy day. If they didn't the body would become over-heated and feverish; they are our escape valves; they make it possible for us to cool down. The hotter we get, the more we perspire. As the air around us is warm, so the perspiration evaporates, drawing the heat from the skin and thus cooling it.

Our skins are left with the residue of this process on their surface. The *Eccrine glands* of the soles of the feet, the head and the hands leave a residue of salt. But when this mingles with the dirt and dead skin of the hair, the socks and shoes, and all the things that the hands touch, the result can be very unpleasant. The residue from the *Apocrine glands* is more unpleasant. These glands are situated between the legs and under the arms and only become active when you reach puberty. You will learn all about this in Chapter 13.

This residue consists of lactic acid, fatty matters and proteins. None of these smell unpleasant, but as soon as they are exposed on the skin bacteria get to work on them and they decompose. This is when, inevitably, offensive odours are caused. They are accentuated by the fact that the circulation of air is very restricted in these areas, and any clothes worn there will smell as unpleasant as does the skin.

These facts, plus the rather obvious one that we get dirty anyway, every day, should have by now convinced you of the necessity to wash—often, thoroughly and regularly! The Elizabethans were never convinced of this necessity, so instead they swamped themselves in perfumes made from musk, civet and frangipani! Even the Victorians were only partially convinced, and they relied on lavender water, lavender sachets and pot pourri to disguise their bodily odour. Judges, even today, are presented with miniature posies of sweet-smelling herbs, a relic of the days when scents were needed to prevent the odours and germs from the prisoners and court in general from reaching their judicial noses!

Today we know that cleanliness is vital for health as well as for companionship. A shower every day is ideal. The water should be fairly hot to loosen the grease particles which hold the dirt to the skin. Make yourself soapy enough to emulsify them. Failing this, have a bath, wash down or dry towelling each day. The special areas already mentioned (except for the head) need a very thorough wash at least once a day. Even after a bath at night, you need a wash in the morning to remove the residue of overnight perspiration. Strangely enough scientific progress has made this problem more acute because now we have better heating in our houses and use such things as electric blankets. We also wear synthetic fabrics which do not absorb perspiration and so we must be especially careful to stay fresh. Luckily progress can help us here.

Special measures

Usually in our teens we begin to realise that even though we wash thoroughly and often, this is not enough to cope with the decomposition of the residue from the Apocrine glands. To help, there are soaps, such as Clearasil or Valderma or D.D.D., which help to remove the bacteria from the skin, preventing decomposition and odours. This help, however, is only temporary. Many teenagers and most adults find they need even more protection. Deodorant and anti-perspirant preparations can be used. Both are safe, providing you have a non-allergic skin. Try a little on your wrist first, to make sure. Then use one or both as well as, not instead of, washing!

The deodorant

This will be sufficient if you only perspire a little. It does just what it says; it removes the odour from the skin and will last from 8–12 hours.

The anti-perspirant

This deodorises and at the same time prevents any excess perspiration. It is stronger than a deodorant alone (the two are often combined) and will last from 8–24 hours. It is an essential for those who perspire a lot, or those of us in hot sticky jobs. Do not be put off by the old wives' tale that it is bad to stop yourself perspiring under your arms. Remember you have about two million sweat glands working for your good, putting a few out of action will not hurt—it will be much more pleasant all round. However, the skin round your vagina is so delicate that washing and talcum powder are the best answer for this area.

For under the arms, Cool, Mum and Sure are reasonably priced. Luxuriously scented but more expensive are Revlon, Yardley or Houbigant.

Boys and men too should be encouraged to keep themselves fresh in this way. Several deodorant and anti-perspirant preparations are on the market just for them which are without scent or with a special male tang—for example, Right Guard and Us. Encourage them while they're young. You may be washing their shirts and sweaters one day!

Your hair

Wash it frequently. Twice a month should be sufficient for dry hair but wash greasy hair twice a week. Brush out the tangles each day. Remember that back combing, effective though it is, is really creating tangles. Brushing will help the surface appearance of the hair, but it cannot help the health of your hair. Feed your hair, not with lotions or expensive shampoos put on from the outside (hair is dead apart from the roots, that is why you can cut it without hurting yourself) but from the inside, to feed the roots. The roots are fed by the blood stream which carries nutrients from your digestive system. It is a good mixed diet that will help you, not sprays, and mists and magics! Have a spotlessly clean brush and comb too and keep them to yourself—this isn't being selfish.

Dandruff

Recognise this for what it is—a fungus infection easily passed on. So be careful about using other people's combs. Seek your doctor's or chemist's advice if the attack is severe. You may need skilled treatment.

Hands

Always keep your nails scrubbed and clean. If you have dirt in them, you will have bacteria in them. Scrub your hands and nails before touching food or cooking and serving utensils, before giving first aid, before applying make-up, and after using the toilet. Try not to bite your finger nails; it spoils the look of your hands. The use of nail varnish may help you to stop; if you use it have it either on or off—not half and half!

Teeth

Care for your teeth, as you care for your hair. Brush them regularly night and morning, and, if possible, after every meal. Brush up and down to get into the crevices, and round the back, which most people forget. Never mind about toothpaste being expensive; if you brush thoroughly it doesn't matter if you are using it or not, although the brands containing fluoride may do something to prevent decay. Your toothbrush will need replacing regularly.

Chewing gum may help to clean your teeth and does not harm them as much as lollies, fruit gums and gob stoppers. It is the long drawn-out flow of sugar round the teeth that encourages decay. The acid in fizzy drinks is particularly bad for the teeth. Nuts, apples, celery and carrots are better to crunch with milk to quench your thirst.

Your clothes

You will probably change your outer clothes very frequently—they can be seen so you are conscious of them. Underwear sometimes gets neglected, especially the poor old girdle which most people think you need only buy singly. Briefs and tights should be washed every day. Bras, slips and vests every two to three days, and pantie girdles at least once a week, more often if worn next to the skin. This is your job, not your mother's. With easy drying fibres and non-iron finishes you can do a quick wash each night, and always be fresh underneath. Don't wear very tight clothes; they will cause over-perspiration and considerable discomfort.

Shoes

Have your foot measured—while standing on it—by an expert. Choose a shoe which does not cramp your foot, or throw all the weight on to part of it. Fifty-six per cent of all 15-year-olds examined in 1964 were suffering from corns, bunions or hammer toes. Do not join their number. Avoid pointed or narrow toes, high heels and insufficient side and arch support. Remember your weight through a stiletto heel equals the weight of an elephant on that tiny area. This weight destroys flooring. It mashes up composition and lino floors and dents and scratches wood floors. Have you the right to do this to the homes of your friends, or to public buildings? Platform soles not only look clumsy but cause sprains, weakened ankles and damaged pelvic girdles. This can affect child-bearing. Is it worth it just for a passing fashion? Wear sensible shoes while your feet are still growing. Then at 18+ you can wear what you like but be careful even then. Do not wear uncomfortable shoes just because they are fashionable—if you must, wear them for short periods only.

Posture

If you heed all these reminders you will have reason to hold your head up high. Have a good look at yourself in the mirror. Are you standing correctly or do your shoulders droop, and does your bottom stick out? A good plan is to imagine that you have a tall friend who is gently lifting you up by the hair! You have got to stand and be tall to stop this hurting. Imagine it and try it. The effect will be to pull your stomach in, straighten you up and flatten your buttocks. Now put back your shoulders and hold up your head. You will find you can breathe more easily and deeply. You will look better and you will feel better.

Cosmetics

These are used on your skin. They will not look attractive, or improve your looks unless their foundation, your skin, is as healthy as possible. We have already seen which special foods and drinks will help—what other steps can we take?

Your skin

It may be suffering from one of these five troubles:

1. Dryness
2. Greasiness
3. Blackheads
4. Spots—probably acne
5. Superfluous hair

Each condition can be remedied given time, and patience.

Remedies

1 *Dry skin* This is the easiest to put right. Eat plenty of fat in the diet, and cleanse with a gentle baby soap. To remove the dry flakes of skin at night cleanse and soothe with a little skin food rubbed in lightly. For very dry or chapped places use a little lanolin on the affected part. During the day use a fairly rich foundation cream.

2 *Greasy skin* This is more difficult to deal with and it sometimes leads to blackheads. Take heart though—greasy skins wrinkle less easily than dry ones! Cut down fat in the diet. Wash in a thick, rich soapy lather and fairly hot water. Rinse in hot water to ease the grease out of the pores, then in cold to close them. Astringents will help to remove all traces of grease before making up and will assist in closing the pores. You can buy them quite reasonably, or you can use diluted lavender water or eau de cologne (one part perfume to one part water) or you can use witch-hazel.

Use a light foundation cream, and keep some compressed powder handy for touching up during the day.

3 *Blackheads* Blackheads are clogged-up pores. If neglected they not only look unsightly but stretch the pores so much that they cannot close properly, and will give rise to blackhead after blackhead. Steam the skin gently, or attend to these immediately after emerging from the steam of a hot bath. Ease them out equally gently with rounded, spotless finger-nails and very light pressure. If your skin is very sensitive shroud your nails in a tissue first. Once they are out dab the open pore first with a gentle antiseptic such as T.C.P. or diluted Dettol, and then with an astringent, to close the pore.

COSMETICS

4 *Acne* This is sometimes the result of neglected blackheads. It is caused by bacteria which multiply in grease, and the toxins or poisons they produce irritate the skin and cause eruptions. These bacteria are present in most skins, but only attack if there is excess grease and the skin is not as fit as it should be. Both conditions are frequent at the beginning of puberty (Chapter 13) because the skin thickens a little and the sebaceous glands in it become very active. The openings of these glands are the pores. Never neglect blackheads. Wash the affected part as frequently as possible, to remove all grease. Use an antiseptic soap such as Derl or Cidal. Cut down fatty foods. Cut out chocolate, cream cakes and sweets of all kinds. See your doctor if the attack is severe. He may recommend Innoxa 41, a preparation especially made to help to clear acne. Try to do without make-up for a while; certainly avoid greasy creams. Sunlight, or ultra-violet rays will help, taken in moderation. Eat lots of fresh vegetables, salads and fruit. Take especial care not to get constipated. Drink lots of water. Cheer up, it will pass. Cheer others up too. It may be just part of growing up.

5 *Superfluous hair—on the face* We tend to consider this masculine and unsightly, so it must be removed! Bleach these facial hairs so that they will not show; at the same time this process will weaken the growth. Ask your chemist for a gentle bleach, such as hydrogen peroxide, and dilute it two parts water to one part H_2O_2. Do not shave unwanted facial hair, it makes it stubby and increases its growth. If you have a lot, ask your doctor to recommend a good clinic where it can be permanently and painlessly removed.
—under the arms You can choose whether to get rid of this or not. It is a matter of convention. On the Continent women do not shave off their hair, in America women do. In England some do and some don't. As it harbours the residue of perspiration in this somewhat unventilated place, and as it looks rather unsightly, it is perhaps better to remove it. It can be shaved off quickly, painlessly and successfully with a tiny Nymph razor and blade, made specially for this purpose. It costs little and, once you have tried, you get the knack quite easily. Depilatories (hair removing creams) such as Buto or Veet are also effective but expensive. Sometimes they irritate tender skins, so try a little on your wrist first.

Make-up

It should enhance your good points, not disguise them—and you—

altogether. Often senior girls at school are allowed to wear subtle make-up with uniform, as an acknowledgment of the fact that they are growing up. Usually they revel in this privilege for a while and then as they really begin to grow up they stop using it at school. They are mature enough to realise that it doesn't really go with school uniform! They also are sensible enough to save their make-up for a more suitable time.

Foundations Always use one under your powder to protect your skin, and to help to ensure a smooth and even finish. Use one the same colour as your skin, or very slightly darker.

Powder Use this lightly and evenly. Choose a colour to match your skin or one just a little lighter. Powder is absorbent and looks darker on the skin anyway, so do not choose a shade already a little darker.

Lipstick Experiment with small inexpensive types, Outdoor Girl, Rimmel or Gala for example. You have got to compromise between your colouring and what suits it, and the colouring of the particular clothes you are wearing. Pale pinks look fresh and unsophisticated for the young teenager—they are usually a good start. Clear reds are good and gay too, but blue-reds tend to make you look about to have a heart attack, especially if your colour naturally deepens when it turns cold! Orange-reds are difficult to tone with, especially if you have pink cheeks, although they look lovely with blue, greens or gold browns. Put on one layer lightly, firmly outlining the lips and then filling in. Blot with a tissue and repeat the process. You may find you are allergic to lipstick, probably to the perfume or to the indelible factor, eosin, in the lipstick. However, you have nothing to worry about—if lipstick is 'in' you needn't look a 'fuddy duddy' by not wearing it. Several firms, such as Max Factor or Innoxa, make N.P.I. lipsticks. These are not perfumed or indelible but they won't leave you with an itchy, unsightly rash, and they cost the same as a normal lipstick.

Never leave lipstick smears on cups or spoons. If you moisten your lips slightly with the tip of your tongue before you drink or eat you will form a protective layer between lips and china, and your lipstick will stay put. Before trying on a dress, having your throat inspected by the doctor or your teeth by the dentist, wipe away all traces of lipstick with a tissue.

In public

Many people object to seeing others 'make-up' in public. Try not to offend by deciding for yourself what is most important to you and to the people you care about. If you need to powder your nose, repair your lipstick or even wear your curlers in public, it is probably because you are going to see someone later on, whom you really want to impress. If you decide that this impression is more important than the way you look while making-up or wearing your curlers—well, that is your decision. But be sure you have taken the trouble to consider all the implications of your actions.

Eye make-up Eye shadow and eyelash mascara should be used with moderation by the teenager. Lavish applications are better left until you have the maturity of the 18-year-old. Otherwise you may look like an adult imitation. Later, used with care and sensitivity, both can highlight your eyes and indeed your whole face. Mascara or eyebrow pencil used delicately on the eyebrows is very effective. Use a colour to match your own or a shade which is just a little deeper. After powdering run a damp fingertip or brush along both lashes and brows to remove surplus powder. A trace of vaseline also can help to give a highlight.

Bedtime

No matter how tired you are wash all your make-up off carefully. A cleansing milk (for greasy skins) or cream (for dry ones) and cotton wool or tissues will help you to be really thorough.

Finally, when using cosmetics, try to be yourself. Do not copy others—whether they are film or pop stars or your friends. Remember it is simply not true—no matter what the advertisements say—that perfumes, dreamy glows, or dewy looks will win you a boy friend. They may encourage him to look your way, but it is just you, and the sort of person you are that will keep him at your side, or send him packing. Perfumes wear off, personality does not. Some cosmetic firms, however, do a wonderful job in advising teenagers on their colour and make-up requirements.

Further reading

Hygiene in the Home, by Elizabeth Norton, published by Mills and Boon Ltd., at $47\frac{1}{2}$p

Your Looks, by Mary Davis Peters, and *Your Health*, by Kenneth Hutchin, are published in the 'Modern Living' series by Longmans, Green and Co. Ltd. in paperback at $37\frac{1}{2}$p

The Human Body, by Janet Noel, published by Macdonald at £1

Science and Your Body, by J. Gostelow, published by Blond at 70p

Hygiene and Public Health is published by the British Red Cross Society, 9 Grosvenor Crescent, S.W.1, at 30p

The Value of Food, by Patty Fisher and Arnold Bender, published by O.U.P. at 80p

First (and Second) Book of Nutrition, by Matthews and Wells, published by Forbes at 60p and £1.80

Practical work

1 On the tip of each of the four fingers of your left hand write *MEAT, FISH, EGGS, CHEESE* and on your thumb write *MILK* in ink or Biro. Learn them and always remember their importance in the diet. Always have these five at your fingertips!

2 Discuss what use we make of the fact that when liquids evaporate, or change state, they withdraw heat from their surroundings.

3 Take your temperature with a clinical thermometer when you feel hot, and when you feel cold. Does it register any difference?

4 Collect, as a class, all advertisements, labels and packets mentioning food values. Are any misleading? Notice which foods such as margarines and tinned milk have vitamins added.

5 Have a debate in class on 'Women are deceivers ever—especially when they use make-up!'

Questions

1 Give two carefully planned menus for one day's meal for two schoolgirls of your own age. One is trying to lose weight and one is trying to gain it. Explain why you have selected the items you have listed in each case.

2 Why is milk so valuable in the diet?

3 Collect picture advertisements of teenage shoes. Refer to the issue of *Which?* magazine which dealt with this. If not in the school it will be in your local library. Select shoes which:

(*a*) you like, and
(*b*) you recognise as sensible.

How can you compromise between the two? Look especially hard and see if there are some which meet both requirements (*a*) and (*b*).

CHAPTER 9 · CHILD CARE

The unique responsibility of the parents

The most important part of child care is that which only the parents can give satisfactorily—love and security. A child who is well fed, well clothed, sent regularly to school, entertained and indulged, may still be a deprived child—a child who lacks something vital. More than all these material comforts, the child needs to know that he is loved, and that his love is welcomed in return.

38 *A child needs to know that he is loved*

Better off will be the boy in patched jeans, with a not-too-full tummy, if he gets a hug in the morning and a sympathetic audience for his troubles at night. Security need not mean a posh home, or a car, or a television. These may help. But real security comes from having people belonging to you, who you can rely on, a mother who is there at home if she has said she would be, who has that vital clean shirt, mended football socks or picnic lunch ready if she promised them; a father who takes the family out for the treat he has agreed upon, and who keeps his word about punishments as well as pocket money. A family of people who are honest in their words and actions, who can be relied upon to be fair and consistent, who do not go back on promises—such a family gives its members real security. This, with lots of love, shown as well as felt, is the greatest gift parents can give to a child.

Health

The responsibility for caring for children must, of course, always lie with the parents, but the actual job can be made a little easier by various welfare and social services. It is important to know what help is available, and how to make the best use of it. Chapter 15 deals with help for the child up to the age of 5, here we are dealing with the school child. It is in fact through school and the Health Service that help is offered.

The School Health Service

It is the duty of the Local Education Authority (the L.E.A.) to provide medical examinations for all children at schools maintained by them. It is their responsibility to arrange for free medical treatment for any children who are found to be in need of it.

Medical examinations and clinics

Each school child should receive routine medical examinations, on entering school, at five-year intervals and on leaving school. Dental inspections are also given at intervals. Medical and dental clinics are provided to give free treatment, and all dental and minor medical ailments are dealt with at these centres. Parents have the right to choose whether their children should take advantage of these treatments or not. They can even opt out of the examinations if they choose to, but they are then expected to have such an inspection carried out by their family doctor or dentist instead.

The National Health Service

For more serious ailments the clinics pass the children on to the consultative and specialist services provided by the National Health Service, with whom the School Health Service works closely. The National Health Service Ear, Nose and Throat Hospitals, which care especially for cases of defective hearing and sight, treat the cases passed on to them by the specialists. Many L.E.A.s also provide *Child Guidance Clinics* for treating nervous disorders. Sometimes these clinics are used by both the National Health Service—for example as an Infants' Welfare Clinic in the afternoons—and by the School Health Service for school children in the mornings. Staffs are often shared as well as premises and equipment. Both services work together as a team; the use of one in no way prevents parents and children from turning from time to time to the other—mainly to that kingpin of the National Health Service, the family doctor. In fact they are expected to, because the health of many children needs more frequent care than the few inspections during their years at school.

Food and clothing

1 *Milk* We have much to thank the 1944 Education Act for. This Act makes the L.E.A.s responsible for providing milk at every infant school. Each child is allowed, free of charge, one-third of a pint of milk per school day. Older children who are in special need are also entitled to this free milk. At special schools, such as those for delicate children, the allowance is two or three times the amount.

2 *School dinners* The same Act makes it the duty of the L.E.A. to provide school dinners. It lays down that they must be cooked and supervised by trained staff, and should be sufficient in quality and quantity to constitute the main meal of the school child's day. A charge of 12–15p is made, but all these meals are subsidised. When there is real hardship they are provided free.

3 *Clothing* It is the duty of the L.E.A. to provide milk and dinners for its schoolchildren. They are allowed, but not compelled, to assist in the clothing of children, with grants for shoes and clothes. These have to be applied for by parents in need, and the amounts allowed vary from one L.E.A. to another.

Physical training

Recreation and social education must also be provided for children at maintained schools. This, too, is part of the 1944 Education Act.

The employment of children

This is regulated by the L.E.A. and the terms vary slightly from one area to another. Generally no children under the age of 13–14 may be employed during school hours, or for more than 2 hours during a school day. To check that this regulation is observed and to see that children attend school regularly and that there is nothing amiss at home, each L.E.A. employs:

School Welfare (or Attendance) Officers

Such officers are not merely there to prevent truancy, but do provide an invaluable link between school and home. They advise the parents of available benefits and special facilities at school or to be gained through the school authorities. They inform the teaching staff of any special difficulties which occur in various homes—unemployment, loss of near relatives, sickness, etc., so that the children can be treated sympathetically at the right time.

Handicapped children

In England our handicapped children are divided into ten different categories and for each the L.E.A. must provide special educational treatment. These are the ten different groups:

1 the blind
2 the deaf
3 the delicate
4 the maladjusted
5 the physically handicapped
6 the partially sighted
7 the partially deaf
8 the epileptics
9 the educationally sub-normal
10 the handicapped in speech

Information about schools for one of these special groups, of classes in a normal school and of transport run to a special school in a neighbouring county is often given to parents by the School Welfare Officers, the Health Visitors or the School Medical Service.

The Youth Employment Officer

Finally, near the end of a school career, the child will be interviewed by an officer of the Youth Employment Service. These officers carry out three duties:

1 To give job or career (vocational) guidance to those shortly to leave school.

2 To place young people in employment which they will enjoy, which will provide good prospects, and which they are mentally and physically able to manage.

3 To keep in touch with these new, young employees after they have found their first job.

Here the L.E.A.s work with the Department of Health and Social Security to help to provide care throughout adolescence.

So there are many organisations and acts and regulations to help children and young people. But when they are worried or over-tired or under the weather, it is to their parents they turn. How well would you cope as a parent?

Home nursing

Every parent does a spell at this from time to time. It is usually a period of anxiety, involving a lot of extra hard work. Running up and down stairs, to and from a sick child, the extra washing of bed-clothes, soiled nightwear, etc., special meals—on top of running the house for the rest of the family—can be gruelling. Often one child recovers just in time for the next one to fall ill. No one would pretend that rules can lessen the hard work, but often accurate information can lessen the strain. If you know you are doing the right thing in *Home Nursing* you relieve yourself of such a lot of worry. Worst of all is to have a sick child and be uncertain what to do for the best. Even doctors sometimes call in second opinions to verify the best way to diagnose and deal with each illness. To attempt anything of the sort here would be impossible, but it is important to consider the general rules which apply to all home nursing, and to try to understand why illness occurs, as a first step to preventing it. We can turn to the British Red Cross for help. Their summary—the *Golden Rules of Nursing in the Home*—introduces the *A.B.C. of Nursing in the*

Home, which is another excellent small booklet (sister to one on first aid). This provides a wealth of information for only $12\frac{1}{2}$p.

1 *Keep the patient in bed* until seen by the doctor, but be sure that she can attract your attention by bell, stick or whistle.

2 *Keep the patient as quiet as possible.*

3 *Keep a written record* of the patient's temperature, pulse and respiration and be able to report these accurately to the doctor with any other observations you have made. Note any complaints of pain—where and when it occurs and how long it lasts.

4 *Save any vomit* or other discharge that appears unusual to show the doctor.

5 *Encourage the patient to drink plenty of water* unless instructed to the contrary.

6 *Serve meals attractively and punctually.* Try to make the menus as varied and interesting as possible.

7 *Give medicines accurately* at the time stated and report any unusual effects, or any inaccuracy in administration to the doctor.

8 *Carry out carefully any instructions* or advice given by the doctor or district nurse, reporting any mistakes.

9 *Never discuss confidential matters seen or heard in the sickroom* with people other than the family concerned.

10 Be economical in the use of all medical and household goods as illness is always an expensive burden.

Find out where the nearest Medical Loan Depot is situated from which medical equipment (wheelchairs, back rests, crutches, bedpans) can be borrowed at a very low cost (bedpans 1p a week!). The doctor or district nurse will give you the address.

Ill health—what is it?

The saying 'Prevention is better than Cure' is especially relevant where ill health is concerned. But you must know what you are trying to prevent. You cannot prevent measles, for example, in the same way you can prevent food poisoning. What causes ill health? The Greeks and Romans realised that cleanliness and physical fitness had much to do with its prevention. Roman Baths, Olympian Games and Spartan fitness are well known even today. Then came the Dark Ages when 'disease' became the new name for ill health, and was confused with disease of the mind, uneasiness caused by curses, evil spirits and witchcraft. This was a serious step back. Superstitions—some of which still exist today—interfered with the advancement of medical knowledge.

Causes of ill health

Some of the things which were later proved to be the cause of much ill health were tracked down by Jenner in the eighteenth century and later by Louis Pasteur. These are the bacteria and viruses which we commonly call germs. Partly because these organisms cannot be seen (except under powerful microscopes), few people accepted the fact that they existed let alone that they caused illness. Florence Nightingale, for one, never accepted 'the germ theory', but fortunately she, like the Romans, believed that where there's dirt there's disease, and, as bacteria thrive and breed in dirt, her passion for cleanliness achieved much. This summary gives the main causes of the types of ill health you are likely to have to cope with in your own home nursing or when helping others out.

1 *Virus diseases*

Viruses are minute organisms. They find a way to enter the body, they multiply there and in doing so produce toxins (or poisons). If they are present in sufficient numbers, if their attack is strong enough and if the body they have entered has not a sufficient reserve of strength to resist them, disease results. To complete their life cycle the viruses must finally leave the body and pass on to another body.

The following are some of the infections known to be caused by viruses:

Smallpox	Poliomyelitis
Chickenpox	Colds
Measles	Influenza
German Measles	Pneumonia
Mumps	Epidemic Diarrhoea

2 *Bacterial diseases*

Bacteria are similar to viruses, but because they are not quite so minute (though still invisible to the naked eye) they are a little easier to identify. A very few bacteria can form spores which resist their great enemies—antiseptics and heat. In the right conditions such as dirt, warmth and exposure, bacteria can reproduce, each one dividing into two about every 20 minutes. Therefore in one hour one bacterium becomes eight, almost 50,000,000,000 in

39 *In one hour one bacterium becomes eight*

twelve hours. Diseases resulting from these efficient and dangerous micro-organisms include: tuberculosis, food poisoning, diphtheria, dysentery, venereal disease.

3 *Bad weather, exposure, air pollution*

These cause diseases such as bronchitis. They also lower the body's resistance, allowing virus diseases, particularly colds and 'flu, to develop.

4 *Emotional disturbances or stress and over tiredness*

These bring about such diseases as shingles, ulcers, nervous asthma, depression and nervous disorders in general. Their main cause is discussed later in the chapter.

5 *Infected food or drink*

Often cause food poisoning, vomiting, diarrhoea.

6 *Accidents*

See Chapter 10.

7 Low standards of living

Low standards of living, such as cold, draughty or damp conditions, poor or inadequate food, cause diet-deficiency diseases such as rickets, caries (tooth decay) and scurvy. They also worsen, but do not cause, rheumatism, arthritis, bronchitis, coughs, colds and pneumonia.

8 Ignorance, bad habits, disregard of health rules

Lung cancer—the conditions for this may be created by smoking. Overweight (obesity) which is sometimes a fatal strain on the heart is brought about by over-eating and under-exercising. You will suffer with caries (tooth decay) if you neglect to clean your teeth and eat too many sweet and starchy foods. Foot troubles—beware of badly designed shoes.

Prevention of ill health

There are secondary causes behind each of these eight main causes. For example, a certain type of bacterium causes food poisoning, but a secondary cause is the absence of hygiene which permits the bacteria to reach and contaminate the food. Let us now look at a less gloomy side of infection, for with care we can prevent much ill health.

Bacteria and viruses

The minuteness of the virus and the consequent difficulty in identifying it have hindered the discovery of cures for some of the infections it causes. For instance, a cure for the common cold has still to be found. Viruses can only grow in living cells, so illnesses caused by them have to be passed directly from one person to another. You cannot catch a cold by just getting your feet wet. But you can lower your resistance to the cold virus. The first person who sneezes near you and who does not trap the viruses so released in a handkerchief may hand on some very active viruses ready to take advantage of your lowered resistance.

This is true of all virus infections, but the viruses can be passed from one human to another in several different ways. Sneezing and coughing pass on viruses by droplet infection. Diseases spread in this way are:

Colds
Influenza
Sore Throats
Scarlet Fever
Whooping Cough
German Measles

Diphtheria
Mumps
Measles
Polio
Smallpox
Chickenpox

Diseases which affect the bowels

These can be passed on through the faeces, even from dirty fingernails and toilet chains. You must be scrupulously careful when visiting the toilet, after using the toilet or when cleaning it out. Wash and scrub with extra thoroughness whenever the toilet has been used or a child's pot has been emptied. Polio, food poisoning, dysentery, typhoid and diarrhoea are passed on this way. The same cleanliness must be observed in warehouse, shop, kitchen and table where foodstuffs and utensils are concerned. Bacteria can so easily be passed into the body by the mouth.

Flies are another source of this same contamination. The common housefly and the blowfly (or bluebottle) which feed whenever they can on exposed food and drink in our shops, markets and houses, are prolific carriers of bacteria. They do this in two ways:

1 They put their germ-covered legs, which have previously rested on dung heaps, manure or the dustbin's contents, straight on to your meat or sugar.

2 As they feed on these things, they both vomit and excrete, and these two delightful additions to your Sunday joint are full of bacteria!

40 *As flies feed they both vomit and excrete*

Several insecticides, such as D.D.T., will destroy flies, but be careful not to use these powders too generously where children may breathe in the chemicals contained in them. These could have harmful effects.

Food poisoning Some bacteria, unlike viruses, can breed in other as well as in human cells. When they multiply they produce toxins. These cause the headaches, high temperatures and general misery that accompany diseases caused by the bacteria. If the toxins are produced outside the body, the poison may be in a very highly concentrated form and extremely dangerous. Botulism is the toxin from a food poisoning bacterium, and, if eaten in food thus contaminated, can be a killer. How far can we cut down the chances of these infections? Follow these rules:

1 Observe scrupulous cleanliness in the home, especially in the toilet and kitchen, food stores, drains and utensils. Shop only in hygienically run food stores. Always see that the dustbin lid is in place and fits well. Cover all food. Wage war on flies. Be generous in your use of antiseptics and disinfectants.

2 Impose a high standard of personal cleanliness on yourself and your family. Hand-washing habits can be taught from toddler stage.

3 'Coughs and sneezes spread diseases', so use handkerchiefs frequently, burn paper ones at once. See that rooms are properly ventilated. Avoid stuffy crowded places if colds and 'flu are about.

4 Take advantage of any special preventative treatments recommended by your doctor, particularly the immunity from disease given by vaccination or immunisation. The immunity is not permanent, but affords protection through babyhood and childhood, the most vulnerable years of life. The following facts illustrate the effectiveness of immunisation. Until 1942 there were approximately 55,000 cases of diphtheria per year. Of these about 3,000, mostly children, died. In 1971 there were 15 cases and only 1 died. In the years between, there was a national campaign to persuade parents to have their children immunised against diphtheria. The campaign succeeded, diphtheria is almost wiped out, such is the effectiveness of this simple, free, treatment. Yet today many parents do not take advantage of it. They are exposing their children to needless risks.

Here is a table of the illnesses which can be completely or

partially prevented by immunisation and the ages at which the vaccines should be administered.

Disease	1st injection	Later injections	Boosters
Diphtheria	} 3–6 months	5–8 months and then	on starting and on
Tetanus			
Whooping Cough		9–14 months	leaving school*
Smallpox	1–2 years	5 years later	on leaving school
Tuberculosis B.C.G.	To babies likely to be exposed and to school leavers		
Polio	6 months	8 months and then 14 months	on starting and on leaving school
Typhoid	At about 3 years, or when about to go abroad		
Measles	Over 1 year and to all children under the age of 15 who have not had measles		
Influenza	These injections are for adults only and are prescribed if necessary by a doctor.		

* Diphtheria and Tetanus only.

These courses of injections can be carried out by your doctor or by the local clinic. Polio vaccine can now be taken by mouth.

What happens when you are vaccinated?

You will be less anxious about vaccination if you understand what happens. Let us take the diphtheria immunisation process as an example. Firstly, *passive immunity*. This is employed when a person has already caught the disease. We know that the diphtheria bacteria will produce toxins. Such toxins are injected into a horse in quantities too small to cause illness (the horse feels nothing), but sufficient to produce poison-killers or anti-toxins in the blood. The blood is then drawn off in small quantities—just as we give a transfusion—purified, and then injected into the diphtheria sufferer. If the disease has not got too firm a grip, the patient gains immediate immunity from the anti-toxin. Secondly, *active immunity*. If the actual diphtheria toxins are injected—in a very safe modified form—into a baby, anti-toxins will be produced by the baby's blood, ready to fight a serious attack of the disease. The anti-toxins, once created in this way, are there ready should any real attack come. The two later booster-injections will create enough anti-toxin to ensure immunity for life. These particular injections are now combined with those for whooping cough and

PREVENTION OF ILL HEALTH

tetanus in one vaccine—all for a needle prick at three widely-spaced intervals.

If, however, an infectious disease is diagnosed it is important to know about periods of quarantine so that your family is not guilty of passing on the illness. A table at the end of this section is a guide to this.

We now return to further discussion of the causes and prevention of ill-health.

Bad weather

The country loses more working days—28,000,000 in an average year—because of bronchitis, than through any other disease. This disease causes great misery and can even be a 'killer'. The damp fogginess and cold of the British climate aggravates the condition. Smoke, both inhaled from cigarettes and from the atmosphere, not only aggravates, but is probably one of the causes. If the entire country became a smokeless zone, bronchitis would probably decline sharply. It is a poor man's disease, found mostly among the under-privileged, and not enough pressure is brought to bear on industrialists with smoking chimneys to alleviate these harmful conditions. Ignorance, too, is a cause. Old people huddle round a smoking fire, having no idea of the way in which thousands of smoking chimneys are polluting the atmosphere. Sufferers from chest troubles should stay indoors in all foggy weather, keeping warm and keeping the windows closed. If they have to go out, nose and mouth should be covered with a mask or scarf. You should take especial care when you have a cough or cold—these are made worse by cold, damp weather.

Emotional disturbances

The mind and the body are not the two separate things we often imagine them to be. The condition of the one vitally affects the other. We are all aware of what the mental process fear does to us physically. Our flesh creeps, our scalps tingle and our hairs stand on end. We react physically because we are disturbed mentally.

Our minds are affected by the experiences we have had. A disorder of the mind, an emotional disturbance or a nervous breakdown may be the result of brain damage from an accident, or shock from an abnormal experience, or a disease which has attacked the brain. Such conditions may well be the result of more than one of these troubles, for example, from both injury and mental shock.

Acute depression can be as serious an illness as pneumonia and should be treated as such. It does no good to say, 'It's only nerves' or, 'She'll snap out of it'. The basic cause of the depression or disturbance must be discovered and removed. It is often lack of security, or lack of someone to share troubles with. People suffering in this way often get the least sympathy—this is partly because they do not look ill—yet often they are the ones who need the most patience and understanding. Medical advice should always be sought and followed. Don't leave it until it is too late. Get the help of an expert through your doctor as soon as possible.

Infected food or drink

Such foods contain the bacteria that we have already talked about. How can you avoid contaminated food? It doesn't always look or smell bad.

Apart from insisting on personal cleanliness, shop only where you can see that the behind-the-counter handling of food is as good as in front. Pre-packaged foods, wrapped pies, packeted ham or bacon is often safest. Be careful to eat the contents before the date specified on the packet. Ready cooked meat and fish are far the most likely sources of food poisoning. Reboil all soups and gravy before use. Take especial care with reheated food. Heat it fiercely enough to kill all the bacteria which have been multiplying in it since you first served it.

Remember that milk is not only ideal for you; its qualities make it equally good for germs. Pasteurised milk is without question the most germ-free. If you have a cool larder or refrigerator make the best use of it. At very low temperatures germs cannot breed and produce toxins. The rule for keeping all food and drink is 'Keep it cool, keep it clean, keep it covered'.

Low standards of living, ignorance and bad habits

These conditions cause diseases which are otherwise easily avoided. For instance, if an expectant mother knew she could influence the pattern of her future child's healthy bones and teeth by including adequate Vitamin D, calcium and phosphorus in her diet, she probably would do so. She may, however, be ignorant of the way to get these, not believe a word of it or be unable to afford them. Many people blindly believe that various diseases are inherited;

with this sort of resigned attitude they do very little to prevent them. A *few* diseases are inherited but there is a great deal of muddled thinking about this. People tend to kill spiders instead of flies, and cases of food poisoning are frequent. People expect bad food to smell bad and refuse to believe that its dangers are sometimes undetectable.

Mothers often talk of 'building up' their children. They mean well, but what they often do is to fatten them up with chips and cakes and sweets, and it is to Father, who does not need it so much, that they give the largest helping of meat. Often they impair their children's health instead of improving it; that extra fatty layer laid down in childhood gradually increases until the heart has to work overtime and is in consequence strained. The same cakes and sweets also damage the children's teeth. There have been great improvements in children's health, but the children in some families still suffer from bad teeth and obesity at an early age.

Advertisements, especially on television, often play a part in encouraging the young mother to satisfy 'half way hunger' with a biscuit, or to give their children the sweet *they* say you can eat between meals, lollies or bottles of pop, which are harmful to children's good health. Advertisements also had much to answer for where lung cancer is concerned. The connection between smoking and this slow and painful killer disease is conclusively established. Yet for the sake of money, the manufacturers continue to badger the public. Worse still, they infer that the young non-smoker is missing the best of life and companionship by not smoking. Fortunately, the young of today are not so easily taken in.

Homes

This country still has many sub-standard dwellings. In them, families, and especially older folk, feel the cold and suffer from draughts and damp. They also suffer from the ill health caused by these discomforts—fibrositis, lumbago, arthritis and rheumatism. This state of affairs can only be relieved by a national programme of research into the causes, and by a re-housing campaign to remove sub-standard dwellings and poverty that exists in them.

To resist ill health the body should be kept as physically fit as possible. This will come with a well-balanced diet, starting even before birth, a clean, well-exercised body, plenty of fresh air and sunshine when possible, rounded off with adequate sleep. All these will help to keep the mind active and alert, and give you the

DISEASE *Notify your Doctor † No need to notify	PERIOD OF INCUBATION, I.E. BETWEEN CONTRACTING THE DISEASE AND FEELING ILL	PERIOD BETWEEN BEGINNING OF ILLNESS AND APPEARANCE OF RASH	PERIOD OF QUARANTINE Patient to be kept apart	PERIOD OF QUARANTINE Patient's contacts to be kept apart
Scarlet Fever *	1–7 days	1–2 days	Take doctor's advice	None
Diphtheria **	2–5		Take doctor's advice	Take doctor's advice
Measles *	10–15	3–4	10 days after rash appears if feeling better	Children under 5, 14 days
				Older children only if poorly
German Measles †	14–21	0–2	7 days from the rash's appearance	None
Whooping Cough *	6–18	—	28 days from the beginning of the cough	21 days from onset of disease for children under 7
Mumps †	12–28	—	7 days from swelling going down	None (except for adult males who have so far not had the disease)
Chickenpox *	11–21	0–2	14 days from appearance of rash	None
Smallpox *	10–21	3	Take doctor's advice	At least 17 days

N.B. Although doctors tell us today that there is no *need* to notify them if you suspect German Measles or Mumps, nevertheless if you are worried, the child's temperature is high, or he is in pain, it is always chance to make the most of all that is good in life; so good, in fact, that the pleasure of it spills over to help those in less fortunate circumstances.

Infectious diseases

Note Incubation. This is a dangerous period for contacts. The child has the disease but it is scarcely if at all apparent. Throughout this time he is highly infectious.

German measles

If any contact is under four months pregnant she must see her doctor straight away. Should the expectant mother get the disease for the first time there is a possibility that the unborn child will be affected. Injections can help here.

Mumps

If adolescent or adult males do not catch this in childhood but contact it later, it can, in a few cases, cause sterility. Therefore it is desirable for small girls to have German measles—and for small boys to have mumps. Some mothers take the chance of deliberately exposing their children—but remember, it is taking a chance, however small.

Further reading

Maternal and Child Welfare Manual is published by the British Red Cross Society, 9 Grosvenor Crescent, S.W.1, at 20p

Welfare Services is published by the British Red Cross Society at $27\frac{1}{2}$p

Family Health, Good Housekeeping, Family Library, Ebury Press at £2·25

Practical work

1 Find out which schools in your area are not 'maintained'. Where is your Local Education Authority Office?

2 Discuss how many medical and dental examinations you each have had. When did you have them? Recently? In Junior or Infants' School? Who examined you, and what were they looking for?

3 Have you attended any local clinics? If so what for? What else is the clinic used for? Does your mother ever go there? Where are the clinics in your area? What is the job of each one?—Go and look!

4 Where is your Ministry of Social Security Office? Pop in when they are not too busy and ask permission to study the posters and leaflet information on show there.

5 Note down one week's school dinners, including vegetables, gravies, sauces, etc. Discuss in class the food value and variety of the dinner. Now draw up a menu that you would like for a week. Now be fair and discuss:

(a) Its food value.
(b) How much it would all cost.
(c) Would it be possible to prepare it on a large scale?

6 Imagine you are a Youth Employment Officer and your friends are leaving school shortly. Draw up a list of questions to ask them, in order to try to help them plan their futures. Try this out.

7 Compare when and where you and the rest of your class had injections. Which ones have you had and why?

8 See what precautions are taken in your local shops to ensure the cleanliness of the food they are selling.

Questions

1 Your sister has recently returned from abroad where her first two children were born. Explain to her what provision she can expect for her children's health while they are at school in this country.

2 What was it that
(a) Jenner discovered and
(b) Louis Pasteur found out?

3 You now know what happens when you are immunised against diphtheria. Find out what happens when the injection is anti-smallpox. Is it an injection?

4 Give concise instructions to someone who has never home-nursed a case of German measles before.

5 Which foods you have seen in shops may have been contaminated? How might this have occurred and how can you prevent it?

6 Find out all you can about *either* the life history and habits of the common housefly *or* smoke abatement in your area. Write an account.

CHAPTER 10 · FIRST AID

A few facts about accidents

The number of children's deaths through accidents per year is approximately four times greater than all other causes of children's deaths put together. In one typical year 4,457 children died from such diseases as T.B., measles, gastroenteritis, etc. In the same year 17,720 died as a result of accidents.

Witnesses of each of these accidents must have been either grateful for their skill in first aid, or deeply distressed by their ignorance—probably the latter. For though we all know that at some time we will be called upon to help at an accident, few of us bother to equip ourselves to do so. Later on it may be our own children who need our help—are we going to fail them?

Here I can only outline the basic principles of first aid, but we need more than this. We need active practice in the skill as well as sound knowledge from a reliable textbook. We can get both through the help of the British Red Cross. Their classes are fun to attend, immensely instructive and always give useful training. A strong sense of team spirit develops among first-aid groups, and as knowledgeable, fast acting teams you can be called upon to help in emergencies. On your own, you have the confidence of your accurate, up-to-date information and practised skill to take the immediate first steps to save a life in danger. Moreover, you will have the authority and knowledge to stop others from causing harm by doing the wrong things. If you move a boy with a fractured rib, it may enter his lung; you—not the initial injury—may be the cause of a more serious injury, or even death. If you had taken the trouble to learn and train, you would have learnt how to detect and deal with a fractured rib. There will be a training centre in your neighbourhood. If you are unsure where it is, write to the address at the end of Chapter 8 and you will receive the information you need. If it is impossible to attend classes, the next best thing is to study the *First Aid Manual* published by the St. John Ambulance Association, the St. Andrew's Ambulance Association and the British Red Cross Society, or the British Red Cross Society's invaluable small booklet, the *A.B.C. of First Aid Treatment*. The *A.B.C.* is up-to-date and comprehensive—all for $17\frac{1}{2}$p. From this booklet I have borrowed the form of the basic principles set as—*Golden Rules of First Aid*.

1 *Do first things first*, quietly, quickly and without fuss or panic.

2 *Reassure the casualty* and those around, and so help to lessen anxiety.

3 *Give artificial respiration* (emergency resuscitation) if breathing has stopped—every second counts.

4 *Stop any bleeding.*

5 *Guard against*, or *deal with*, *shock* by keeping the casualty cool, by moving him as little as possible, and by gentle handling.

6 *Do not attempt too much*, do the minimum that is essential to save life and prevent the condition from worsening.

7 *Do not allow people to crowd around*, as fresh air is essential.

8 Arrange for the removal of the casualty to the care of a doctor or a hospital as soon as possible, and notify the police in the case of a serious accident.

From these rules we can see that it is essential to have knowledge of at least four points of first aid:

Artificial respiration.
How to stop bleeding.
How to prevent—or deal with—shock.
How to send for help.

1 To give artificial respiration

The most efficient way to do this is to lay the unconscious casualty on his back, with his head tilted well back so that the line between the point of his chin, his ear and the back of his head forms a right angle with the floor. This opens the air passages to the lungs. Seal his mouth and/or nostrils with your mouth and blow. When his chest rises remove your mouth and watch for the chest to fall, then repeat the action. Do this five times then continue blowing in one breath about every 6 seconds. Blow gently at a faster rate for a child, whose breathing is quicker and shallower than an adult.

If the chest does not rise it means that air is not reaching the lungs. Check the position of the head and clear any obstruction from the mouth and throat. An adult should be turned quickly on his side and his back thumped; a child may be held up by the ankles and his back smacked smartly between the shoulder blades. Clear the mouth and start the breathing sequence again.

2 To stop bleeding

Provided there is nothing in the wound (e.g. glass), apply pressure directly on the bleeding point; cover with a clean dressing and pad and bandage firmly. Remember there are two sorts of bleeding, external and internal. In both cases you will need to deal with shock, but in the case of the suspected internal bleeding (or if the casualty is unconscious) give *nothing* to eat or drink, and get the casualty to hospital as soon as possible.

External bleeding may be complicated by the possibility of a fracture with the bleeding, or foreign bodies in the wound. Learn to recognise each type of bleeding and how to treat it.

3 To guard against and treat for shock

Do not move the casualty at all if you suspect fractures or internal haemorrhage. Otherwise lay him down. Stop any bleeding and make him as comfortable as possible. Loosen clothing at neck and waist. Keep the patient as *cool* as possible, do not apply extra rugs or give hot sweet drinks. Never give alcohol.

N.B. This treatment is new and is correct. The body needs to concentrate entirely on the circulation between the heart and lungs. If you stimulate the blood to the skin, there may not be enough left to keep the core of the body warm.

4 *To send for help*

Unless a doctor is at hand, dial 999 for an ambulance, or send a reliable onlooker to do so. You will probably have to tell him how to. Reassure him that we all have the right to do so, in an emergency, and it will cost nothing.

To make a call for an ambulance:

1 Lift the receiver and say, or dial, 999.

2 When the operator asks, 'Do you want the Police, the fire service or an ambulance?' Say, 'Ambulance', but do not ring off yet—the ambulance does not know where to go.

3 State where you are and the nature of the accident (serious or not). Still do not ring off.

4 Answer any other questions you are asked, and then ring off.

5 If the accident is serious, dial 999 again, ask for the Police and report what has happened.

Often, in a state of panic, people have phoned, shouted that someone is injured and then forgotten to say where. This is all too easy to do in the heat of the moment.

The treatment of minor ailments (ordinary everyday cuts and bruises)

To treat these effectively you must have a well-equipped *First Aid Box* at home, and one in the car, if you own one. Keep it out of the reach of small children—they might cut or poison themselves, or remove something vital—but where you can easily find it. The top shelf of a kitchen cupboard is a good place.

Its contents should include:

1 Cotton wool
2 Paracetamol
3 Calamine lotion
4 Adhesive plasters of various sizes
5 Bandages of various widths, 1–3 inches
6 A conforming or stretch bandage
7 Sterile dressings for more serious wounds
8 Gauze

ACCIDENTS IN THE HOME

9. Methylated or surgical spirits
10. Paper tissues
11. Soluble aspirin (keep away from children)
12. A small bowl or cup kept specially for antiseptic solutions
13. A clinical thermometer
14. An eye bath
15. Tweezers or forceps
16. Safety pins
17. Scissors
18. Milk of Magnesia or Actal tablets for indigestion
19. Sal Volatile, in case of faintness
20. A triangular bandage
21. Splints
22. Anti-histamine cream, to relieve insect bites
23. An aperient, e.g. Sennacot
24. Your *A.B.C.* or *Manual of First Aid*

Simple treatments

(a) *Minor cuts*

1. Wash round wound thoroughly with soap and warm water.
2. Cover with a clean, dry dressing.

(b) *Minor burns or scalds*

1. Put out flames if casualty is on fire.
2. Immerse burnt area in cool, clean water.
3. Cover with a clean, dry dressing.
4. Unless the burn is very slight, send or take the casualty to the hospital or doctor immediately.

N.B. Never smear with fat.

(c) *Insect bites*

1. Remove stings with forceps.
2. Relieve pain by the application of anti-histamine ointment.
3. Treat for shock. Hot sweet tea for an adult, fruit drops for a child.

Accidents in the home

Of the total of 17,720 accidents among children mentioned earlier in this chapter, only 6,643 were on the road. Eighty-five per cent of all the rest happened in the home; that number amounts to over 9,000 in one year. More, of course, happen to adults, and even more to old people.

How can this happen today—what are the causes?

The main cause of nearly all the accidents in the home is carelessness. We know accidents happen, we see films about them, we read about them, we see television programmes about them. But we always seem to imagine that accidents happen to someone else. Yet the horror and guilt which cloud the lives of parents whose children have suffered in this way are very real and tragic.

People who call themselves 'accident prone' may be more careless than average. But sometimes there is good reason for this—over-tiredness, poor hearing or vision, a nervous disorder. However, unless we all face up to the fact that nearly all accidents are caused by our own carelessness, we will, or more likely our children will, continue to die, be disfigured or crippled by avoidable accidents. Less serious accidents are an occupational hazard for housewives. They occur mainly among women in the age range 20–60. But four out of every five deaths resulting from an accident in the home are those of either the very young or the very old. Fewer accidents happen in a serene, ordered home, where the mother has taken the trouble, in the house, and the father in the garage or shed and garden, to seek out and list the dangers. Once listed and considered, ways can usually be found to lessen the dangers or avoid them altogether.

Here are some general points to consider, though every house has also its own special dangers, such as the drop from a sky light or the depth of a gold-fish pond.

1 *Falls* Be orderly when you plan the position of furniture and playthings. Once they have a fixed place see that they are kept there. Train children from babyhood to pick up bricks, roller skates, balls, etc., before they start a new game, or before they go to bed. Be especially firm about objects left on the stairs. They will soon respond automatically, and you will avoid treading on needles or drawing pins, skating up the passage accidentally or flying down the stairs. Never block your view with your load when carrying things up or down stairs. See that stair carpets and door mats are secure. Check that your floor coverings will not be dangerous when wet. Wipe up water or grease as soon as it is spilt, especially in the kitchen. Be careful about electric lamp cords—don't let them trail

across the floor. See that stairs and dark corridors are well lit, with switches at either end. This is especially important for old people. Provide them, if possible, with hand rails, and a handle and rubber mat to assist them in the bath.

2 *Poisons* See that not only your first aid box, but all medicines, tablets and poisons are out of reach, or locked up. Recently the manager of a well-known chain-store chemist told me that medicine chests are made without locks because there is no public demand for them. He added that the extra cost of a lock would be about the price of twenty cigarettes. It is also unfortunate that drug manufacturers make dangerous tablets look just like Smarties. Iron tablets, which are often a chocolate colour or pale green, strengthen adults, but may fatally poison a child. And how attractive some of the little bomb-shaped Sulphonamide capsules are! What does you good may harm a child. Do not give or take tablets in the dark. Read the label, learn the dose and stick to it. Throw old medicines down the sink and burn or dissolve away old pills. Disinfectants, hair preparations, cleaning agents, e.g. salts of lemon or oxalic acid, may also be poisonous. Keep them out of reach, and never put them in bottles which have once contained squash. Some weed and vermin killers are deadly poisons. They may contain arsenic, phosphorus or strychnine. These must be locked away and handled with the greatest care. Check your garden for poisonous berries, deadly nightshade, laburnum, and so on.

Lead is a poison which has caused many small children death or given them mental abnormalities. Nearly all children come into contact with it through paint with a lead base. Such paint on toys, cot rails or walls is dangerous. A little boy of 2 recently suffered brain damage through lead poisoning, because he ate the flakes of paint which came off the walls in the entrance hall of his home. I wonder how his parents feel about this as they visit him in the mental hospital? I wonder how the paint manufacturer would feel if it had happened to his son? Make sure there is no lead in paint which may be within reach of your children. It will state on the tin if it is lead-free. Do not just accept the word of an inexperienced or unconcerned shop assistant.

3 *Dangerous weapons* Scissors, knives and razors are dangerous. Set an example yourself and train your children to carry them by the handles and pointing down. Then if you slip and fall the point will go down into the floor, not up into your eye or back or into your

hand. Put especially sharp ones, such as the carving knife, well out of reach. Tumblers, glass oven ware and vases seem less dangerous, but a child running with a glass in his hand may end up with a severed artery. Stick to plastic or china. Razor blades are often left around, so are handsaws and chisels.

MATCHES are always irresistible to the young. Why did a toy manufacturer package his toys in boxes like them?

PLASTIC BAGS are also killers; once over the head, suffocation follows. For a young child there is an overwhelming fascination in trying one on to become a Spaceman.

SOFT PILLOWS, carelessly placed carricots or plastic cot linings can also cause suffocation. Never fall asleep—or risk doing so—with a tiny baby in bed with you. You cannot be sure that you will not roll over on top of it in the night.

4 *Electricity and gas* Both can be dangerous. Gas taps should have safety devices so that the child cannot turn them on. This is especially important in the living room where there may be a gas tap near naked flames, for a gas poker. Manufacturers should move the controls of gas cookers from toddler level. Until they do, the main tap should be switched off when the cooker is not in use. Never look for a gas escape with a naked flame—you might easily cause a fire.

ELECTRICITY Unless you have been trained to carry out repairs, do not attempt any. If you are competent to mend a fuse, or to connect a plug, do so only after switching the power off at the mains. Check all plugs and switches from time to time to see if any fitting has become loose, or if the insulated flex has become threadbare. Remember that if too many appliances are plugged in on an adaptor from one socket, you may be overloading the wires and so cause fires. Never touch any electrical apparatus with wet hands. Water conducts electricity so easily that this is most dangerous. The shock could kill you. There should be no power plug in the bathroom, nor should you be able to touch the light switch. This should be within reach, and operated by a cord not by a normal switch. Record players and radios which run off the mains should never be taken into the bathroom. Touching them with wet hands could cause a fatal accident.

Leave plugs in wall sockets so that inviting holes are not visible for the experimentally-minded to insert knitting needles. Choose a cooker with controls well out of a child's reach. Warn children about pylons—they often look just like climbing frames—and tell them about electric rails. Check carefully to see that electrically controlled toys are safe. Be very careful with an electric blanket—it is better to remove it as you say goodnight.

FIRES It is thoughtless and foolish and a legal offence to have an unguarded fire where there are children under the age of 7. Often the main coal fire is guarded, but oil heaters, gas and electric fires are forgotten. By law, all fires should be guarded. The guards should not only be big enough but fixed firmly, and give protection at the top as well as the front and sides. Otherwise the inquisitive child will merely move it, or throw things into the fire from the top.

This seems commonsense yet many families take a chance. If real hardship exists, fireguards can be borrowed, either from the local council office, or the nearest Red Cross branch. The Welfare Clinic will advise.

MANTELPIECES Now let us look at a typical shelf over the fireplace. In the middle we usually have the mirror, there is a space for the clock, perhaps a photograph or picture, and one or two pretty ornaments. Often a toy or sweets that have been taken away

41 *A typical mantelpiece*

as a punishment are put on the mantelpiece. From the child's point of view this place, probably the most dangerous in the home, holds more fascinating objects than anywhere else in the house. The mirror reveals a small mischievous-looking face peering back at the child, the clock hands move round and tick and chime, the pretty objects are more fascinating because they are probably forbidden playthings. And the sweets, tucked away behind the photo, are an overwhelming temptation once Mummy's back is turned. The teenager in a flouncy party frock will peer at the mirror, and Granny in her trailing skirts will lean forward to see the time. None of these objects should be anywhere near the fire; yet there they are in home after home. *Inflammable materials.* You can further secure your child against fire accidents by insisting on

42   *Would* you *dress* your *child in inflammable materials?*

non-flammable (or non-inflammable) material for your child's clothes. If you cannot afford the dearer, safer materials, put your little girls into pyjamas. They are warmer than nighties, anyway. If you must buy a nightie, avoid untreated cotton or rayon or, worst of all, winceyette. All of these flare and envelop the child in flames. Cotton or rayon net is especially dangerous; it not only flares but is often made to flounce and billow out. Nylon net is safe; it merely melts. It is now illegal to sell children's nightdresses of flammable material, but unfortunately you can still buy the material to make up a flammable garment in attractive nursery designs.

Note. The words flammable and inflammable mean the same thing —burnable; only non-flammable or non-inflammable means non-burnable or flame resistant.

5 *Cigarettes* Smoking, apart from being bad for the health and an awful waste of money, is the third greatest cause of fire in the home. If the people around you smoke, see that they are provided with plenty of ash trays, and avoid the flat types where, when cigarettes are forgotten, they can topple as they burn and drop out of the tray. This often happens in bedrooms when people fall asleep with a cigarette still alight. Do discourage this. Smoking in bed is a common cause of fires and resultant burns. Be careful, too, about leaving waste paper in bins where people may flick burning ash.

Smokers are also guilty of leaving matches and lighters about, within easy reach of children. This is a temptation and a danger for young children. Over 23,000 fires were caused by children with matches in what is described in the *United Kingdom Fire Statistics* as a 'typical' year.

6 *Scalding* Often scalds, especially from steam or chip fat, are even worse than burns. There are *five* main ways in which they are likely to happen.

(i) BATHS are filled with hot water and children or old people either fall or step into them by accident.

Safeguard: always put the cold water in first, then the hot. This way no one can get scalded. Do not leave baths, buckets, or kettles of water unguarded on the floor.

(ii) HOT TEA POTS or cups of tea are placed on the edge of the table, with the fringes of the cloth hanging over. One tug, and the child is scalded.

Safeguard: have a cloth which just fits the top of the table so that tassels and corners do not dangle. A Formica top and no cloth is safest. Any vessels containing hot liquid should be placed in the middle of the table. When the toddler sits up to the table make sure that nothing dangerous is within reach. His skin will scald far more readily than yours.

(iii) SAUCEPANS AND FRYING PANS are left with their handles

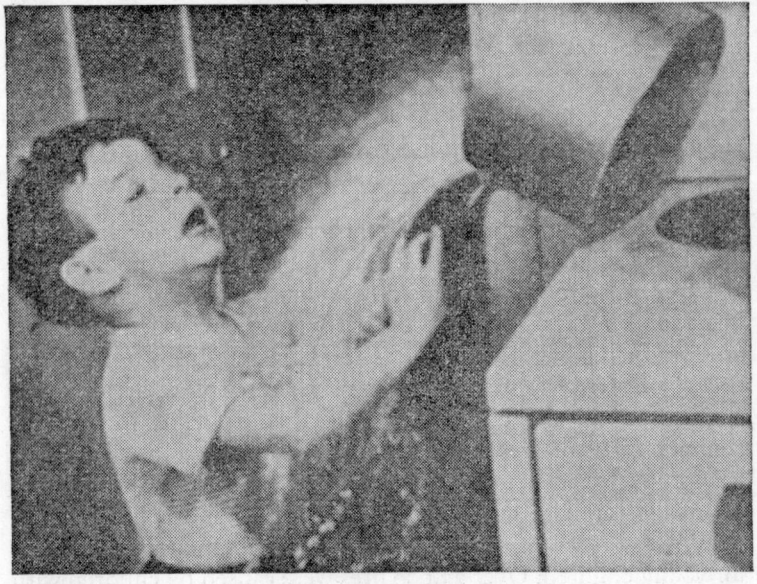

43 *What a moment's thought could so easily prevent*

projecting over the edge of the cooker or kitchen table. Often these utensils make interesting bubbling, frizzling noises and small hands reach up to investigate. The pan's entire contents may tip right on to their upturned faces.

Safeguard: whenever possible cook on the back burners. Turn all pan handles inwards. If possible buy a cooker with a built-in safety device for saucepans, e.g. a Cannon Gas Cooker.

(iv) KETTLES The flex from an electric kettle is often left dangling. The child trips over it, or pulls it experimentally.

Safeguard: if it cannot be put completely out of reach, either shorten the flex or fix it round a hook well out of reach.

(v) THE CHIP PAN Smoking hot fat or oil is so dangerous that it probably causes more kitchen fires than anything else. It does not merely catch fire if spilt or allowed to boil over; it can light spontaneously if overheated.

Safeguard: never leave it unattended. Do not try to make chips if you have several small children hanging round your skirts. Do not put too many chips into the fat at a time and make sure they are

ACCIDENTS IN THE HOME

dry, otherwise the fat may boil over and ignite on contact with the gas flame or hot plate. Should it catch fire do not pour water on top; do not open a door or window, the draught will make matters worse. Instead, exclude the air by covering the pan with a lid or plate. Nothing can burn without the oxygen in air.

'*Accidents will happen* . . .' They needn't. But if they do give first aid at once, and if the result is serious, send for help. If someone is actually on fire, exclude air, and try to smother the flames. The foam from a fire extinguisher will do this, or nearer at hand, roll a rug, blanket, or coat round the burning person. Never open doors or windows. If the house or room is on fire, get the people out. Do a quick mental check of those at home. Never mind about money or jewellery. Do not allow a child to go back for a pet which will probably escape on its own. Dial 999 and ask for the Fire Service. Give the address.

Poisoning

If someone is poisoned, call the doctor or ambulance, and while waiting try to find the cause. Different poisons have different remedies. Discover the cause quickly for every minute counts, and it will be the first question the doctor asks. If he has drunk paraffin you must try to make him sick, but not if he has drunk a disinfectant. To do this push your index finger right down his throat, pressing the tongue down as you do so, or make him drink strong salt water.

Electric shocks

Turn the electricity off at the mains before you touch the patient, or pull him away from the source of current with a wooden tool or stick, never a metal one. Make sure you know the position of your fuse box and main switch. Then treat for shock. If breathing has stopped, apply artificial respiration. Send for medical help.

Finally

1 Warn small children of dangers in a calm sensible way. Warn them often and make sure they understand and remember. Do not be sensational about it. This will only make them want to experiment.

2 Do not be afraid to forbid them from touching certain things,

e.g. wall sockets, gas taps, car controls. Do not shirk from punishing them severely if they forget or disobey. You may hurt their feelings (and their bottoms) at the time, but you may be saving their lives.

3 Always set a good example. A 'do as I say and not as I do' attitude will make a child distrust you.

4 Be warned by the pictures and posters and statistics of accidents.

5 Are your pets a potential danger? Does the dog sleep on the stairs, or could the cat lie on a baby's face in pram or cot? Cat and insect nets are a protection.

Go right round your house, shed and garden searching for dangers. Look for the faulty gate latch that will allow a toddler to run out into the road, for a loose paving stone that will trip you in the dark, for a high unbarred window (can children reach it?), for toys which have sharp edges and are inflammable. Do Teddy's eyes come out? Could they be swallowed? Is it a good idea to have highly polished lino? Could your youngsters safely nibble those pretty white snowball berries? Take the trouble to find out. Take the trouble to make your home accident-proof not accident-prone.

Further reading

First Aid Manual is published by the British Red Cross Society, 9 Grosvenor Crescent, S.W.1, at 30p

First Aid Questions and Answers, from the Order of St. John, 1 Grosvenor Crescent, London SW1X 7EF at 30p

Protect Your Home, free from Her Majesty's Stationery Office

Practical work

1 Get into groups and imagine one of each group has met with an accident. Treat according to your diagnosis of the trouble. Check with the casualty afterwards to see if your diagnosis was right. Let the other groups watch and criticise your treatment.

2 Look in your library for first-aid manuals. Check at home and school to see where first-aid boxes are, and if they are well stocked. At school you could offer in groups to be in charge of the various boxes and keep them clean, tidy and well stocked.

3 Draw a diagrammatic sketch of the human body. Find out where the arterial pressure points are and fill them in, carefully labelled. How do you apply pressure to each? List and learn the things to be remembered when stopping bleeding.

4 Finish the essay, 'There was a screech of brakes and then a scream—no one else was in sight——'

5 Find out where your local Red Cross Depot and Headquarters are. Is there one run by the St. John Ambulance Brigade as well? Where do you see their uniformed representatives? Why are they there? Ask them about their work.

6 Assess the dangers of the room you are now in. List them and see what positive steps you could take to avoid them.

7 In groups enact various accidents in the home, showing how you would deal with them.

Questions

1 Find out the exact terms of these three Acts:

(a) 1952 Heating Appliance (Fireguards) Act.
(b) 1961 Oil Heaters Act.
(c) 1961 Consumer Protection Act (Flammable Clothing).

Do these go far enough in protecting the public?

2 If you could introduce one act to assist in reducing accidents in the home, what would it be?

3 Do you consider that parents, whose children die or are injured as a result of their carelessness, should be punished?

4 Go round your own home making a list of potential dangers. Can any of them be removed?

5 Plan an accident-proof kitchen, imagining that you have a 2-year-old and a 4-year-old.

6 Granny is coming to stay. What special care will you take to keep her safe and sound?

CHAPTER 11 · WHEN AND WHERE TO GO FOR HELP—OFFICIAL ORGANISATIONS

Official organisations

Often when people are in need of help, are ill or anxious, bereaved or worn out, they are least able to consider clearly where they should turn for help. Usually help is available. This country has some wonderful organisations dedicated to service and basically most people are kind—if they are given the opportunity.

It helps if you know beforehand about these organisations, about services you are entitled to turn to, about those who will help you if they can, and about those who dedicate much of their spare time and energy in the service of others.

Firstly, everyone can turn to the Department of Health and Social Security. This now embraces several sources of help:

The National Health Service

We pay for this and we are entitled to make full and sensible use of the services it offers. Often we are unaware of the scope of these services. We pay for them in several ways mainly from general taxation, a small part from National Insurance Contributions (see Chapter 2) and an even smaller part from our rates.

Its history and purpose Before 1939 the care of the health of this country's inhabitants was a precarious business. The well-to-do could afford doctors and specialist services, hospital beds and surgical care. Some employers subscribed to an early form of National Insurance. The less well-to-do people were 'panel' patients who paid a regular subscription to insure their health. The poor who could not afford this went without medical care—sometimes until it was too late. The Second World War brought full employment and a realisation that neither the soldiers nor the women of the country (whose task it was to make munitions and do the jobs the enlisted men had vacated) were as fit as they might have been.

Rationing of food helped in some measure. It ensured a fair sharing of nutritious foods—proteins and vitality foods, and the bulk foods which poorer people had previously relied upon for sustaining their hunger were either non-existent, such as cakes, or rationed and scarce such as biscuits and confectionery. Bread was rationed but fortified with Vitamin B and calcium. Therefore more vegetables were eaten, and advantage was taken of every drop of milk and ounce of cheese and all the meat and butter available. This restored vitamin deficiencies to some extent, but did not provide a cure for more malicious forms of ill-health. So, in 1946, the National Health Service came into being with these as its aims:

(i) To ensure that everybody in the country, irrespective of means, age, sex or occupation, shall have equal opportunity to benefit from the best and most up-to-date medical services available.

(ii) To provide, therefore, for all who want it, a comprehensive service covering every branch of medicine from the care of minor ailments to major medicine and surgery; to include the care of mental as well as physical health and all specialist services for ailments such as tuberculosis, cancer, and for infectious diseases, fractures, orthopaedic treatment and maternity; to include all normal general services, the family doctor, midwife and nurse, the care of the teeth, of the eyes, the day-to-day care of the child; and to include all necessary drugs and medicines and a wide range of appliances.

(iii) To provide the service free of charge (apart from certain possible charges in respect of appliances) and to encourage a new attitude to health—the promotion of good health rather than the treatment of bad.

These three aims are taken from the White Paper of 1944. The Act that followed 2 years later tried to carry them out as far as was then possible. It was hoped that the aims could gradually be extended as the country became more prosperous in the post-war years. But the country's economy fluctuated. When it was necessary to make financial sacrifices sometimes it was the National Health Service that suffered. The care of teeth for instance is one of the services we now have to pay something for, except those under 21 and expectant or nursing mothers who are treated free of charge. Adults pay for medicines on prescription at 20p an item, but children under 15, people over 65, the chronic sick and expectant and nursing mothers get theirs free. We have a Health Service to be proud of—perhaps one of the finest in the world.

Charges Dental treatment and dentures, spectacles and some special appliances have to be paid for. But anyone in real need can get help from the Department of Health and Social Security. No other payments, stamps, contributions or fees have to be paid. If you wish you can pay for your doctor, specialist or private bed in hospital.

What does the Service consist of?

1 General Medical Services. These are the Family or Group Practice Doctor, the Dentist, the Pharmaceutical and Supplementary Ophthalmic services (chemists and opticians).

2 Hospital and Specialist Services

3 Local Health Services

4 The Mental Health Services. In April 1974 the Regional and Area Health Authorities are due to combine.

The family doctor

Because of the pressure of work doctors usually work (or practise) in pairs—as partners—or in teams in a Group Practice. We can choose our doctor by finding one near our home and asking to be placed on his register. The doctor has the right to accept or refuse a patient. Once you have registered the doctor will be paid for his services to you whether or not you are actually making use of his services. So that should you move say from Cornwall to Durham, you should re-register *at once* so that the doctor you may actually have to send for at midnight is the one who is actually getting paid for such services! You can change your doctor but you must apply to the Executive Council to do so, and your medical records will be passed on to your new doctor. You should not keep changing, for your doctor should know you and your family, and have first-hand experience of your past health to make the greatest use of his skill in treating you. He will pass you on to various other services within the National Health Service if he considers it necessary. He will also make use of the local pathological laboratories, bacteriology departments and blood transfusion units if he needs to. His name will appear on your National Health Medical Card.

Your medical card

44 A medical card

Each member of your family will be issued with one of these at birth. Keep them safely, and make a separate record of the number on each in case they become mislaid. This National Health Service number is important—your dentist will want to know it when you visit him, and should you have to visit a strange doctor—perhaps on holiday—he too will want to know it. On your card you will find the address of the Local Executive Council to whom, as we have seen, you write if you wish to change your doctor. You will also find a series of instructions on how to do this, and much more important, how and when to call your doctor when you need him. Finally there are instructions about what to do when you move house.

The dentist

You can choose your dentist but there is no need to register with him as with your doctor. Because many dentists are very overworked it is a good idea to register unofficially with one in the neighbourhood. You may find you have to wait weeks or even months for an inspection, and then a further period of time for treatment. Once you have left school you will be charged for artificial dentures and after your 18th birthday you will have to pay 50 per cent of the scale fees up to a maximum of £10 for all dental treatment.

The Supplementary Ophthalmic Services

These cater for testing sight and for the fitting and supply of glasses. Serious defects are treated by specialists at the Local Eye Hospital. The family doctor examines the patient first and recommends a visit to the specialist at the Local Eye Hospital or, if the defect is less serious, a visit to any ophthalmic medical practitioner or ophthalmic optician who has joined the National Health Service. A list of their names and addresses is obtainable at the Post Office or the Executive Council Office. Probably your doctor, when he gives you a letter of reference, will recommend one. No charge is made for testing sight, but at present there is a charge for spectacles, frames and lenses.

Pharmaceutical Service

Chemists are an important link in the National Health Service. They read, interpret and make up the prescriptions made by family doctors for medicines and tablets. One in each area stays open late at night to do this. A list of which shops are open on which nights is usually displayed in each doctor's waiting room. Some doctors in remote areas dispense their own drugs, many keep a few in stock for emergencies.

Hospital and Specialist Services

The Minister of Health must supply for each area three amenities to meet all reasonable requirements:

(a) Hospital accommodation.

(b) Medical, nursing and other services at the hospitals.

(c) The services of specialists, whether at a hospital, a health centre or a clinic or at the home of the patient.

Almost all contacts with hospital and special services are made through the family doctor. If he considers that hospital treatment is necessary he will give you a letter for the specialists and book you an appointment. Then you become the responsibility of the hospital, which reports back on your progress to your family doctor.

The Out-patient

If, after examination by a specialist, you are told you need treatment of some kind, a series of appointments is made for you and you attend the hospital as an out-patient. At the end of the treatments you will be re-examined and either discharged or given further treatment. No charge is made for this unless you are given special appliances.

The In-patient

If your examination shows that you are in need of an operation, or hospital care, you will be taken in if there is a bed vacant. How long you wait depends on how serious your condition is. No charges are made unless you choose to be a private patient. You may also be offered an 'Amenity bed'—these are in side, or small wards and a charge of £1–£2 a day is made for the extra privacy they allow. Your doctor can send you straight into hospital if he considers your condition serious enough, and if a bed is available. Emergency beds are kept for serious cases.

Casualties

In case of accident you can take the patient straight to the casualty department of the nearest hospital. You can do this either by dialling 999 (see Chapter 10) and requesting an ambulance to come, or by driving straight to the hospital. If a child has cut his wrist badly and the blood is spurting from it, you must get him to hospital at once and as quickly as possible. If he has a less serious accident, is neither bleeding nor in acute pain, it is better to seek your own doctor's advice first. Don't send for an ambulance unless it is essential, otherwise you may deprive someone in desperate need of its services.

Convalescence

In certain cases, this is part of in-hospital treatment. Because of the shortage of staff or beds patients are often kept in hospital for a minimum period. If it is obvious that a patient is not yet physically or mentally fit enough to cope with home circumstances, a stay in a convalescent home can be prescribed. Unfortunately, these homes are few and far between and only cases in serious need are sent for this extra recovery-care. Home helps are available (see Chapter 15) when the patient must return home but is not yet fit to run the house. The social worker will take care of this. She is the link between the hospital and the patient's rehabilitation at home. It is her special job to see that the patient gets all the financial help and care he is entitled to when he leaves hospital. Once home, the patient again comes under the care of the family doctor who will have been informed of his progress, and may even have found time for a hospital visit.

Mental health

The mentally ill may be treated at out-patient clinics, at in-patient or day units in general hospitals or at psychiatric hospitals. Though compulsory powers can be exercised to see that patients of this category receive care and treatment, normally they are treated on an entirely voluntary basis. The recent change in public opinion towards mental suffering has encouraged many patients to seek help.

Since 1960 the Mental Health Act has directed local authorities to make the following arrangements to assist the mentally ill:

1 To provide residential accommodation.
2 To provide centres for training and occupation.
3 To appoint mental welfare officers.
4 To provide ancillary services for those who suffer or who have suffered from mental disorders.

More help needed There is a serious lack of trained staff; there are not enough doctors, dentists, nurses, midwives, health visitors, radiographers, physiotherapists, social workers, etc. For many years these dedicated people have been overworked and underpaid. Now doctors and dentists are beginning to get a better deal—let us hope that eventually all will be treated fairly. At present many voluntary workers try to make life easier for them (as we will see in Chapter 12). Often, long illnesses, or injuries can so disrupt a family's organisation that they begin to need more help than their National Insurance or National Health entitlements can cover. They need then to turn to the Department of Health and Social Security. It has been fairly said that no one today who lives within the care of our Welfare State need lack the means by which to live. However, many people either do not realise they are entitled to seek this extra help, or they are too proud to do so. This pride is false because National Assistance is not charity; it is paid for out of general taxation. We ourselves have been paying into it ever since it was started in 1948 and so are fully entitled to our share when in need.

The National Assistance Act of 1948

The passing of this Act established for the first time in this country a single comprehensive system of financial help for those in need. Before this various Poor Law grants provided by Local Authorities and paid for out of the rates were used to help those in need. As often the recipients of this assistance did not pay rates and were made to feel they were receiving charity and, as they were also subjected to a means test to see if they needed help, only those who either were hardened, or were really desperate, applied, and so many suffered real hardship. Still today, however, a horror of the means test, poor law and the workhouse persists and many old people suffer cold and hunger to preserve their pride. The Act was administered by a Board covering England, Scotland and Wales. Northern Ireland had its own Act and Board. This is now the responsibility of the Department of Health and Social Security.

The Department of Health and Social Security

Its duties as laid down by the Act are:

1 'To assist persons in Great Britain who are without resources to meet their requirements, or whose resources (including benefits

receivable under the National Insurance Act 1946) must be supplemented in order to meet their requirements.'

2 '[To] exercise its functions in such manner as shall best promote the welfare of persons affected by the exercise thereof.'

Who are these 'Persons'? Anyone over the age of 16 may apply for supplementary benefits, provided they are in need, whether on account of old age, sickness, unemployment, or because they have to stay at home to care for young children. As you cannot leave home under this age, it is assumed that parents will apply on your behalf if the need arises.

If you are in full-time employment there should be no need for you to apply, so grants are not available, nor are they to those in full-time training, such as university students (who are entitled to grants of another kind) nor will they be for *you* if you are a worker on strike, although your dependants may qualify. If the strike is official, your trade union will finance you. (See Chapter 2.)

How the grant is assessed Certain scales are laid down to assist those in differing circumstances. For instance, if an older person receiving a pension and supplementary benefits goes into hospital, the supplementary benefits stop for the period he is in hospital, for during this time the State is fully keeping him. However, if he has to continue paying rent he will get enough to help with this. If he is married, and the rent, heating, food and lighting bill, etc., have to be paid on his wife's behalf, she will continue to receive full assistance. Special grants can be made for dentures, spectacles and even fares to and from the hospital. The leaflet A.L.18, which gives details of current grants and scales, is available at Post Offices and Social Security Offices.

These two organisations, the National Health Service and the Department of Health and Social Security, are the official bodies to whom we can turn for help. They are financed partly from rates and partly from Government funds. Other services which are financed entirely by our rates, plus the Government grant made by exempting rates from general taxation, include:

1 The Police Service
2 Local Courts, Tribunals and Justice
3 The Fire Service
4 Sewage and refuse disposal
5 Local amenities such as roads, lighting

We will look at several of these more closely to see exactly what we can expect from them. Without the financial backing of our rating system they certainly would not exist. So we see that our rates are partly a means of providing us with people and organisations to turn to when in need.

Rates

These are a local tax on land and property. Property that is used for human occupation—not farm land for instance, only the farmhouse—would be rated. The tenant in a rented property or a council house has to pay rates. In a block of flats either the landlord pays the rates or the rates are divided between the tenants. Offices and shops pay rates, and these are substantially higher than those for houses.

How are rates assessed? Each building with its surrounding land is separately assessed by the local Valuation for Rating Department. New valuations on all property were carried out in 1972/3. The Rateable Value, commonly abbreviated R.V., is assessed according to the amount of land; the position of the property; whether the house is detached, semi- or terraced; whether it has a garage, a greenhouse, a shed, etc. The average R.V. for a 3-bedroomed semi with detached garage is around £30.

The local rating authority may be a County Borough, such as Sheffield, a Metropolitan Borough, such as Battersea, a Borough, such as Enfield, an Urban District, like Gosforth, or a Rural District like Ennerdale.

The authority calculates how much money it needs to pay for all the services it wishes to provide. It will also know the value of the rateable property in its area. By dividing one into the other it can tell how much to charge each rateable property to provide the money it needs. For instance, if it needs £100,000 and has property to the rateable value of £66,000, it must charge £1·50 in the £1 on each of the £66,000 to obtain £100,000. This means that, for every pound at which a property is rated, the occupier must pay £1·50—i.e. 50p per £1 more.

Therefore a man in a small terraced house with a rateable value of £30 pays £30 plus 30 × 50p per year = £15 so that he will pay £45. The man in the semi-detached whose R.V. is £40 will pay £40 plus 40 × 50p, i.e. £60 a year.

Usually these rates are paid quarterly or half yearly but in most areas they can be paid monthly if you wish. Council house tenants pay a portion each week or fortnight with their rent. This is really the best way to do it—whereas it is only a small amount a week it is an awful blow to receive a rates demand for £20 to £25 a half year! Try in any case to put it aside regularly, you have no option but to pay.

How are the rates spent? This varies from area to area but there are certain services every area is committed to provide, the cost of which is covered partly by the rates and partly by a grant from the Government.

Let us look at the total expenditure of Local Authorities for a 'typical' year—the amounts given are in million pounds.

Local Authorities' Expenditure 1960

		£ million
Police and Justice		99
Social Services, i.e.		
Education	692	
Child Care	23	830
Health	90	
Aged, Handicapped, Homeless	25	
Basic Local Services, i.e.		
Roads	118	
Public Lighting	22	254
Fire Service	29	
Sewage, Refuse Disposal	85	
Town and Country Planning, Parks		42
Other (rate collection, agricultural services, land drainage)		100
Total expenditure on goods and services		1,325
Housing Subsidies		26
Current Grants to persons, i.e.		
School meals and milk	59	
Scholarships,		98
Grants to Universities	39	
Debt Interest, i.e.		
To Central Government	123	289
To others	166	
Current Surplus		218
Total		£1,956

A total of £1,956,000,000! Where do we get such a vast amount to spend? In the typical year quoted this is where it came from:

	£ millions
Receipts from Rates	764
Grants from Central Government	741
Income from House Rents	229
Income from other land and building	133
Gross trading profits	52
Interest on Investments	37
	£1,956

As we see, nearly half the money is provided by the Government. The National Health Service is supported to only a very

45 *What the rates help to pay for*

small extent by the rates. To the £25 million shown for the aged, handicapped and homeless a further £172 million came from the Government for National Assistance. Often Local Authorities borrow money for building schemes, swimming baths, museums, etc., hence the amount shown as debt interest. A surplus is shown too, which is a necessary nest egg.

Often within an area a County Council is responsible for major services,[1] and rural and urban boroughs responsible for minor ones.[2] In this case the rate allocation is divided between them. This is sensible and economical and leads to efficiency. If each small area

[1] Such as schools, libraries, police forces, roads, sanitation and fire brigades.
[2] Including street lighting, parks, refuse collection and playing fields.

wanted its own ambulance and fire engine and its own garages and stations to house them in, the rates would shoot up. Obviously they must co-operate. An adequate section of the rates must be allocated for two of the most important services: The Police and The Fire Services. I visited local headquarters of both these services recently to make sure I knew exactly what they had to offer in the way of help.

The Police

I didn't get a very clear answer to my questions, how, where and when do you help the public? The reason for this I gradually realised is that anywhere and everywhere, at any hour of the night or day, the Police will tackle any problem of any kind. If the job is too specialised for them to handle alone, and you are not able to cope, they will fetch the specialist to help you. Here are some of the tasks, apart from routine duties, that one branch tackled during a Christmas week in a town of about 27,000 people in answer to appeals for help, emergency calls and as a result of observation.

1. Old lady falls in bathroom, gashed head. Doctor called.
2. Youth trampled to death in excited crowd leaving dance hall.
3. House flooded during Christmas night, old couple desperate. Plumber knocked up and fetched—happy Christmas after all.
4. Middle-aged couple in shooting tragedy—both found dead.
5. Numerous car offences.
6. Various drunk and disorderlies.
7. Four people injured in car crash.
8. Schoolmaster unable to find his keys.
9. Wife calls for protection at home from drunken husband.
10. Evidence given in court concerning attack on a toddler by a large Alsatian. (No injuries sustained.)

The Police don't boast, but gradually the extent of the care they take of us is revealed. Nothing is too much trouble, no child is too small to be listened to, no adult too old or disreputable not to matter. A tramp has the same rights as a tailor—the welfare of all of us matters to the Police. Their lives are neither quite as dramatic as 'Z Cars' portrays, nor as homely as that of Sgt. Dixon, but a mixture of both. It is quite clear that they take pride in not leaving us with our problems unsolved or our questions unanswered. They can be very good friends, so go to them in trouble. If they can't help they'll put you in touch with those who can. At all times they will listen sympathetically—ignore this silly idea that they are there to be avoided, and bring your children up to regard them as friends. Then your children will turn to them in trouble, and your children will be safe.

Dial 999 in an emergency. Report events that look suspicious and co-operate with the Police whenever possible. They never let us down and, we, the public, let them down every hour of the day. We melt out of sight rather than give evidence, rather than get involved. We watch them maintaining order instead of helping them. A group of youths once watched a young constable being kicked to death—they didn't want to get involved! A woman refused to give evidence, and the next time the man involved attacked a child, it was criminally assaulted—her reason?—she had an appointment at the hairdresser's. Such things as these happen all too often. Don't ever have any such event on your conscience— if you cannot give immediate assistance, run to the nearest telephone—help the Police to help you.

The Fire Service

Chapter 10 tells you *how* to call them. A local Chief Fire Officer tells me that *when* to call them is as early as possible. Call, he says, even if you just suspect fire—remember—where there's smoke—— Once fire gets a hold its destructive power is unbelievable. Because of this be sensible, take precautions.

We know the services of the Police are free yet there is a widespread belief that you pay to have a fire put out. The only payment you make is through your rates. No fee is ever asked for putting out a fire, whether or not it is your fault that it started.

Other services

Because they have hoses firemen are sometimes asked to help with drainage, pumping a cellar dry, etc., and a small charge may be made in this case. Often they are asked to rescue kittens from trees or children with their heads stuck somewhere. This is humanitarian and there is no charge.

Auxiliaries

Both Police and Fire Services are considerably under-staffed. Either would be grateful for your services in a part-time capacity when you are a little older.

Women Special Constables These do a valuable job. They are only called on for duty a few hours a month, plus special occasions. They get a smart uniform free, all expenses paid and an interesting training.

46 *A Woman Special Constable—All part of the job*

The rates alone would never meet the bill for all these services. You have seen that the Government grants a sum to each area almost equal to the rate receipts.

These Government grants come mainly from Direct Taxation. Indirect Taxation also plays a part here. This includes the tax on licences of all sorts, purchase tax and death duties—these last are taxes paid on property belonging to a person who dies, over and above the first £4,000's worth. The profits from Government trading, the Crown Lands and the money for National Savings,

Trade unions

In the nineteenth century conditions in many jobs used to be unbelievably bad, and there was no possibility of leaving and changing your job because there were many applicants for every vacancy. It was work or starve. Boys were used to sweep the large old-fashioned chimneys. Often, because the work was so hot, they worked naked. Their bodies were affected by the soot, so that if they escaped being overcome by the heat and fumes they might die of skin cancer or tuberculosis. Another form of cancer, phossy jaw, was prevalent among workers who made matches from phosphorus. The dust of coal mines caused silicosis, a disease which cripples and kills. Children were employed to run underneath dangerous machinery if the spaces were too small for adults, and often got caught, injured or killed. Girl seamstresses had their eyes and chests permanently weakened by poor light and cramped, damp conditions. In 1864 seamstresses were paid only $1\frac{1}{2}d.$ for making a shirt.

Men used to watch their families starve and were helpless to better their position. In these desperate conditions the workers began to unite into small unions. But fear of an uprising similar to the French Revolution led the Government to pass laws making

47 *A nineteenth-century chimney sweep*

unions illegal. Not until 1825 were these laws repealed, and even then there was great opposition to trade unions. At last, in 1871, they gained legal recognition until today nearly half our working population belongs to a trade union of some kind.

There are three main kinds:

1 *Craft Unions*, where a skill or training is the common link between the members of the union. Such unions may be as large as the Amalgamated Society of Woodworkers, with 191,726 members or as small as Equity, the British Actors' Union with some 9,000 members.

2 *Industrial Unions*, where a common industry gives the union members a link. Some of these unions are very large and powerful, such as the A.E.U. or Amalgamated Engineering Union, which has 907,673 members.

3 *General Union* The workers belonging to such a union are often unskilled and they band together in many groups within the union. The largest is the Transport and General Workers' Union which has over 1,000,000 members.

The professional associations are similar in structure to the craft unions and, although often smaller in size, are sometimes very powerful. The B.M.A., British Medical Association, is one and the N.U.T., National Union of Teachers, is another. Employers too can join organisations so that they can meet the union representatives jointly for discussions and negotiations.

Today the work of the unions includes such things as:

1 Bargaining for fair wages. This is complicated by such things as piece rates, overtime, holiday pay and differentials. If the pay of an unskilled worker who once was paid two-thirds the wage of the skilled worker is raised, the wages of the skilled worker must also be adjusted to make the whole wage structure fair. This is known as maintaining differentials.

2 Bargaining for good working conditions. This includes the fencing of dangerous machinery, the extraction of fumes and dust, the provision of adequate space, heat, light and ventilation for the employees to work in. Protective clothing must be provided, safety regulations must be displayed and observed, and the provision of refreshments, medical facilities and rest rooms is expected.

3   Fair treatment for its worker members is jealously guarded by the unions and watch is kept to see that no one is wrongfully dismissed or victimised.

The elected representatives of the unions do the on-the-spot checking for the unions and these are called shop stewards. Officials are also elected to draw up and carry out union policy. These are usually working full time for the union and so are paid by the union. It is a most important part of union life that all members should attend meetings to express their opinions and then send forward the members they really wish to represent them at a higher level. A union must be a thoroughly responsible body if it is to win the respect of the employers and country. Unfortunately after the harsh treatment of employees in the last century the unions, or at least some of them, struggled for the betterment of their members at any price, and sometimes the price was too high to pay. It is wrong to insist on higher wages unless they are linked with higher output. Of course, if the employees are earning large profits for their bosses they, too, should benefit, but the bosses have to expand production to make more work so that more employees benefit. If the workers claim higher wages irresponsibly, production costs rise, the goods they produce become dearer and the orders for them fall.

When bargaining fails, unions can call for a withdrawal of labour. This can be just a ban on overtime, or a strike to stop work altogether. This is a last resort and is resorted to only in dire circumstances. If the workers have a legitimate complaint and negotiation fails, the union officials should examine the facts and then grant official recognition to the withdrawal of labour. The strike is then an *Official Strike* and the workers receive from their union a financial allowance during the period of the strike. Other unions sometimes rally round and support the strike with money or by striking in sympathy. *Unofficial* or *wildcat strikes* occur when workers strike without the approval, or sometimes even without the knowledge, of their officials. These do a great deal of harm. This is why it is so important to see that the union representatives are men and women of integrity and common sense.

The Closed Shop   It is sometimes felt that if a worker accepts the good wages and conditions which have been fought for by a union he should be *made* to join and support that union. When all members of a firm are required to join the union, it is called a 'closed shop'. Any new worker refusing to join may find that the rest of the workers strike in protest. On the other hand, one of the freedoms of the worker may be considered to be the freedom to decide whether to join a union or not.

Today, employers and trade unions are beginning to work together, not only for their own good but to plan for the good of the whole industry of which they are part, and for the country which needs their support.

Further reading

Maternal and Child Welfare Manual is published by the British Red Cross Society, 9 Grosvenor Crescent, S.W.1, at 20p

Welfare Services is published by the British Red Cross Society at $27\frac{1}{2}$p

Signpost to Welfare is published by the British Red Cross Society at $7\frac{1}{2}$p

A Citizen of Today, by Michael Hansen, published by Oxford University Press at 40p

Guide to National Insurance is available from Her Majesty's Stationery Office, Cornwall House, Stamford St., S.E.1, at 4p

Practical work

1 You are part of the *first* generation of this country to have been born into the Welfare State. Your children will learn only from textbooks what the country was like before. You still have the chance to find out first hand by asking your parents or your grandparents what such things as a visit to the doctor, an operation, being on the dole or needing dental treatment, meant to a family before the last war.

Find out before it is too late and they have forgotten. Talk to the oldest people you know and see what things were like in their day. Pool the information you collect and compare it with conditions today.

2 Was there a workhouse in your district? If not, where was the nearest one? What date was it built, for whom did it cater and, if still in use, what is it used for now?

3 The Family Doctor is a thing of the past. Debate this subject, taking these points into consideration:

(a) Is he being replaced by a health centre or a group practice of doctors?
(b) Is he far busier than he has been before? Why?
(c) How important is a 'bedside manner'?

4 Find out how other countries, such as France, Canada, West Germany, Eire, China, Russia, Spain and the U.S.A., look after the health of their nation. Is it true, for instance, that in Canada many families are still paying for the nursing home expenses at the birth of their first child when the third arrives? Is it true that in the U.S.A. seriously ill cases are turned away from hospitals unless they can prove their ability to pay? Is the Dr. Kildare image a factual one?

5 Do you know a member of a trade union? What about your parents? Find out to which trade union any friend of yours belongs. How much do they pay per week, per month or per year in union fees? Do they go to union meetings? If so, what happens there?

6 Would you, as a woman, join a trade union? Would you in order to get equal pay with men? Can you think of any reasons why you shouldn't?

7 Debate whether or not a wife should support her husband who wishes to take part in the official strike at his works.

Questions

1 Who was the man behind the White Paper of 1944 whose clear and imaginative report led the way to the Act of 1946 which brought into being our National Health Service? What else was his report concerned with?

2 Are there any ways in which you would like to see the National Health Service (1) improved; (2) curtailed?

3 Write an essay beginning, 'I opened my grandmother's door and was sure I could smell smoke . . .'

4 Ask either at home or at your Local Government Office for a rates demand. Does it tell you how your rates are used? If not, find out, and write an account of 'Where the rates go—in my area'.

5 Write an essay on 'The History of the Trade Union Movement'.

6 Which novels have you read which reveal the plight of employees of the past?

7 What is the T.U.C.? What is the connection between the Trade Unions and the Labour Party? Why does this connection exist?

CHAPTER 12 · WHEN AND WHERE TO GO FOR HELP— UNOFFICIAL ORGANISATIONS

Voluntary organisations

When we read about the official services there are to help us, and, when we think of the numbers of people who need help, of the tremendous variety of their problems and of the unavoidable rigidity of official services, it is clear that something more is needed.

This 'something more' is supplied by many voluntary organisations too numerous to list; but the most important can be mentioned here.

1 The Citizens' Advice Bureaux

These were started during the last war as an emergency service to supply information and advice on problems arising from war conditions. They dealt with 10,000,000 enquiries during the war period. People were faced with a flood of forms, permits, coupons, ration books, milk tokens, holiday coupons and coal tokens, etc. To many people it was confusing. The C.A.B. sorted out people's troubles and sent them away informed and reassured. At the end of the war the value of this service was recognised and it was continued. The local Government Act of 1948 provided legislation for aiding and financing this service.

48 *The sign of the Citizens' Advice Bureau*

Its purpose is stated as: 'To make available to the individual, accurate information and skilled advice on many of the personal problems that arise in daily life; to explain and to use wisely the services provided for him by the State, and in general to provide counsel to men and women . . .'

Its structure At present there are 438 C.A.B. in England, Scotland, Wales and Northern Ireland, established in nearly all the big cities and in many of the larger towns. Some bureaux are directly administered by local authorities, but most are controlled by voluntary organisations working with the local authority. Each is an independent local unit, all are non-political. They are partly financed by the local authority and partly by voluntary funds raised locally.

Staffing Some bureaux are open full-time and some part-time, depending on the local needs. Most of them are staffed by trained voluntary workers but the larger bureaux have a paid professional social worker in charge of a team of volunteers. In addition, there is normally a panel of consultants, such as the local probation officer, a lawyer and a moral welfare worker, to give specialist or professional advice.

Its work You can go into any Citizens' Advice Bureau and ask for information which will be given you in the strictest confidence and absolutely free; the answer, in short, to almost anything.

What exactly can you ask? The C.A.B. deals with all enquiries relating to travel, emigration, postal information and sending gifts abroad. Also queries about apprenticeships, evening classes and community and youth activities. You may ask about employment, medical facilities, property and land, the armed services and trade. If you have any problems concerning insurance, pensions or more personal matters such as making a will, marriage and divorce, or if you just want some information about places and events, go along to your nearest C.A.B.

As you see, the C.A.B. is invaluable. The address of your local bureau can be obtained from the Headquarters at 26 Bedford Square, London, W.C.1.

2 The Women's Royal Voluntary Service or W.R.V.S.

This is another organisation which emerged from the last war and continues to do valuable work.

49 *The sign of the Women's Royal Voluntary Service*

Their record now Their work is vital, and always of a consistently high standard. It may take the form of rallying to the call of *World Refugee Year* (1962) when the W.R.V.S. processed 2,458,977 garments to bring relief. It may take the form of bringing cheer and sustenance to our old age pensioners here in England. The W.R.V.S. now runs 2,000 Darby and Joan Clubs with a membership of more than 150,000. Many of these old people are also lucky enough to receive a hot nourishing midday meal from the *'Meals on Wheels' scheme* The meal, costing 5p to 7½p, is delivered to the old person's doorstep. Sometimes the National Assistance Board subsidises the cost. The regular visits from the W.R.V.S. are a check on the old folks' well-being. In 1972, 12,480,547 meals were being delivered. Luncheon clubs have recently been formed by the W.R.V.S., because many old people are badly in need of company as well as nourishing meals. In an increasing number of areas they can now meet two or three times a week for a meal and a chat. In 1972, 2,840,248 such meals were served at about 15p per head.

You will find the W.R.V.S. green uniform almost everywhere where there is worthwhile work to be done—visiting families of those in prison, helping at clinics, sending magazines to our services abroad, visiting the lonely and sick in hospital, running canteens in out-patients departments.

3 The British Red Cross Society

This is a member of what is probably the most famous, the busiest and one of the most wonderful organisations in the world. It was founded in the nineteenth century by Henri Durant, a citizen of Geneva, where the international house of the Red Cross is still situated today.

50 *The sign of the Red Cross*

The Red Cross at present There are 111 Societies from different nations with a total membership of about 214,000,000. Throughout the world they aim 'to relieve all kinds of distress and need, and to inculcate the idea of service'. The British Red Cross Society now has 137 branches. As a voluntary body the Society is dependent on contributions from the public. Not only have we come to rely on the Red Cross in times of emergency but we also count on it to carry out many everyday tasks and to fill many of the gaps left in the Welfare State. To meet these demands the British Red Cross has a nucleus of specially qualified full-time paid workers, so that the voluntary body—the heart of the movement—can provide a service of a professional standard. This it achieves by intensively training large sections of its workers in first aid and simple nursing. *Voluntary Aid Detachments* are made up of men trained in first aid and women trained in nursing and first aid. Today, they are not only quickly on the spot after an emergency, they are present and on duty wherever one is likely to take place, on football fields, in cinemas, near crowded beaches, on the T.T. circuit at the Isle of Man, and at all public events where crowds gather. Their biggest task is to supplement the National Health Service in hospitals. We have already talked about the shortage of nursing and other hospital

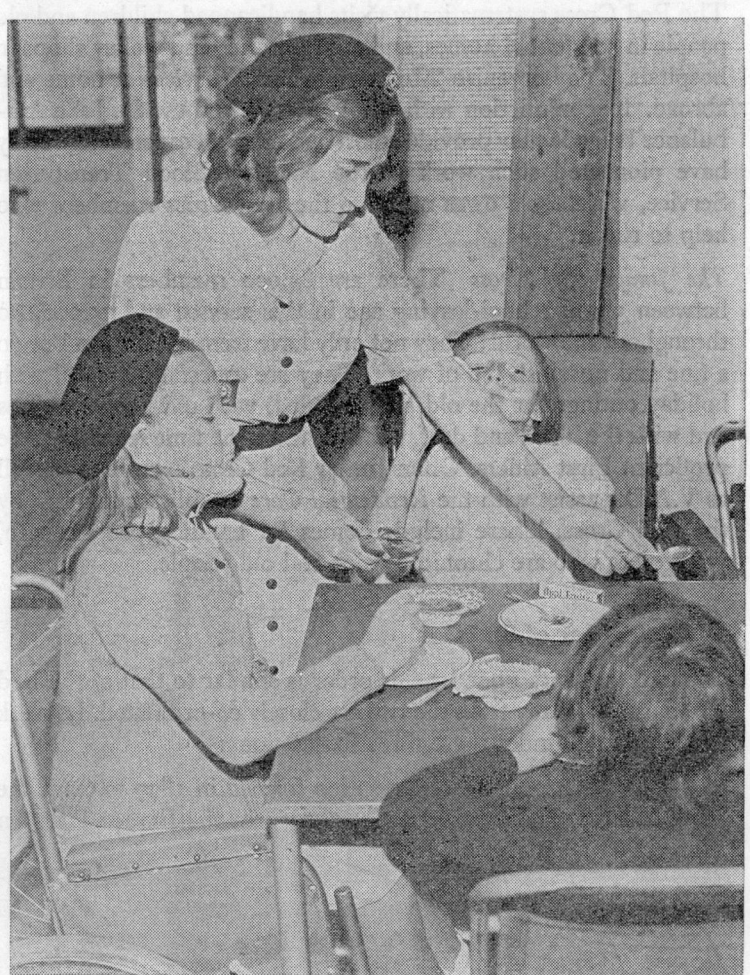

51 *The Junior Red Cross Club in Ottershaw was founded by fit cadets and handicapped children as a result of a holiday camp held by the Surrey Branch of the British Red Cross Society at Barnett Hill in the summer of 1959. The club meets fortnightly on Saturday afternoons*

staff. Many a ward would be on the verge of closing without the devotion and reliability of its V.A.D.s. In Britain over 32,000 women and 8,000 men are trained V.A.D.s. In overseas branches we have another 3,200. Is it any wonder the Red Cross is turned to in an emergency?

Members in Groups There is much work for these people too. The Red Cross systematically visits handicapped children and old people in residential homes, and runs libraries and trolley shops in hospitals. They organise 'Meals on Wheels' services at home and abroad. In conjunction with the W.R.V.S. and the St. John Ambulance Brigade they provide escort and hospital car services. They have pioneered such work as the National Blood Transfusion Service, which still owes much to the Red Cross members who help to run it.

The Junior Red Cross There are 84,000 members in Britain between 5 and school-leaving age in this service and 75,000,000 throughout the world! They not only have tremendous fun but do a fine and unselfish job of work. They are especially helpful with holiday outings for the old and disabled, with old people's clubs and with the blind and deaf, while at the same time training to be proficient First Aiders. Often Junior Red Cross members as well as V.A.D.s assist with the *Residential Care* establishments run by the Red Cross. These include homes for handicapped children, youngsters who are chronically sick and old people.

4 The Order of St. John

Some of the work done by this order is similar to that of the Red Cross, and in many tasks the two are closely co-ordinated. Its work has developed under these three foundations:

(i) St. John Ambulance Association formed in 1877 to teach the First Aid that had been so badly needed in the Franco-Prussian War.

52 *The sign of the Order of St. John*

THE ORDER OF ST. JOHN

(ii) St. John Ambulance Brigade formed in 1887—a practical expression of this teaching.

(iii) The Hospital in Jerusalem—its roots deep in history, its use as an Ophthalmic Hospital right up to date due to the fact that about 95% of all Middle East children suffer from eye diseases before reaching the age of 10. Now the virus of *trachoma*, the most damaging and widespread of these diseases, has been isolated and a vaccine is being developed.

At home

The St. John Ambulance Brigade is a voluntary uniformed foundation devoted to the following special duties:

1 *First Aid* Under the guidance of doctors and State Registered Nurses members are trained to give prompt and skilled help that may save life and relieve suffering in the many accidents that occur in day-to-day life, at home, at work and in major disasters. They also regularly give their services at national and public functions, sports meetings, cinemas, theatres, etc., and staff first-aid posts by

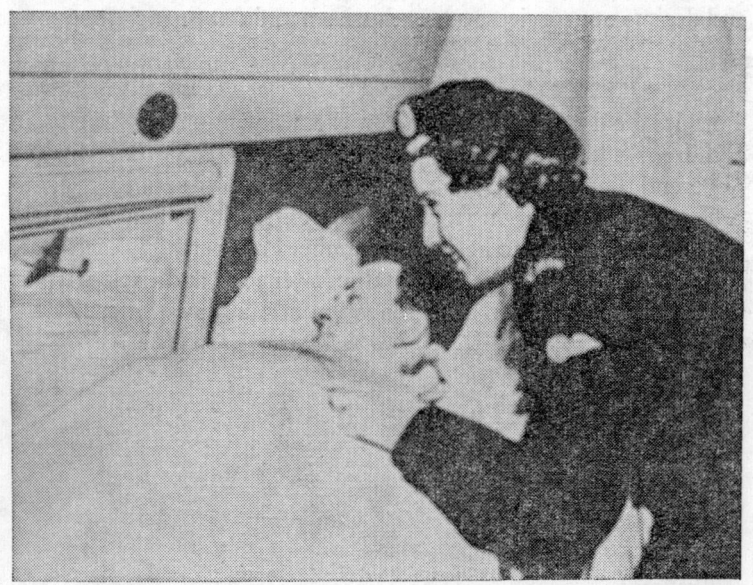

53 *St. John Ambulance at work*

the roadside and on the beaches. Their skill is re-examined every year, they never become out-of-date.

2 *Nursing* Voluntary nursing aid under the District Nurse is given to patients in their own homes and part-time nursing is undertaken in all types of hospitals and clinics, extended help being given in emergencies and epidemics.

By joining the National Hospital Service Reserve (including mobile first aid units), the Queen Alexandra's Royal Naval Nursing Service Auxiliary Section or the Royal Naval V.A.D. Reserve, members have opportunities for special training and experience.

3 *Welfare* This includes the care of old people and the physically and mentally handicapped and welfare duties in service and civilian hospitals and in homes for the elderly and disabled, such as Hospital Library and handicraft services. Also Meals on Wheels and Medical Comforts Depots for the loan of sickroom equipment.

4 *Special duties* Special duties covering first aid in industry. Voluntary escorts of the sick and injured by land, sea and air. They run ambulance services voluntarily and as agents of local authorities. Training of national importance in the Civil Defence Services.

This is yet another voluntary organisation which is in need of and desires our services, our enthusiasm and our financial support.

5 The N.S.P.C.C.

This is the National Society for the Prevention of Cruelty to Children. This was started 87 years ago, in July 1884, by the Reverend Benjamin Waugh, when there was a serious need to protect children—often from their parents. Since then 7,000,000 children have received help. The number grows steadily each year, a matter for pride in the organisation's tenacity and tireless work, but for infinite sadness at its reflection of our way of life.

54 *The sign of the N.S.P.C.C.*

THE N.S.P.C.C.

In 1884 there was one centre, 175 children received help and this was all the work of one inspector. In 1972 at various centres, 320 inspectors supported by visitors dealt with 62,227 children. These were from new cases; 8,342 cases were already being dealt with. It is not that there is more cruelty nowadays, but that more cases are being discovered. People are more public spirited about reporting cases and our standards of humanity are now much higher. A vivid example of changing attitudes comes from China. Not many years ago it would have been cruel *not* to bind a Chinese girl's feet so tightly that she would totter on them for the rest of her life, for no Chinese girl with average, let alone big, feet would have had a hope of marriage. Now, mercifully, this is forbidden, but the social attitude had to be changed as well as the law.

Even in Britain today the N.S.P.C.C. inspectors come across some horrifying cases such as that of Molly, an infant girl. She was admitted to hospital three times in the first 18 months of her life. The first time she was suffering from a broken collar bone and a fractured skull. A few days after her discharge she was back with her skull so severely fractured that she nearly died. After a long recovery and discharge, back she came with a black eye and scratches which looked as if they had been inflicted by human nails. At last the N.S.P.C.C. had some evidence that her parents were responsible. Then, particularly her father—a man in his early twenties—pretended to know nothing of the causes of the injuries. He was charged, found guilty, and given a prison sentence. Molly was carefully looked after, and eventually recovered.

Rehabilitation

If you are uncertain whether to report an incident to your local branch or not, remember that 98% of an N.S.P.C.C. Officer's work and 100% of a Woman Visitor's work is rehabilitation, that is helping, sorting out, cleaning up, giving physical and financial help. Only 2% of the cases end in court. The N.S.P.C.C.'s instructions are clear:

If you know of a child:

Who is being ill-used or neglected;
Who is being denied necessary medical treatment through the negligence of his parents;

Or of a parent who is worried about any matter concerning his, or her children and needs advice;

you will be doing a kindness if you will communicate at once with:

The Director, N.S.P.C.C., 1 Riding House Street, London, W.1. (Telephone 580 8812) or you can get in touch with any of the Society's Inspectors. Their addresses are in the telephone directory.

Since 1963 the Inspectors have a clear Act, the Children and Young Persons Act (see Chapter 15) to assist them. You have the Society's absolute guarantee that your name will never be revealed as being in any way connected with a reported case of cruelty.

What should you report? Not one case of screaming all night—we all get toothache!—or bruising or fractures. We all have accidents. But if the crying or screaming is persistent—night after night—report it at once. Two cases spring to my mind. The first, an Air Force Officer's children who screamed persistently at night. After the house had caught fire and the children were only just rescued in time, the neighbours admitted that they knew those children were locked in and left alone every night while the parents went

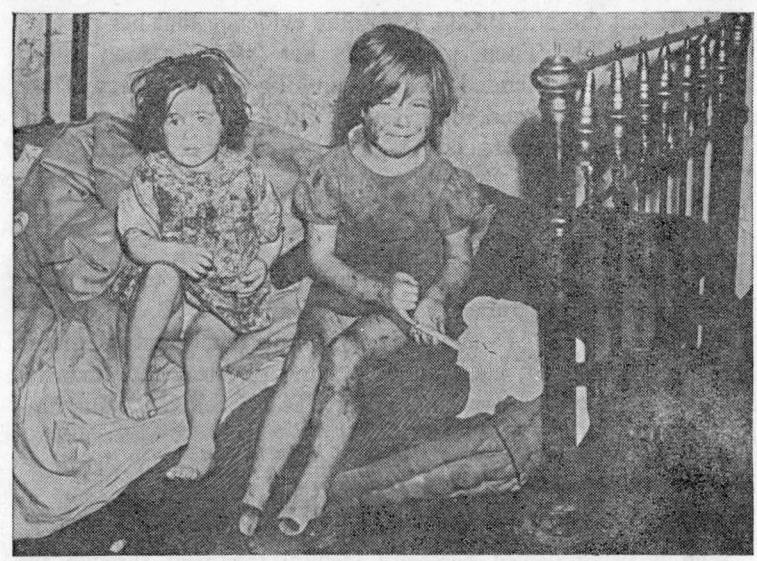

55 You *can help prevent suffering like this*

out. They also knew that the children (aged 2 and 4) were frightened at night. *Yet they did nothing.* The second case is of a baby screaming in the early hours every night and bitter quarrelling between the parents. It was reported, and this was the outcome —a rare stomach disorder, which the local doctor had not recognised, was diagnosed by a specialist. An operation was carried out and the little baby began to sleep soundly at night. The young couple, no longer distracted with weariness and worry, stopped quarrelling. No court case, just a helping hand leading to a happily sorted-out tangle.

Report bruising, if it is extensive and happens often. Should you ever see an act of cruelty, which you cannot deal with yourself, phone your local N.S.P.C.C. Inspector at once. If you do not know his number, dial 999 and ask for the police. They will advise you. *Never* do nothing. Report neglect—children left alone at night, no fireguards, inadequate and dirty clothing. The mother may desperately need help, and the N.S.P.C.C. will be only too glad to give it.

Neglect and ill-treatment are the two commonest causes of cruelty. These figures are for January–December 1972.

	Number of Cases
Neglect—lacking physical care	2,668
Emotionally disturbed	2,640
At risk, without symptom at present	47,352
Assault or ill-treatment	492
Not living at home	1,686

Many of these children were very young. Of the new cases, 25,965 were under the age of 5, and 23,786 in the 5–11 age group. However only 146 cases had to be brought to court, and an increasing number of parents now voluntarily go to the N.S.P.C.C. for help and advice—as many as 10,490 in 1972.

You can see what a formidable job the N.S.P.C.C. has. It is a voluntary body supported by the public and by grants from each Local Authority, some more generous than others. It has no direct Government Grant. Some of its workers are voluntary, but its Inspectors are carefully selected and trained for their job. They need our help and co-operation. Our children need our love and security. We as parents must not only be above reproach, but we must set an example of firmness with gentleness, fun with consistency, spontaneity with security because we know what we are doing. Not all parents do, and many should have our sympathy—and help—rather than blame.

6 The National Marriage Guidance Council

This is made up mainly of voluntary Counsellors, who help people with problems concerning their marriage, or the marriage of their parents or children. And when you come to think of it, this means just everybody—young and old! But most of the people who seek help are of course couples who find problems within their own marriage.

They can find the address of their nearest branch either in the local paper or in the telephone directory (under Marriage). They can then write or phone for an interview, or just go along in the hope that someone will be on duty. When they do meet their Marriage Guidance Counsellor, they will find they are meeting a very sympathetic, understanding person who has spent at least two years in part-time training and who was very specially selected to do his or her job.

If you ever need to go, you will be able to talk about your troubles, knowing that nothing will be repeated or discussed without your permission. The interview is entirely confidential. If another person is causing your unhappiness your Counsellor will, with your approval, seek an interview with that person. It is surprising how many problems are solved by talking it over. When you are emotionally involved with someone, disagreements tend to get heated. But if you consider the problem sensibly and calmly with someone who is not closely involved, you have a wonderful safety valve. Not all problems can be solved just by talking about them, but often just by doing this, you find they are not as serious as you thought and, because your Counsellor will listen to you and not lecture you, you will find his or her help infinitely valuable. If you cannot find the local address, write for it to the Council's national headquarters (address below).

7 The Samaritans

This voluntary organisation was set up in 1953 by the Rev. Chad Varah. It is not, however, a Church-sponsored or religious organisation, and its help is available to anyone of any age. This help can be immediate or long-term. Whereas the N.M.G.C. tends to help people who have long-standing problems and more usually family problems, the Samaritans help with literally anything, and are especially careful to see that anyone who rings them up will be helped *at once*, if the problem is urgent.

Their branches and telephone numbers are to be found in local papers or in the telephone directory. Help can be obtained by visiting them with or without an appointment, or by giving them a ring. If needed they will then send someone immediately to the telephone box or home of whoever is in distress. Sometimes problems of all kinds pile up and the lonely, the hurt or the physically or mentally sick feel they just cannot cope any longer. A call to the Samaritans brings to their aid without delay someone who cares. Often people just want a chat over the telephone, sometimes they need physical help and sometimes, over a cup of tea, they can share their troubles.

All cases are treated confidentially—even names need not be given. Whenever possible, the same Samaritan will follow a case through from beginning to end. This service is given for up to twenty-four hours a day depending on the area, but there is always a telephone number given to the caller and a flying squad is available to go to the aid of anyone in urgent need of help.

Needless to say, Samaritans are very carefully selected for this work, and are equally carefully trained. These men and women come from all walks of life and are responsible for having brought many almost suicide cases back from the brink. Last year 17,000 people were helped in this way. But the aim is not just to keep people alive but to try to give them a reason to be *glad* to be alive. As this is a voluntary body, each branch has to be self-supporting. Voluntary contributions are always needed to keep this splendid organisation going. Help them; one day you may need them to help you.

8 The R.S.P.C.A.

Last, but still important, the birds and animals. The Royal Society for the Prevention of Cruelty to Animals exists for their protection. This vigorous, well-supported and hard-working society was founded in 1824 by the Reverend Arthur Broome. The interest of Queen Victoria, who became the Society's Patron, was of considerable help, and help was badly needed in those days of bull-fighting, dog-fighting, and cock-fighting—some of the sports of nineteenth-century Britain.

56 *The sign of the R.S.P.C.A.*

Today the R.S.P.C.A. is the largest animal protection society in the world. It has many branches in England and Wales and 228 trained Inspectors. It provides these various amenities for the 350,000 animals who benefit from them each year:

Clinics for all animals.
Shelters for dogs, cats and birds.
Homes of Rest for horses.
The Airport Hostel for animals in transit.
Overseas branches. There are Inspector/Organisers in many parts of the world, e.g. Malta, Nigeria.
Special services. Veterinary surgeons, lawyers, etc., are employed in the service of animals.
Finance It is an entirely voluntary organisation and has no public grants. Its trained officers are paid and professional, but it is supported by many voluntary helpers and by the money you give.

These facts will show how this organisation is needed and what an efficient job it does. Let us take the year 1972:

R.S.P.C.A. Inspectors investigated 26,638 complaints of cruelty to animals. Their investigations led to:

- 801 convictions, 6 imprisonments and 238 disqualifications from keeping pets.
- 193 admonitions issued by R.S.P.C.A. Headquarters.
- 4,427 verbal cautions administered by Inspectors.

Some animals that are genuinely lost are taken to the R.S.P.C.A. Many others arrive having been turned out or abandoned by people who are selfish enough not to care about the suffering they are causing. Often a pretty kitten or lovable puppy is given a home, but as soon as the pet becomes grown up and needs food and room and attention, or the dog licence has to be paid, the sad little animal is just turned out. Some people even abandon animals just in order to enjoy themselves on holiday! In 1972, although homes were found for 48,612 dogs and 25,585 cats, another 288,788 rejected pets had to be destroyed. Think carefully before you offer a home to an animal. If you really want one and decide to care for it unselfishly, you might be able to save a life by asking your nearest R.S.P.C.A. branch if they have any deserted animals in their kennels.

These Seven Methods are the R.S.P.C.A.'s carefully planned programme of campaign against this cruelty.

METHOD 1   *Education.* Lectures to schools, Animal Defender Groups formed.

METHOD 2   *Maintenance of a Corps of Inspectors.* Vigilance day and night, prompt action taken.

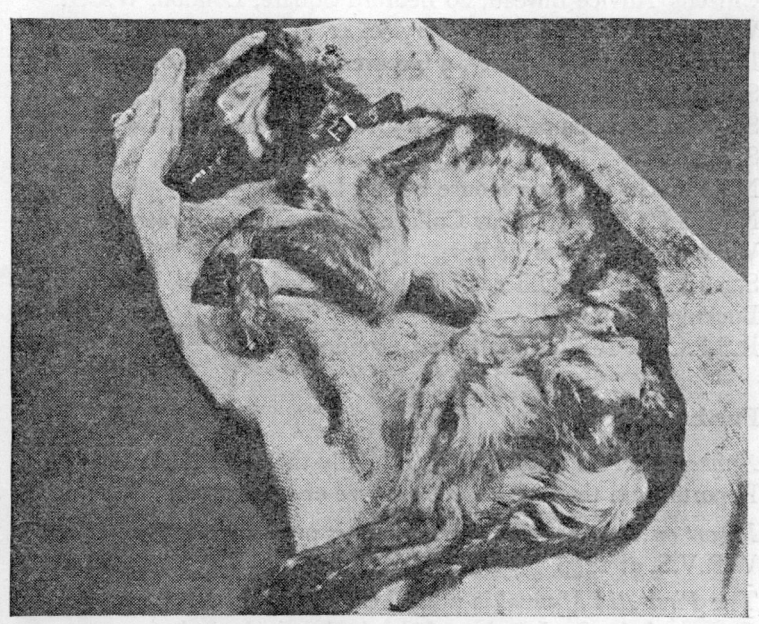

57   *Will* you *try to stop such cruelty?*

METHOD 3   *Free Veterinary Treatment* in permanent or mobile clinics. 247,139 animals treated in 1972, homes found for a further 81,714 animals.
METHOD 4   *Promoting Humane Legislation.* Several bills passed.
METHOD 5   *Advocating Humane Methods* when food animals are to be destroyed—two Acts passed.
METHOD 6   *Helping Humane Work Overseas.* The R.S.P.C.A. has 12 branches in the Commonwealth and is associated with 46 animal protection societies throughout the world.
METHOD 7   *Spreading Humane Knowledge.* Giving advice through films and magazines, *Animal Ways* for children and *Animal World* for adults.

There is less cruelty to animals nowadays than in 1824, and with your help and support, the society can continue to educate people to a greater understanding of the needs of animals.

Where to go for help—Addresses

Citizens' Advice Bureau, 26 Bedford Square, London, W.C.1.
Women's Royal Voluntary Service, 41 Tothill St., London, W.1.
British Red Cross Society, 9 Grosvenor Crescent, London, S.W.1.
St. John Ambulance Brigade, 8 Grosvenor Crescent, London, S.W.1.
N.S.P.C.C., 1 Riding House Street, London, W.1.
N.M.G.C., Herbert Gray College, Little Church Street, Rugby, Warwickshire CU21 3AP.
Samaritans Head Office, 17 Uxbridge Road, Slough, Buckinghamshire.
R.S.P.C.A., 105 Jermyn Street, London, S.W.1.

Further reading

Animal World is published monthly by the R.S.P.C.A. at $2\frac{1}{2}$p
Reports from the N.S.P.C.C. are free on application

Report on Twenty-Five Years' Work is published by the W.R.V.S. at $12\frac{1}{2}$p

The *First Aid Manual* is published jointly by the British Red Cross and the St. John's and St. Andrew's Ambulance Associations

Practical work

Organise yourselves into groups and adopt one of these 'Big Six' voluntary organisations. The first four you know about:

1 The British Red Cross
2 St. John Ambulance Brigade
3 The N.S.P.C.C.
4 The R.S.P.C.A.

Add any two others such as:

5 OXFAM, 274 Banbury Road, Oxford
6 The Save the Children Fund, 29 Queen Anne's Gate, London, S.W.1, or any other your group fancies

Now—work like blazes for it!
How?—give them some of your free time—plan how to raise funds for them.

7 Where is your nearest W.R.V.S. Depot? Pay them a visit, find out what special jobs they are doing. Can you help?

Questions

1 Should there be a place for voluntary organisations within the Welfare State? Try to give both sides of the picture.

2 Write an essay explaining why you have selected your particular organisation.

3 Find out where your nearest Citizens' Advice Bureau is. Write to them, or better still, visit them and see if they carry out all the jobs mentioned in this chapter. Remember to go back there for Consumers' Advice, if necessary.

SECTION IV · TEENS, TWENTIES, MARRIAGE AND MOTHERHOOD

CHAPTER 13 · TEENS TO TWENTIES

One day you will leave your childhood illnesses behind—mumps and measles will have come and gone. You are far less prone to infectious diseases in your teens. But at the same time your body takes on new responsibilities.

Our rate of growth and development is controlled by the hormones which act as message carriers. Hormones are produced by the glands. Glands are organs which we only become aware of, as a rule, when they become swollen and painful. Then we wish we were without them. But it is just as well we are not, for they carry out many complicated tasks for the body. You probably know something of the salivary glands in your mouth. These produce saliva to moisten and begin the digestion of your food. You can feel it pour on to your tongue when you smell something delicious. These glands have ducts, or outlets, through which the saliva flows. Similarly, the mammary glands, commonly known as the breasts, have ducts through which milk is secreted when it is needed.

Some glands have no ducts; instead of secreting liquids, they secrete hormones into the bloodstream. The blood carries these hormones to the parts of the body which are in need of the 'message' or stimulation which the hormone carries. For example, how does the breast know when to start producing milk for a new baby? A hormone from one of the endocrine glands of the new mother has stimulated the breast to do so.

These endocrine glands include:

1 the Adrenal glands which lie just above the kidney. Among other things, their hormones control the rate of our heart beat. The drug Adrenalin is injected to stimulate the heart in emergencies;

2 the Thyroid gland in the neck produces hormones which control the growth of the body, and the pace at which we develop. If inadequate thyroid hormones are produced growth will be slow, and the body sluggish. If too many are produced the effect will be the opposite.

Both these glands—and these are just two among several—start to work from the time we are born. Others lie dormant, or asleep, until we are ready to grow up. In fact, when these wake up you are at the beginning of a series of mental and physical changes that result in your maturity, and adulthood. The beginning of these changes is known as the onset of *puberty*, and as you gradually develop and mature you are passing through a stage usually known as *adolescence*.

Two of the glands which lie dormant until this time are the ovaries in girls and the testes in boys. Both are signalled into action by hormones produced by the vital control gland called the *pituitary* gland. This is very small—about the size of a pea—but it controls the work of all the other endocrine glands. It lies just beneath the brain. You can compare this gland system to a school. The pituitary gland is the Head who sends out messages to his teachers (the other endocrine glands). They, in turn, send out instructions for various jobs to be done. All the messages and instructions are carried not by pigeons or the telephone, but by hormones!

Teens to Twenties for a girl

At some stage, just before or at the beginning of her teens, such a message is sent from every girl's pituitary to stimulate her ovaries. She then experiences the beginning of a pattern of actions which will go on for about 30 years in her life. At about this time her breasts will have started to develop, and hair will be growing under her arms and between her legs. She has reached the stage known as 'puberty'. She is leaving childhood to start to become a woman.

Puberty

A girl knows exactly when she reaches this stage because for the first time an ovum—or egg—which has lain dormant among many others in her ovary since she was born, reaches maturity. The mature ovum takes just over a week to pass from the ovary along the fallopian tube, leading to the uterus or womb from whence it is discharged from the body with the lining of the uterus. This lining breaks down at this time and is passed out of the body accompanied by varying amounts of blood. We know this as menstruation, or having 'a period'.

Menstruation

Call menstruation by its proper name—*mensis* is Latin for month. This function is as normal and natural as any other function of the body—eating, sleeping, perspiring or breathing. Treat it naturally, talk about it normally, neither make a great thing about it nor try to pretend it doesn't happen.

The onset—or start

Some girls start to menstruate very early, in some cases as early as 8 years old. They often get worried if they do not know what is happening. Once explained it is all so simple. But if your periods have started early be sure that you understand this—they have done so because one of your glands has stimulated another into action. It has nothing whatsoever to do with you as a person. Ignore all suggestions that early starters are girls who are forward (meant in the 'precocious' sense). People who make such suggestions are speaking out of ignorance.

The Menstrual Cycle

Unless illness, pregnancy or emotional disturbances upset us, we menstruate roughly once every 28 days. This varies from girl to girl and from age to age. Your periods may be irregular at first, but they should settle into a pattern of roughly 28 days from the beginning of one period to the beginning of the next—each period lasting from 4–6 days.

1	
2	
3	MENSTRUATION
4	
5	

For about the first 5 days you are menstruating. This means that the ovum and uterus wall lining are being expelled, together with blood.

6
7
8
9
10
11
12

For about the next 7 days—day 6 to day 12—the new ovum travels from the ovary through the fallopian tube to the uterus.

13
14
15

On about the 14th day, the ovum is ready in the uterus for fertilisation. This is called *ovulation*.

16
17
18
19
20
21
22
23
24
25
26
27
28

If the ovum is not fertilised it remains in the uterus for a further 13–15 days. Then it is expelled during the following 5-day period of menstruation.

1	
2	MENSTRUATION
3	
4	
5	

Menstruation.

What happens in those 28 days?

So your menstrual period does not just happen accidentally, it follows a regular cycle of events and arrives to carry out a necessary, regular function. This diagram shows just where your reproductive system lies and what happens when you menstruate.

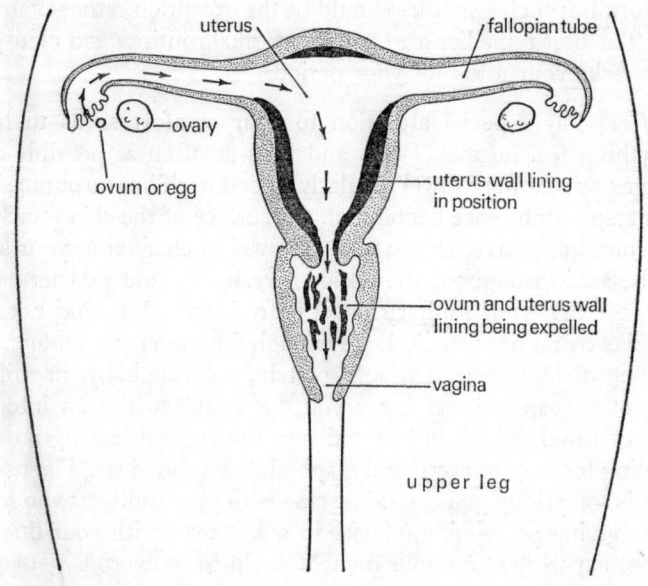

58 *Menstruation*

You may feel unwell at these times, but be sensible about it—you are not suffering from the 'curse'. Before people understood the menstrual cycle all sorts of 'old wives' tales were told and believed—some still are. Girls used to be kept hidden indoors, they were not allowed to handle meat, and were even forbidden to wash! Now we realise that this was due to sheer ignorance. In fact, there are few times when you need to wash more often. But, to be quite honest, it is all a bit of a nuisance.

A nuisance not a curse Just before a menstrual period we may feel a bit touchy or depressed. Keep a note in your diary to remind you when your period is due, so that you are prepared for it. Some girls get a little pain or discomfort just before the start of the bleeding, or for the first day or two. This will pass—try to make the best of it—not the most of it! Sometimes constipation is the cause. Any blockage near your uterus—through which the blood will pass—will prove unhelpful. Eat plenty of roughage—fruit, vegetables, salads, wholemeal bread and cereals. Drink plenty of water—this will help.

A hot bottle, hot drink, lie down or soluble aspirin may also bring comfort, but such remedies should be the exception rather than the rule. The best remedies are exercise, normal routines and plenty of fun to take your mind off your period.

Comfort Pay especial attention to your comfort so as to help everything feel normal. Wash and bath as often as possible and change your sanitary towel regularly. Blood itself has no odour, but like perspiration, once bacteria on the surface of the skin attack it, it becomes offensive. If you allow a towel to chafe you, your skin will be sore throughout the period. Wash, dry and powder carefully, see that your sanitary towel is fresh and clean and not too big. Size 0 or 1 are usually large enough for teenagers. Do not use a strong or highly scented soap or talc; a gentle baby, or mildly antiseptic, soap is best. Later you may want to use an internal sanitary towel, which is inserted into the vagina, leaving an end dangling for easy removal and disposal down the toilet. The use of these is something you should discuss with your mother, who may, before giving permission, choose to talk it over with your doctor. Do not experiment on your own; it could be dangerous.

Not an illness Because menstruation is not an illness it is only occasionally that a doctor's advice is needed. But if your periods are very irregular, really painful or your loss of blood very heavy, do not hesitate to go and see him. Many girls do not like to talk to their doctors about menstruation. Others cannot bring themselves to ask a male chemist for sanitary towels. If only these girls remembered as they mingled with others in the street, that one out of every five women they pass is in the menstruation period and that all sensible girls and women discuss their periods and buy sanitary towels, they would then realise how silly it is to be shy about something so commonplace.

During menstruation everything except swimming can go on normally. Have plenty of sleep, though, as you may tire a little more easily. Wash your hands each time you touch or change a towel. Wrap them carefully and burn them as soon as possible. If

59 *Don't make the most of it—*

this is impossible, buy soluble ones and break them in small pieces before flushing them—a little at a time—down the toilet.

Puberty—boys as well as girls The onset of menstruation is one of the signs that your body has reached puberty. It is also a sign that your body is now beginning to get ready to reproduce—when you need it to. *Pubes* is Latin, as many medical terms are, and means the extra hair grown by an adult. This pubic hair grows in similar places for boys as well as for girls, but boys also begin to notice hair on their faces and possibly on their chests. These changes are also started and controlled by hormones.

Growing up

You could not expect such considerable changes to take place in your body without its affecting you considerably in other ways. You will find that your attitude to the other sex gradually changes. Boys are no longer other children. They become more interesting and fun to be with. You will probably find this is especially true of boys one or two years older than yourself. Girls mature more

60 —*make the best of it*

quickly than boys, so that the boys of your own age during early and mid-teens will seem, on the whole, much younger than you are. By the time you are approaching 20, the boys will have caught up and those of your age will be as mature as you are.

You will find, too, that your enjoyment of mixed company increases, and that you start to consider your relationship with boys a little more seriously. Unfortunately, just as you begin to want to look your best you sometimes find yourself developing spots, putting on 'puppy fat' or shooting up and becoming lanky. You may also find that you are a little self-conscious and blush easily. Boys also have worries. One of their changes is the breaking of their voices. As this deepening takes place they cannot always control their pitch and this can cause them considerable embarrassment. They too are often plagued by skin troubles at this stage—the advice in Chapter 8 may be of help here.

In-betweens Often these little irritations cause tension. You feel that not only have you at last begun to grow up, but that you seem to be the only one aware of this tremendous development! At home and at school you are often still treated as a child. Moreover, no matter how big your bust development is, they will continue to treat you as a child until you have won enough of their respect to prove that you are growing up mentally and emotionally, as well as physically. Now this is the difficult thing to do. Puberty is automatic. You will develop physically whether you wish to or not. Growing up demands much more than this. A young adult must accept some of the responsibilities of adulthood and behave accordingly. The in-between stage of having developed fully physically, and having only partially developed mentally and emotionally, is one we all go through, and one we have to make a real effort to cope with. As you learn to cope you may find yourself prone to moods—great depression one minute and great jubilation the next.

See-saw moods These ups and downs are very difficult for your family to bear. Remember this and try to act accordingly. When you are happy be considerate; when depressed, busy yourself with something constructive—bake a cake, run errands, try a new hair style. You would be surprised how much irritability you can work off while you are creaming! Share your troubles with your friends and listen to theirs. You'll be surprised how similar they are. Watch the behaviour of other young people of your age. Which do you want to be like—that silly girl who giggles and whispers endlessly, or the serene girl who has something interesting to talk about? Where has she learnt about her interesting topic? She has listened, or looked or read.

Boy/Girl relationships The girl who is interesting will be popular both with girls and boys. She need not be beautiful or even pretty, provided she takes sufficient interest in herself to make the best of her good points. No matter how much we think looks should or should not matter, they are the first things we see in other people, and these first impressions either interest us or not. My very first boy friend was introduced to my family just after a game of football. They noticed how muddy and windblown he looked—*I* had only noticed his black curly hair, but 'Scruffy' was their nickname for him ever afterwards! First impressions are important. You seldom get to know if people are interesting or not if you are not sufficiently attracted by them to start a conversation—and vice versa!

It is easier now than ever before to get to know the boy who interests you because there are so many mixed social gatherings and youth clubs. Dancing is informal; you do not have to wait anxiously to be asked but can dance in a group, or just dance. Drawing attention to yourself by showing off is the best way to lose a boy's interest. They hate to be shown up by girls who make an exhibition of themselves, or who over-dress, or who plaster themselves with make-up. Such flamboyancy may be bearable at a party but boy/girl friendships become deeper and more personal than this, and a young couple needs much more in common than just being extraverts.

Boy friends Choose your boy friends carefully. While it is fun to have lots of them, think how complicated this can make your leisure hours. Certainly you should not tie yourself exclusively to one too early. If you have had several boy friends and have discovered the qualities that you will need in a husband to match your own qualities, then you will be in a position to decide later on if you have yet found the one you wish to marry. You may need a quiet sensitive boy, if you too are reserved; or an organiser if you are scatterbrained, and so on.

Value each experience and remember you will be judged partly by the company you keep. If you are 'anybody's girl' you will be treated as such, and when you have gone the rounds there will be loneliness ahead. An interest in the opposite sex is important and normal and natural. But keep it in perspective. There are many other things for a teenager to concentrate on as well. There are examinations to be tackled, school work to make the most of, and games and sports to enjoy. Your girl friends should still be important to you, and your family even more so. A girl who drops everything to concentrate on a romance may find herself with nothing when the romance ends, as it may well do, because no boy wants to be swamped with your attentions. He will respect you far more if you have other interests, and he will enjoy sharing or discussing them with you. Don't go boy-mad and so become narrow and boring. Make the most of your adolescence in every way.

The final stage Eventually you will find a boy with whom you want to share the rest of your life. Committing yourself too soon is a pity. A period of courtship, of getting to know one another really well, and then a further period, of engagement, are good safety valves. During this time you get a chance to see your fiancé in all winds and weathers! You will see him at work, at play, ill and well, in good and bad tempers, in his home and in yours.

This last point is important. We will see what a marked effect our parents and our upbringing have on us. The way your fiancé responds to his parents and your family is significant. Probably consideration is the greatest single asset in a husband. This means

61 *Probably consideration is the greatest asset in a husband*

kindness, sympathy, thoughtfulness and unselfishness. To be treated in this way when you are in need of such consideration, is to be, and to be made to feel, really loved. However, you will not get such treatment unless you deserve it; and you must be equally considerate in return. You must never abuse love; never use it for your own ends or exploit it. Engaged couples sometimes do this—'He loves me enough not to mind'—is an excuse for being selfish. If you really love him would you be selfish? When you have spent the money you saved together for furniture on a pretty dress, is it true that, 'He'll get over it'? He won't. He will probably forgive you but it won't be quite the same as before. You may turn out to be the wife who spends the grocery money on Bingo! Try to make as much effort in every way—your looks, your dress, your punctuality and so on—not only throughout your engagement but later throughout marriage. Don't take one another for granted. Before you act, ask yourself, 'Would I like to be treated like this?'

Absolute honesty is essential in a serious relationship. This begins with honesty about yourself. We all tend to show our best side to someone we are trying to impress. A period of courtship gives a young couple the chance to see the 'other' side. Make sure you really know your fiancé. Whether you attract one another physically is easy to judge. But what are his attitudes towards other important issues?—your job or career—sharing chores—having children—in-laws—pay packets—the home you hope to have? Get all these things sorted out long before you think about a wedding dress. What about his religion, his interests, his hopes and ambitions? Can you share them or will you have to find a compromise?

Finally, can you no longer visualise a life without him? Is he as important to you as that? If so, you have indeed found someone you love. Wait to be sure that you mean as much to him. And then, in all confidence, you can go ahead and plan for the big day, whether you are 18 or 28.

Further reading

Your Looks, by Mary Davis Peters, and *Your Health*, by Kenneth Hutchin, are published in the 'Modern Living' series by Longmans, Green and Co. Ltd. in paperback at $37\frac{1}{2}$p

Questions

1 Your younger sister is away from home and has started to menstruate. She has written very anxiously to you for an explanation. Answer her letter, explaining carefully to her what is happening and giving her advice.

2 Find out all you can about the endocrine glands, and write an account of three of them.

3 What qualities do you look for in a boy friend? Which do you think it would be sensible for him to look for in you?

4 For how long do you consider a young couple should get to know one another before:

(*a*) starting to 'go steady';
(*b*) becoming engaged; and
(*c*) getting married?

Give careful reasons for your answers.

5 Do you think an engagement ring is necessary, if so why? Would you wish your fiancé to wear one? Explain your answer.

6 Give all the pros and cons of a white wedding. In order to do this find out first how much it, and other types of weddings, cost.

CHAPTER 14 · MARRIAGE

When you are a child you have the opportunity of seeing how your parents' marriage works. You obviously have no way of telling how their early struggles were resolved, but now you are in an excellent position to watch and to understand the sacrifices each is making for his home and for his partner in marriage. Parents make sacrifices for their children because they choose to do so, and often this makes them feel happier. They should, however, think carefully before reminding their children of these sacrifices. Even more often they glow later in the reflected glory of whatever their sacrifice has accomplished. I remember a hard-up couple who sacrificed clothes, holidays and many luxuries to pay for ballet lessons for their small dainty daughter. At 18 (and weighing $9\frac{1}{2}$ stone) their formerly small dainty daughter joined the Land Army and learned to drive a tractor. At 22 she married a farmer and now happily raises her own family, and dozens of pedigree pigs! If you try the 'I nearly died——' routine on your daughters, they may answer airily 'Why, didn't you learn your relaxation exercises properly?'

If your parents have to try to win your sympathy and consideration in these ways, it is probably high time you took a look at how considerate you are being. Are you treating them in the way you hope one day your daughter will be treating you? Remember that their marriage is of the utmost importance to them. They will be together long after you have left home. Are there any ways in which you can lessen the strain that occurs from time to time in any marriage? Money is nearly always a cause of strain. Sometimes the anger that greets your request for yet more nylons, a new dress or a shop hair-do, springs from the fact that Mum would love to be able to treat you, but there just is not enough money. Of course, she wants you to look as nice—or probably nicer—than anyone else's daughter, but there is the gas bill to pay, and young Johnny has just 'gone through' the seat of his trousers! Your Mother is probably as upset at having to say 'No', as she is angry with you for asking. Should she be angry with you at all? Did you notice Johnny's trousers? Have you noticed how often, or seldom, she has had new clothes?

Were you really silly enough to say, 'All the other girls have one'? This last remark is never true. You would never find even two girls whose parents were in exactly the same financial position.

In the Left corner—Mum!
In the Right corner—Dad!

Have you ever tried to wheedle them into this position? Have you ever tried to get your own way without caring what it does to their relationship?—— 'I know Mother will say "No", but I'll try to work on Dad.' They should end by disliking you; but they won't, of course, because they are your parents, and you are counting on this. But they will respect you less. And what about you? Are you proud of yourself?

Why not try to do something constructive instead? Remind each of them quietly when birthdays and anniversaries are due. Share your love and loyalty equally between them. Respect their privacy —this is most important. Encourage them to go out, and enjoy one another's company; leave some coffee hot in a Thermos as a surprise to greet their return. If they can get away for a holiday on their own and they want to, be ready to stay with friends during their absence.

The number of chores there is to get through is another cause of strain. We will talk about sharing this when we deal with your family—your own new family.

Your own marriage

The courtship that we have discussed will, if all goes well, lead to a deep and lasting relationship which may in turn lead to marriage, and we have seen exactly what we mean by 'if all goes well'. So many people talk of a young couple 'starting a family' when a baby is on the way. Surely you start a family when you marry; is your young husband just an outsider? If you are ever silly enough to treat him as an outsider he will stay as such; some young husbands, not realising the responsibility of a family, will like this. But many will feel thoroughly snubbed and out of it. Neither attitude will help your marriage to start off well.

What is marriage?

It is a union of two people and this means the two people become one and share in every way. Most young couples accept this eagerly. They share that most important part of marriage—their physical love; they share their honeymoon, their new home, their breakfast table, their entertainments. Everything is wonderful! These are all enjoyable things and they are fun to share. But there are many less pleasant sides to marriage which should also be shared.

The 'working wife'

There must be many wives who stay at home. Young farmers' wives must surely take on greater responsibility than many a career girl when they begin to run a farmhouse, and they often work much longer hours. But normally the young bride runs her new home and still goes out to work. It is obvious that she should not be expected to do two jobs to her husband's one, and, indeed, most young husbands would be horrified of the thought of her doing so. But when it actually comes to sharing out the chores, these noble thoughts sometimes disappear!

The trouble at the beginning of marriage is that we women have two special snags to contend with:

SNAG 1 We are so busy maintaining the rosy glow left over from the honeymoon that we tend to spoil our young husbands. 'You sit down darling, I'll do it,' is all very well when you are 20—but at 40 you will wish you had not eased him out of the kitchen! A better approach might be, 'Let's get the kitchen sorted together, then we'll have more time to ourselves when it's done.'

SNAG 2 Often young couples are busy redecorating, and making do and mending at first. The husband usually has the main responsibility for this while you settle for the chores. The trouble is that he will eventually come to the end of his 'do it yourself' campaign, but you will never come to the end of your daily chores! So before he becomes engulfed in the evening paper, try to interest him in those witty sayings on the modern tea towel!

Seriously, you must try to share all the household duties fairly and happily—and this includes the kitchen. While you have an outside job as well as running the home, your various activities—the shopping, washing, ironing, cleaning, cooking and washing up—must be shared. Clearly, if one works longer hours than the other, or has further to travel, so that there is a time lapse between your arrivals home, the picture is slightly different. But remember there is nothing in a woman's physical make-up that fits her better than a man for any of these chores. It is simply that she has had more practice at most of them than her husband, and has been *conditioned* to accept that this is her work. By conditioning I mean that a baby girl is given a doll, a pram, a pastry set, a toy dust pan and brush, and so on as she grows up, whereas a small boy is given none of these, even though, should he choose not to marry, he may one day be doing all his own cooking and cleaning. In some parts of the world the men run the house and the women go out to work. Not long ago in Scotland it was considered unmanly to carry a shopping basket or to push a pram. How it could ever be considered manly to watch a woman struggle with either, I do not know, but the men and women had been conditioned to think this way and no woman would allow her man to be seen doing such chores!

Try to get together on this well in advance of the wedding. Forget what your friends do, or what was good enough for your parents or what you imagine the neighbours will think—what does it matter? Plan your routine so that neither of you will get overtired or frustrated, so that nothing is unfair. Should anything go wrong —shift work can play havoc with the best of schemes—discuss it together. If, in a fit of resentment, you discuss it instead with mothers-in-law or neighbours this usually only makes matters worse. If they side with you, you feel even more hard-done by, and if they side with your husband, you resent them too! Moreover, you will probably bitterly regret having told them.

'*His and Hers*'

Another subject which should be discussed before the marriage is money, and budgeting. This is not always discussed as openly as it should be. The only secrets in marriage should be the exciting surprises planned for a birthday or anniversary. All money is jointly earned, so it must be jointly discussed, budgeted and shared. If you are at home all day with your small children you are really earning part of your husband's wages. Without you he would have to be paying for a housekeeper to cook and clean and a nanny to care for his children. For this he would pay at least £8–£10 a week, plus keep. Do you hope to get that to spend on yourself? Of course you don't, but if you did the same job for anyone but your husband, you would receive as much—so do not underrate your earning power. He is not keeping you. You are doing your share of keeping him and the children. Both of you are earning. 'His' or 'Hers' is all right for towels, but never for wage packets or salary cheques. Disputes over money probably cause more unhappiness in marriage than any other single issue.

62 *'His' and 'Hers'—all right for towels, but not for wage packets or salary cheques*

In the marriage vow you promise to share. The vow should be honoured in every way. Your home and children are yours jointly. You belong to one another and the money you both earn belongs to both of you. This is the only way to real trust and love and happiness. *'The Non-working Wife'*—this is a quote from a daily newspaper and it makes me want to hoot with laughter (or quietly despair, if I cannot manage to raise a laugh). It refers to the wife who stays at home, bears children and looks after them and her husband. I would not expect the title to convey this meaning to you because when her children are small this woman probably works harder for longer hours than almost anyone else.

If she has a baby of 6 months, a toddler of 3, and a new school boy of 5 who has to be taken to and from school, she probably needs her husband's help even more than the 'working wife' whose flat will stay clean all day because there is no one romping around in it. But if she has only one small child, or if her two or three are older, at school all day and encouraged to pull their weight in the home, she will have more time to herself. Certainly her husband would expect to give less help in these circumstances. It is as foolish to take advantage of a husband's willingness as it is never to enlist it at all. If he helps willingly, be glad and show it—and bring your own sons up ready to play their proper part in the home. Their wives will probably also want to make the most of their jobs or careers, and will be deeply grateful to you if your sons are as adept with the dish mop as they are with the spin drier or egg timer!

Your baby

Try to plan for the arrival of your baby. You will need advice so go to your doctor or priest or family planning clinic about this. Make sure that you are fit and well, and that both you and your husband want a baby before you conceive it. I would never say 'Wait until you have enough money', because many young couples would wait for ever. Do not wait too long. A child brings more lasting happiness than a television set or a car. A life with your children, and their children's children, will be full and happy.

As I say this I know that one out of every three teenage brides is already pregnant when she marries. This girl has little time to adjust herself to marriage before her baby comes. She needs all the help and understanding that can be given. So does her husband, who has stumbled into the responsibility of a family, probably long before he was ready for it. This young couple should not be singled out for special attention, nor for ill-informed advice. They will appreciate it if someone could baby-sit regularly and let them enjoy a bit of the fun together that they would otherwise have missed.

The arrival of the baby

The baby belongs to both you and your husband—together you created it. Its arrival is a wonderful moment for you both at the end of 9 or 10 months' worry, wonder, discomfort and excitement.

You will have prepared all the material things for your baby— the pram and cot, the knitted and embroidered garments, and blankets and coverlets. If you are wise, you will have gone to classes for instruction in the art of relaxing (see Chapter 15) so that your muscles are well trained to cope with the baby's birth. You will also have taken expert advice from your doctor, ante-natal (before birth) clinic or midwife about your weight and diet, your rest and exercises and all the extras which your body needs so that you do not suffer dietetically when feeding your unborn baby.

Both you and your husband should try to prepare yourselves mentally. Recognise the difference that your baby will make to your work routines and leisure time. For every minute of entertainment you may lose temporarily, you will gain hours of enjoyment and fun later on. A question which faces parents-to-be is, 'Shall we share the moment of birth, or is this an occasion just for the mother?' If the baby is to be born in hospital or at a maternity home, the father will probably be allowed to be present at the birth of his child if he wishes. Many hospitals permit this, but not all. Find out about yours in good time. If the baby is to be born at home, in the presence of a midwife, and perhaps a doctor, of course the father can be there if he wishes.

If you decide hastily or wrongly about this you may have regrets all your lives, so weigh up the question carefully. Firstly, take no notice of parents' or neighbours' unpleasant experiences. No two births are ever identical. What happened to them has nothing whatsoever to do with you. If a young wife finds that clasping her husband's hand gives her strength and reassurance at other times, this may be the time she will need him most. If, on the other hand, he faints when you have a nose bleed you are probably better off without him! But the moment your baby is born should be one of the most wonderful moments of your life. You may feel it could be twice as wonderful if it was shared.

The new family member

He or she will be 6–9 lb. of squiggle and squawl, almost permanently damp at both ends and taking up—to begin with—nearly all your physical and mental energy. It will take your body months and months to recover completely from the job of having produced a baby. A full-time job, would you say? If you allow it to be, your marriage will deteriorate. At this time you have got to make an almost superhuman effort.

To understand the reason for this, try to put yourself in your husband's place. All through your pregnancy you experienced many things which he could only share second hand. It was your womb which was kicked at the fifth month, reassuring you that all was well. He could only be told about it. You did not feel like going out as often as you did before pregnancy, and you were probably preoccupied by your condition. Perhaps you were even tempted to make the most of it—up with feet and you dream up a strange fancy for expensive chocolates!

Then on the day it is you who is surrounded with flowers and greetings. Occasionally someone remembers to congratulate poor young dad! No sooner has this died down than you are engaged with nappies, feed times (at the oddest hours!) and rose hip syrup. Who is getting left out? Who, if you have forgotten to make your superhuman effort, is feeling just a bit jealous? Often a baby's feeding routine is 2 p.m., 6 p.m., 10 p.m., 2 a.m., 6 a.m., 10 a.m., to begin with. If your husband gets home at 6 p.m., for goodness' sake push the feeding times forward by 30 minutes and have most of the messy part done by the time he arrives. Then let him share the contented gurgles and pop the baby back into bed for you. Once done, let him see that he still comes first. Babies are much easier to come by than loving husbands. Not only do you want to be secure in his love; you also want him to love the little one, not be jealous of it. It's up to you!

It's up to you

It is going to be up to you where your children are concerned for about the next 5 years. There is a saying—'If you educate a woman, you educate a family'—which is largely true even though husbands are coming to accept more and more responsibility in this direction. So your education, as a woman, is of the utmost importance. Are you making the best use of it?

Your small children may still be in bed when your husband leaves for work, and they will probably be washed and dressing-gowned by the time he returns. Their primary upbringing is in your hands. What happens during these first 5 years? It is this period which has the greatest influence on your children's lives. Their rate of physical and mental growth is at its greatest; they learn quickly, easily and are readily influenced. They absorb, copy and experiment. They start off as little intake and output vegetables and end up as small unique people.

Your example

What a responsibility you have taken on. Sometimes parents hope that at the secondary stage, at school, their children will change for the better. Often it is too late by then because the child's behaviour pattern will already be set. It is easy enough to provide for their physical needs; there are countless leaflets, books and magazines with feeding tables, charts and advice, so it would be pointless to repeat their contents here. But there are emotional needs that are less easy to understand. We seldom realise, for example, what a strong influence we as parents have on our children; and the children are themselves unwilling to recognise this because they like to feel independent. But we can recognise quickly enough how our friends' children take after their parents! They resemble them not only in looks, height and build, but also often in their ways, habits and personalities. This is partly conditioning. The children unconsciously imitate their parents and repeated imitations can soon become a code of behaviour. If a red-haired father always gets his own way because of a fiery temper said to match his hair, his small red-haired son will soon see the advantage of having a temper and may develop one of his own! Probably some red-haired great-great-grandfather started all this, and the myth grew up that red hair and bad temper go together.

What are you passing on?

Fears are very quickly copied. A baby creature has no fear. If it cannot find its mother, it will waddle hopefully to the nearest object confident of being mothered. One tiny duck, whose mother was run over within an hour of his birth, took to a large turnip, and had to be reared in the turnip's company! But small animals and babies soon learn fear from their parents. Of course, if they did not acquire a healthy respect for such things as fire, roads and heavy feet there would be even more early tragedies than there are now.

But needless and senseless fears are also passed from parents to children. Make sure that you recognise what a deep impression you leave on a child's mind when you say, 'I hate the dark', in casual conversation, or 'Don't do that or I'll call a policeman!' A child is not able to stop and consider that 'the dark' contains some very real dangers—such as falling over objects, or knocking your shins. Instead the child is likely to believe that if the dark is hateful, it must be fearful, full of things to be feared. When the lights are switched off and a child cries, the mother who had previously placed the fear in her child's mind now says, 'Don't be silly'. I have also heard parents tell their children to go to the police station if lost or in trouble. Yet when the same children were making a lot of noise in their own garden they had been threatened with the police. Were they supposed to think of the police as friends or foes? Be sensible and consistent in dealing with your children, and be strictly truthful. Few parents really hate the dark, and most would be as horrified as the children if a large policeman did turn up to deal with noise in their own back garden!

If you lie to them, even in fun, they will copy you. If you send them to the door to say you're 'out' when an unwelcome visitor calls, you are starting a code of behaviour which may well get out of hand.

Your and their fears

Try always to be honest with them and they will respect you. Sort out the things they really must be careful about, and forget the silly little fears, even if they are real to you. So many of these are communicated from one generation to another and it is often mothers who are guilty of this because of their close association with their under-5s. Let us take an example. Many people go through life fearing small things that creep or run. They are completely incapable of explaining this fear. Because of this hundreds of spiders meet their death daily. Children have been taught by the attitude of their mothers to fear them. Yet, though its web may be unsightly in the house, the spider's one aim in life is to destroy flies, the carriers of dirt and disease. The fly is vaguely flicked away and the spider feared and destroyed. If you have such a fear try not to pass it on. Reason it out instead, like this:

Can any of your local spiders bite?—*No*
Can they harm us in any other way?—*No*
Are their webs dust traps?—*Yes*

Is it better to remove the web—or to scream and fuss and kill the spider? As the last action is both pointless and cruel, obviously you just scoop up the spider and drop it out of the window—this won't hurt it.

If your child finds out that there is nothing to fear about something you regularly make a fuss over, he may doubt your judgment

63 *Just scoop up the spider and drop it out of the window*

about other things. Therefore, make sure you do not communicate other more serious fears unless they are well and truly justified.

Your responsibility

The heavy responsibility of setting an example to your children falls upon you, as parents. Examine all your own proposals and suggestions you make to your children to be sure they have real value, and cannot be misunderstood. This is probably one of the most difficult things in life to do. Almost every day parents must ask themselves—'Ought I to tell my children this?' 'Should I warn them about that?'—'How can I say "no" to them, even though I know it is wrong, when every other child in the road does it?'

As you grow older, certainly as you approach and climb through your teens, you must try to understand the difficulties your own parents face. It is not easy being a parent! Your success will often show in the sense of *security* your children can enjoy.

Time for securing security

Children are always far happier if they know where they stand in their family circle. Let us see what security we have tried to give them so far:

1 Love that is real to them in active affection, not just loving words.

2 Consistency in our treatment. Not a slap one day, and nothing the next, for the same offence.

3 Promises and threats which are always carried out—a child needs to be able to trust your word.

4 The truth. They must be able to respect your statements and views, which must be free from white lies, evasions or whims and fancy fears.

5 They must be able to trust your example. Remember that young people will say, 'The folks do it, so it must be O.K'.

6 They must be able to see your happiness and teamwork as husband and wife. They will understand your differences and arguments, and appreciate you as human beings, but bitter squabbles in front of them can be very damaging. Avoid this at all cost.

7 They must be able to have confidence in your fairness. (No one member of the family working much harder than the rest—fair shares all round in chores as well as treats!)

How do you find the time for all this? Point 7 will help to show a way. We have already seen that at certain times the husband's help is vital in the life of any married woman. The help of her children is important for their sake as well as hers. Just as a 'happy ship is an efficient ship', so it is with a happy home. But efficiency does not just happen. You are not able to help by answering the door if you are smothered with shampoo, nor should any child be asked to 'pop round to the shop' in the middle of homework.

So we are back to planning—inevitably—because you have to plan to get fair shares. At some stage in running the home shares should be allocated, agreed upon and accepted. It is a good idea to write them down—like this:

DAD AT WORK 8.30–5.30	MUM AT WORK 11–3 (part-time)	TEENAGER AT SCHOOL 8.30–4.30	JUNIOR AT SCHOOL 8.45–4
Chops wood	Main shopping	Washes up tea things	Lays breakfast and tea table
Fetches in coal	Cooking		
All gardening	Cleaning	Some cooking at weekends	Sometimes wipes up
Odd jobs, e.g. joinery	Washing	Makes own bed and cleans own room	Makes own bed
Cleaning windows	Ironing		
Sometimes wipes up	Washes up breakfast		Runs errands

This plan may suit this one particular family, but it would suit very few others. The teenager might hate cooking but be willing to do the ironing; there may be no garden; or it might be too far and too dangerous for the junior to run errands. Each family needs to make its own plan to fit its own special needs.

Reality

It all sounds so easy and ideal until you try to get your family to sit down and do the planning. If they get used to the haphazard running of a home without a routine, you will probably have trouble in starting one. So try to start as you mean to go on. Tiny children love to help. Encourage them without overdoing it, and if you are ever silly enough to treat your small boys differently from your small girls in this matter, you are the one who will suffer later, and your daughters-in-law won't thank you either! The success of your marriage and of your family relationships will depend on how much thought you put into them, how hard you work at making them a success and how well your example inspires your family to work at it too.

Practical work

1 Marriage is, in law, a legal contract. It can also be—and usually is—a religious one too.
Find out exactly where you can be married and by whom in your area. Who gives authority to marry couples?

2 What is a marriage licence, who issues it, and how much does it cost? Where does the money go?
What are banns? Why are these 'called'?
  Find out about the other legal requirements to be satisfied before a marriage ceremony can be carried out—minimum age, parental consent, blood relationships, witnesses, etc.

3 Notice where you can get expert advice on ante- and post-natal care for a mother and baby. Are there clinics in your area? Which books and magazines are helpful?

4 Imagine three different families, one with a wife out at work, one with a wife working in a part-time job and one with a wife at home all day. State the ages of the children in each family, and then plan a Work Share Routine for each of the three families.

Questions

1 When you marry do you plan to stop work, change your work or continue to work full- or part-time? Write a short essay explaining reasons for your decisions.

2 How much do you think that you as a teenager—in your own special home circumstances—should help with chores? Make one list of what you actually do, and another of the things you think you ought to do.

3 Give examples of unexplainable fears which you suffer from. Where have you got them from? How will you try to avoid passing them on?

4 What things do you consider it is right to teach a child, under the age of 5, to fear? What other dangers should you warn an older child against?

5 How has conditioning affected you so far? What sort of behaviour have you been told is unladylike? What is your attitude towards this?

6 (i) Do you think that:

(*a*) small boys should be allowed to play with dolls, pastry sets, etc., if they wish to?
(*b*) boys should be allowed to learn cookery at school?
(*c*) husbands should help with the chores?

(ii) Do you think that:

(*a*) small girls should be allowed to play with cricket sets, cowboy outfits, etc., if they want to?
(*b*) training in wood or metal work be made available at school for girls?
(*c*) women should expect equal pay for doing exactly equal work with men?

CHAPTER 15 · THE MATERNITY SERVICES

The expectant mother

As soon as a young wife suspects that she is pregnant, and her doctor confirms this, she can begin to receive help and care from the National Health Service. This confirmation is usually possible about 6–9 weeks after conception. An unmarried mother is entitled to exactly the same help and care, and in many areas extra help is at her disposal if she needs it.

Welfare foods

Free milk, liquid or National Dried Milk, and free Vitamins A, D and C, are available to low-income families and families with three or more children under five. Leaflet W.11 from the Department of Health and Social Security gives all details.

The expectant mother's doctor will probably recommend iron tablets.

Many doctors like to supervise the pregnancy of their patients but some prefer to send them to the nearest ante-natal clinic, which is run by the National Health Service, and to which several doctors, health visitors, nurses and voluntary helpers will be attached. Some women prefer to visit these clinics because they can do so with friends who are also expecting. Often cups of tea are served and the atmosphere is informal—certainly more so than in a doctor's waiting room. At the clinic they are taught how to prepare for their babies, what to eat, and what to expect when the birth approaches and arrives. But it is absolutely vital that an expectant mother, whether she is preparing for her first or fourth baby, regularly attends either her doctor or her ante-natal clinic (or both) throughout her pregnancy.

Health

Pregnancy is not an illness. Apart from some discomfort because of the extra weight, many women feel fitter while expecting than at other times. This is, of course, if they have the sense to rest, to sit or lie down for considerable periods and to eat sensibly. The young mother will be advised whether it is necessary for her to have her baby in hospital, or whether she can have it at home. Her wishes, and her husband's, will also be taken into consideration of course. Sometimes during the 9 months of pregnancy she is sent to a specialist to check on possible irregularities—such as twins! Her weight and blood pressure is always very carefully checked, as is her blood count and group and her urine. This is to keep a check on her heart, to discover whether she is anaemic, and which type of blood she must have in the very rare case of needing a transfusion, and to check on her kidneys. As the confinement time draws near, she will attend her clinic or doctor more frequently. At first, the visits are monthly, then fortnightly, then weekly and towards the end possibly every few days.

Where to have the baby

1 *Hospital*

If she chooses, or is guided, to have her baby in a hospital or nursing home, her bed will be booked well in advance—though precise dates cannot always be kept to. Babies arrive when they are ready, not necessarily when there is a bed free! Sometimes there are clinics attached to maternity hospitals or homes to which the mother-to-be is transferred from her local clinic, so that when she moves in she will know some of the trained staff who attend her.

2 At home

In this case, instead of booking a bed, she will book the services of a midwife. The local Health Authority is required to provide help and advice for expectant and nursing mothers, and part of this help depends on the Midwifery Service.

Midwives A midwife is a fully-trained S.R.N., C.M.B.—a State Registered Nurse, who has the additional training, qualifications and experience of Maternity and has been examined by the Central Midwives' Board. Usually several midwives work together as a team and, of course, their services are free. The one chosen and booked by the expectant mother will visit the home regularly during the months of pregnancy. She carries out brief examinations and makes sure the mother is attending her doctor or clinic. She advises on diet, rest, layettes and exercises and is generally there to turn to in need. By the time the baby is due the mother usually knows her midwife well.

If the mother-to-be has a house to run and perhaps other small children to look after, she will need help immediately after her baby is born. Often relatives are at hand to do this, but if not the *Home Help Service* is available. Again, it is wise to book your home help as soon as you know when the baby is due. This service is not free; you pay for the help by the hour, but it is heavily subsidised when this is necessary. You can decide how many hours per day to employ one help, and whether you will need her for 7 or 10 or 14 days. This is difficult to decide in advance. Before the birth of the baby you cannot be sure how well you are going to be.

If the birth is easy the mother will soon feel much better. This is often made possible by learning the art of relaxing at the birth. To do this she must already have learnt and practised relaxation at classes, probably held at the clinic. Should the birth prove difficult, both the hospital and the midwife can supply analgesics—injections or gas—to ease pain. Should an emergency occur, the mother who is in hospital can be attended to on the spot, but the home-confined mother can be removed to hospital with the utmost speed. At home she has the advantage of freedom from hospital rules and regulations. Her baby can be with her all the time, and she can choose her own visiting times. But it is probably better to be in hospital for the birth of your first baby.

Premature babies

These are babies who arrive before the date expected. They are usually less fully developed and more fragile. They are therefore in need of special care, and are usually born in, or transferred to, hospital. But most local Health Services can now supply special equipment and staff to assist mothers to care for these tiny babies in their own homes.

Post-natal treatment

The midwife visits mother and baby regularly—once or twice a day—for the first fourteen days after the birth. She also visits hospital-confined mothers who have been sent home within 2 weeks of their babies' birth. Some are sent home only 3 days afterwards, due to lack of hospital accommodation and staff. During the 2 weeks, the midwife makes sure by regular weighing, that the baby is progressing. She encourages the mother to feed the baby herself, and sees that she begins to get up when she is fit enough and not before. She lays down clear rules of diet and hygiene, and teaches the mother to change nappies and bath her baby. At the end of the 14 days, the midwife gives way to the Health Visitor who visits far less regularly. The mother should also consult the post-natal clinic for help and guidance in recovering successfully from her baby's birth.

Health Visitors

These are specially trained and very experienced nurses. They have both S.R.N. and C.M.B. qualifications as well as Health Visiting training. They were first introduced in 1862 in Manchester. Then the service was voluntary and the visitors untrained, but they managed to teach some rules of health and hygiene in the more squalid homes and, as a result, fewer babies died. Since then they have done wonderful work in very difficult circumstances. Nearly always, like the midwives, they are overworked and have large districts to supervise. They attend and often run the clinics. When there are diphtheria or polio injections to be administered, the Health Visitors publicise this, and try to get the young mothers to co-operate.

They visit as often as they can while the children are from 2 weeks to 5 years old. They look out for deficiency diseases, poor health on the mother's part and general troubles arising from these in the home. In thinly-populated areas the Health Visitor, the Midwife and the District Nurse are often all one and the same person. She also looks after old people, and arranges for them to have home helps if necessary.

She is available at the *Infants' Welfare Clinic*. These are usually open once or twice a week. They may be in a specially-equipped building, or in a caravan which goes from village to village. The mothers have the right to have their babies examined by the presiding doctor if they wish it, and if the Health Visitor, when she weighs and looks at the baby or toddler, feels an examination is necessary, she will advise it. At this stage the welfare clinics fulfil a special function. You would not, as a rule, take a healthy baby to the local doctor just to make sure that progress was normal. But at the clinic this is the expected and accepted routine, and is a reassuring way of seeing that everything is all right. You will be reminded about vaccinations and immunisations and these can either be carried out by your doctor or at the clinic. At the clinic toddlers do not have to be restrained quite so much as they do at a doctor's surgery.

Play is a child's 'work'

Children learn through play. It is not enough to fill their tummies, love them and clothe them. They must be allowed to express themselves, to experiment, to create and construct. This can cause havoc and ruin your new decorations; or it can, if organised, perhaps on the kitchen floor, in the sink, or in a sandpit or play pen, be fun and of value. Not all of us are 'born mothers'—but some of us take to it and love it. Some, especially if trained for a specialised job or profession, love to have children, but also miss going out to work. The frustration welling up from this sometimes does no good to the mother or her children. She may find more happiness by taking her toddler to a Day Nursery; her toddler will too, very probably, especially if he lives far from other children of his own age.

Day Nurseries

The more enlightened authorities, such as those of London, Nottingham, Derbyshire and Manchester, run these Day Nurseries under the National Health Service. They are staffed by specially-trained Nurses under the supervision of State Registered Nurses.

Children are accepted from 7 a.m. to 6 p.m. on weekdays, from the age of 6 weeks to 5 years. Many attend part-time, and the hours and the age range are extensive, to meet all needs. Such day nurseries are vital for the widow or widower with children, or for the unmarried mother. They are important for the mother whose husband is temporarily incapacitated or out of work. They are also a great help to the mother who wishes to return to work.

Providing that the children are loved by their parents, welcomed home at tea-time and given lots of individual attention at weekends and during the holidays, they gain through the social and community training they get at the Day Nursery. It is much more fun playing 'Ring a Roses' with a group of toddlers of your own age and size than just with Mum! And it is also fun having toddler-sized toilets, wash basins and tables and chairs.

There may be high secure fences round the Day Nursery, but within those barriers the children have far more freedom than in a flat, for instance, where there are dangerous stairs, windows and fires. The toys are simple, large, and substantial—orange boxes, slides, large sandpits and climbing frames. They enjoy good, balanced meals; they rest on little beds and play together under careful supervision. The babies are bathed, weighed, changed and their nappies washed by skilled staff. Orange juice and cod liver oil is given to them, and the doctor is on hand for advice or help. The charges depend on the income of the parents and range from £1·03 to as little as 5p (or sometimes nothing) a day. Those in need are subsidised by the State.

Some Day Nurseries are privately run. These have to be registered and inspected so that their standards of hygiene, safety and their staff ratio can be checked.

Child minders have also to be registered with the State for the same reason. These are women willing to look after other people's children.

Play groups are often run by groups of mothers who take it in turn to mind and play with the children. No meals are provided, the idea being to let the children play together for brief periods while most of the mothers have a break for a hair set or an unencumbered shopping trip. These groups, too, must be registered.

Nursery classes

These are run by the Local Education Authority in areas where they are lucky enough to have school staffs and premises to spare, to extend the scope of the infants' school, to which they are usually attached. The children receive normal milk and school dinners and a rest in the afternoon. As in an infants' school, the parents pay only for the dinners.

64 *Milk at school*

You may decide that the age of 5 is young enough to part with your child for several hours per day. In fact, many people believe that 5 is rather too young. So much depends on the individual child and family. We must all make up our own minds and act accordingly, being sure of course at all times we are acting in the best interests of our particular children. We are responsible for their arrival and we must be responsible for their happiness and safety.

Whatever you decide, the care and advice of the Welfare Clinic is available until your child starts school at 5. Then the School Health Service takes over, as we have seen in Chapter 9. All the way

The dentist

The one service that is not always used to its full advantage is that of the dentist. Dental care should start before a baby is born. But many young mothers take little or no care to ensure that their children's teeth have a good start and that their own do not suffer from pregnancy. The rapidly-developing embryo or unborn child will withdraw enough nutrients from its mother to damage her teeth unless she takes steps to prevent this, by supplementing her diet with the main tooth-builders—Vitamin D, calcium and phosphorus.

The nursing mother, who is feeding her newly-born baby directly from her own food intake, needs $2\frac{1}{2}$ times as much of these particular nutrients as does her husband. The expectant mother—whose baby is, of course, less developed and demanding—still needs twice as much. Milk and cheese contain all three nutrients and if taken plentifully and reinforced with cod or halibut liver oil, with butter and eggs and liver, neither the teeth of the baby nor the mother will suffer. Yet often the extra eggs and cheese go to the husband—this is not being unselfish, he can just as well fill up on extra bread or potatoes—your baby can't, it *needs* its tooth builders and so do you!

Your doctor will check to see if you are short of calcium. He will also tell you to visit the dentist during pregnancy, and, if necessary, afterwards too. These visits, at this time are vital, and they are free. You pay no fees from the day your pregnancy is established to one year after the date of birth of your baby—make the most of it.

The growing child and the dentist

If you are feeding your own baby, keep to a nutritious diet. Drink lots of milk, wean your baby on to milk, then gradually on to solid foods. But keep milk at the core of his diet, for this is the best single bone and tooth builder. Every toddler who is given tea or pop is being robbed of these building materials. Give them as a treat, if you want to, but let milk be the habit. Better still let treats consist of cod liver oil and malt, scrunchy apples, sticks of raw carrot or celery instead of lollies and sweets. He will thank you later on, and you will save yourself endless painful trips to the dentist. Your growing child needs twice as much calcium as an adult and four times as much Vitamin D—so see that he gets it.

Good habits Toddlers love to copy, so let them brush their own teeth just as you do, as soon as they are able. Eighteen months isn't too early. A visit to the dentist should be a special outing for the toddler between the ages of 3 and 4. Then visit as often as the dentist advises. It is quite free for children, right up to school-leaving age. Later the school dental service is available, but at least one visit before your child is 5 is advisable.

A child will only fear this visit if he has been led to, probably by thoughtless remarks at home. His first visit—if you have taken care—should be just a routine inspection, which he may enjoy. He'll love the dentist's swivelly chair and his gadgets. Later, when treatment is required, new instruments such as high-speed drills have taken much of the pain from having teeth filled.

Dental decay, or caries, is on the increase. Most of it is due to ignorance and laziness. Fluoridation of water would help but it is being fought on very questionable principles. Only half the people of Great Britain, we are told, own a toothbrush. You would think that false teeth and toothache were popular in the country!

Financial help

As we have seen in Chapter 2, our National Insurance Benefits include special grants and allowances for the birth and care of children. This is divided into three parts.

1 *The Maternity Grant*

This is a lump sum of £25 granted after the birth, provided that either the mother or the father has paid at least twenty-six insurance contributions before the birth of the baby. More is paid if twins are born. It is granted to the parents no matter where the mother chooses to have her baby.

2 *Maternity Allowances*

This allowance of £3·60 a week is payable before and after the baby's birth. It continues for 18 weeks, starting 11 weeks before the baby is due and for 7 weeks after the birth. Not all mothers are entitled to it, only those who were employed up to 11 weeks before the birth and who were paying full national insurance contributions until that time. This allowance is paid to enable mothers to give up work in time to have a rest and feel fit before they have their baby, and not to return to work too soon afterwards. If they do return to work during the 18 weeks they receive no allowance. Extra allowances are available for dependants.

3 *The Family Allowance*

This is payable for the second child and subsequent children. The entitlement is 90p per week for the second child and £1 for each of the subsequent children. This allowance is continued until the children leave school, whether this is at 15, 16 or 18 years of age.

All the allowances and grants mentioned are received after application is made to the National Insurance Office. It is a very sound idea to visit this office when you think you may be entitled to benefit. You will be listened to sympathetically, in private if you wish.

Special laws relating to children

Many laws have been passed to safeguard the young. We have seen in Chapter 12 the N.S.P.C.C.'s part in this. Here are some other regulations:

1 If it is considered by a Local authority, who is informed by such qualified people as a Health Visitor, Police Constable, School Welfare Officer or Doctor, that a child is 'in need of care and protection' the child can be brought before a Juvenile Court who will then take one of four courses open to them under the Children and Young Persons Act.

(*a*) Commit him to an Approved School—that is a special school for unfortunate children of various kinds.
(*b*) Commit him to the care of a 'fit person' for this purpose.
(*c*) Order the parent or guardian to exercise proper care and guardianship, or
(*d*) Place him under the supervision of a probation officer or other person appointed by the court.

2 Restrictions on the Employment of Children (these are listed in Chapter 9).

SPECIAL LAWS RELATING TO CHILDREN

3 Protection from moral danger. It is an offence:

(*a*) for anyone who is in charge of a girl under the age of 16 to place her in any kind of moral danger;
(*b*) to allow children between the ages of 4 and 16 to be in a house of ill-repute, such as a gambling house or brothel;
(*c*) to give intoxicating liquor to a child under the age of 5;
(*d*) to allow anyone under 16 to be in a licensed bar while open;
(*e*) to cause anyone under 16 to be used for begging.

4 Prevention of Cruelty (see Chapter 12).

5 *Protection from physical danger*. It is an offence:

(*a*) to train a child under 12 to take part in performances of a dangerous nature, or, without a licence to employ a child under 16 for such performances;
(*b*) to fail to provide for the safety of children at entertainments;
(*c*) to fail to provide guards for fires where there are children under the age of 7.

6 *Foster Parents and Adoption Acts*

These are to ensure that children are placed in suitable homes where they will be happy.
Two points need clarifying. Firstly the definition in law of:

(*a*) *a child* is 'a person under the age of 14';
(*b*) *a young person* is 'one who has attained the age of 14 but not yet 17'.

Sometimes the latter is extended to 18.
Secondly, what exactly is meant by a child or young person being 'in need of care and protection'? This is the definition:

(*a*) If he has no parent or guardian, or his parent or guardian is either unfit to exercise, or does not exercise proper care and guardianship, and the child or young person is either falling into bad associations, exposed to moral danger or ill-treated or neglected in a manner likely to cause him unnecessary suffering, or injury to health.
(*b*) If certain offences have been, or are in danger of being committed against him—mainly offences relating to cruelty or moral or physical danger.

(c) If he has been prevented by a vagrant parent or guardian from receiving efficient full-time education.

Warning. If you think carefully about all these points you may realise that some of them are not so far from our own doorstep as we may imagine. Do you know any parents, for example, who refuse to let their children have inoculations, or to let them be treated by the school dentist—and then don't get round to seeing about it themselves? This is, in fact, causing 'unnecessary injury to health'.

Do you know any parents who keep their children away from school unnecessarily?

Do you know any homes where the children under the age of 7 live—without fireguards? Parents therefore have a legal as well as a moral duty to care for their children. Their carelessness which is the cause of many of the accidents and injuries their children suffer, is thought by some to be sufficiently serious to treat as criminal.

Further reading

Maternal and Child Welfare Manual is published by the British Red Cross Society, 9 Grosvenor Crescent, S.W.1, at 20p

Welfare Services is published by the British Red Cross Society at 27½p

Guide to National Insurance is available from Her Majesty's Stationery Office, Cornwall House, Stamford St., S.E.1, at 4p

The Newborn Baby from the Consumers' Association, Fine Books Ltd., 8 Lorenzo Street, London W.C.1 at 85p

Practical work

1 Divide into groups, each with the assignment to find out as much as you can about the work of one of the following in your area:

(a) The Medical Officer of Health
(b) The Midwife
(c) The Home Help Service
(d) The Health Visitor
(e) The District Nurse.

2 Find out where there are:

(a) Maternity hospitals
(b) Maternity wards in hospitals and
(c) Maternity homes in your area.

Discuss in which—or at home—you would prefer to have your first child.

3 Write to as many firms as offer this service, e.g. Heinz, Trufood, Cow & Gate for advice on Baby Care. Compare the answers, and the value of their service.

4 What is added to our water before it reaches us? What is fluoride? Should it be added to our drinking water? Debate, 'chemicals should not be added to our water'. Think carefully before you take sides.

SOME BOOKS WHICH MIGHT INTEREST YOU

The Consumer Council's publications, including a series of brief reports called 'Consumer Contexts', are still available from 3 Cornwall Terrace, N.W.1.

Among those published are:

1. *Hire Purchase*
2. *Guarantees*
3. *Flammable Clothing*
4. *Travel Agents*
5. *Door-step Selling*
6. *Deaf Aids*
7. *Consumer Education*
8. *Consumer Protection Act 1961*
9. *Consumer Research*
10. *Insurance of Hired Cars*
11. *Medicines Legislation*

They are all free.

'Special Studies'

Some booklets already published by the Council in this series are:

Stamp Trading (20p)
Furniture Trade and Consumer (25p)
Information for Consumer Education (10p)
About Shopping (2½p)

Free leaflets:

How to Say 'No' to a Doorstep Salesman
Making a Nightdress?

Other titles to follow:

About Buying Furniture
About Buying Toys
About Buying Food and Drink

The Consumers' Association (14 Buckingham St., W.C.2) not only publishes *Which?* monthly, but also booklets:

The Law for Consumers
The Law for Motorists
The Travelling Consumer
The Legal Side of Buying a House
Radiation, Part of Life
Ailments and Remedies
All at 40p

The Research Institute for Consumer Affairs (address as above) publishes a series: 'Essays and Enquiries'.
Some booklets already published are:

Estate Agents: a consumers' assessment (17½p)
General Practice: a consumer commentary (17½p)
London Stations: a users' assessment (20p)
British Co-operatives: a consumers' movement? (20p)
Children's Toys: the trade assessed (17½p)
Butchers' Shops: the customers' view (20p)
Consumer Education: conceptions and resources (22½p)

SOME BOOKS WHICH MIGHT INTEREST YOU

Fair Trading: protecting consumers (20p)
Town Planning: the consumers' environment (22½p)
New Nations: problems for consumers (20p)
Elderly Consumers: the problem assessed (25p)
Car Defects: a consumer investigation (22½p)

All the above-mentioned publications can be purchased at a discount if ordered in bulk, so the more of you who want them, the less each of you will have to pay.

Other interesting sources of consumer information:

The Spectator runs a regular feature, 'Consuming Interest', *The Guardian* runs 'Consumers' Viewpoint', *At Your Service* (17½p), by Elizabeth Gundry, is published by Penguin Books Ltd.

INDEX

accidents, 213, 217–27, 234
accommodation, 63–86
acne, 191
Acts
    Children and Young Persons, 306
    Consumer Protection, 20, 227
    Education, 197
    Food and Drugs, 20
    Foster Parents and Adoption, 307
    Heating Appliance, 227
    Hire Purchase, 20, 52–4
    Labelling of Food, 212
    Mental Health, 235
    Merchandise Marks, 19–20
    National Assistance, 236
    Oil Heaters, 227
    Protection from Eviction, 75
    Sale of Goods, 18, 19, 52
    Supply of Goods, 22
    Trade Descriptions, 21
    Weights and Measures, 21

adhesives, 120–1
adolescence, 186, 191, 272–80
Adoption Act, 307
adrenal glands, 272
ambulance, 216, 234
anaemia, 184–5
apocrine glands, 185, 186
approved schools, 306
arthritis, 203, 209
artificial respiration, 215
asthma, 202
auxiliary services, 243

babies, 288–90, 295, 299–301, 308
bacteria, 185, 188
bacterial diseases, 201–2, 203–5
banks, 43–7, 59
B.E.A.B. sign, 13
birth, 289, 298–300
blackheads, 190
bleeding, 215
blinds, window, 174

board and lodging, *see* accommodation
botulism, 205
bowels, diseases of, 204
boys' clubs, 98, 99
boyfriends, 278–80, 282
British Standards Institution, 13, 131, 137, 138
British Thermal Units, 166–8
bronchitis, 202, 203, 207
budgeting, 3, 29–37, 286–7
building societies, 78–9
bulk buying, 8, 9

calcium, 304
Camping Club, 95
cancer, lung, 203, 209
carbohydrates, 181–2, 209
care-labelling, 24–5, 111, 113–14
carpets, 109, 129–32
cars, 311, 313
central heating, 165–9, 176
chemists, 233
chicken pox, 201, 204, 210
Child Guidance clinics, 197
child minders, 302
children
 care, 195–212
 conditioning, 291–6
 employment, 198, 306
 in families, 88–90, 288–95
 handicapped, 198
 health, 196–201, 304–5
 illnesses, 200–12
 protection, 300–2
Children and Young Persons Act, 306
chores, *see* housework
Citizens' Advice Bureau, 19, 64, 100, 251–3, 266–7
City and Guilds, 96
cleaning equipment, 108–10
cleanliness, 185–8, 194, 205
clinics
 ante-natal, 297–8
 child guidance, 197
 infants' welfare, 197, 221, 297–8, 301
 post-natal, 300
closed shop, 246–7
clothes
 buying, 14–16, 24–5, 27, 30, 31
 children's, 197, 222–3, 311, 312
 washing, 111, 113–14, 188–9
clubs, 95, 98–9
colds, 201, 203, 204, 205, 207
conditioning, of children, 291–6
confinement, 289, 298–300
Consumer
 Council, 20, 55, 311–12
 education, 311–12
 protection, 12–26, 59, 227, 311
Consumers' Association, 18, 141, 312
co-operatives, 57–8, 312
cosmetics, 189–94
credit, 8
 notes, 16
 sales agreements, 54
C.U.C. sign, 13
cupboards, 150–1
curtains, 140–1
Cyclists Touring Club, 99

damp, causes of, 128–9
dandruff, 188
date-stamping, 22
deaf aids, 311
decorating, home, 124–8, 142
deficiency diseases, 203, 230
dentists, 231, 233, 304–5
deodorants, 186–7
depression, 202, 207–8; *see also* moodiness
Design
 Centre, 137, 138, 176
 Council of Industrial, 138
detergents, 107–8, 110, 116–17, 119
diarrhoea, 201, 202, 204
diphtheria, 204, 205–6, 210

INDEX

diseases
  bacterial, 201–2, 203–5
  childhood, 200–11
  deficiency, 202, 207–8
  virus, 201, 203–5
doctors, 231–2, 247–8, 312
double glazing, 170–3
dry cleaning, 115
dust, 106–7
dustbins, 160, 176
dysentery, 202, 204

eccrine glands, 185
Education
  Act, 197
  Authority, Local, 197–9, 211
  further, 96
electric
  central heating, 166–9
  fires, 164
  repairs, 121–2, 141
Electrical Association for Women, 176
electricity and accidents, 215
emotional disturbances, 207–8, 275, 278–9
employment of children, 198, 306
endocrine glands, 272, 282
energy, 181–2, 184–5
engagement, 280–2
entertaining, 93–5
estate agents, 80–1, 312
eviction, 75
exercise, 185, 190
eyes, 183, 193, 233, 257

fabrics and fibres, 20, 111–18, 129–31, 138–41, 222–3
Fair Trading, 312
family
  allowance, 306
  life, 87–90
  planning, 288
fats, 181–2
fears, children's, 291–3, 296

fibres, *see* fabrics
fibrositis, 209
fire guards, 123, 164, 221
Fire Service, 242
fires
  dangers of, 221–3
  electric, 164
  gas, 163–4
  oil, 164, 227
  solid fuel, 162–3, 175, 221–3
first aid, 213–27, 254, 256, 257, 267
flats, *see* accommodation
flies, 204–5, 212, 292
flooring, 129–33
fluoride, 188, 305, 309
food
  budgeting, 31, 33, 312
  labelling, 21–2, 209, 212
  poisoning, 204, 205, 208, 212
  school, 197
  values, 180–5, 194
Food and Drugs Act, 20
Foster Parents Act, 307
friendship, 91–2, 99–100
furniture, 134–8, 312

gas
  central heating, 165, 167–9
  fires, 163–4
Gas Councils mark, 13
gastro-enteritis, 213
G.C.E., 96
German measles, 201, 204, 210–12
germs, *see* bacteria
glands, 185, 186, 271–2, 282
grease, 103–4, 107–8, 116
guarantees, 22–4, 52, 56, 134, 311
Guardian, The, 313
Guides, Girl, 99

hair
  care of, 182, 187–8
  superfluous, 191

handicapped children, 198
health, 179, 194, 196–201, 211
Health
   and Social Security, Dept. of, 191, 212, 229, 236–7, 297
   Visitors, 198, 300–1, 306
heaters, safety, 20, 227
heating, 161–71
   central, 165–9, 176
hire purchase, 20, 45, 49–54, 311
hobbies, 96
home helps, 235, 299
hormones, 271–2, 277
hospitals, 234, 288
hostels, 69–70
house
   buying, 77–83, 312
   decorating, 124–8, 142
   planning, 141–2
   running, 30, 33, 103–43
housework, 71, 103–9, 285–6, 294, 295–6
hygiene, 10, 185–8, 194

illness, 200–12, 312
immunisation, 205–6, 212
income, 31–2, 287
   tax, 34
incubation of diseases, 211
inflammable materials, 20, 222–3
influenza, 201, 204, 206
insecticides, 205
insulation, 169–70
insurance
   car, 49, 311
   companies, 78
   endowment, 49
   house, 48–9
   life, 48
   National, 34–5, 47, 236, 247, 308
roning, 118

Juvenile Court, 306

kitchen
   accidents in, 223–5
   equipment, 145–7, 152–8
   orders of work, 146–9, 175
   storage space, 150–1
kitemarks, 13, 131, 137

labels, 11–14, 19–20, 24–5, 27, 111, 113–14, 131, 137
Labour Exchange, 35
Land Registry Office, 81
launderettes, 114–15
laundries, 115
laundry, *see* washing
leisure, 95–100
lighting, 173–4, 175
linen, household, 132, 138–40
linoleum, 132
list, shopping, 3, 6, 7
Local Authorities, 197–9, 211, 238–41, 301
lodgings, *see* accommodation
love, 195–6, 281, 293
lumbago, 209

mail order firms, 11–12
make-up, 189–94
marks, merchandise, 19–20; *see also* labels
marriage, 283–96
Marriage Guidance Council, National, 262, 266
maternity
   allowance, 305–6
   grant, 305
   see also birth, motherhood
measles, 201, 210, 213
Medical
   Card, 232
   Loan Depot, 200
   see also dentist, doctor, health, hospitals, illness
medicines legislation, 311
menstruation, 273–7, 282
Mental Health Act, 235

INDEX

mental illness, 207–8, 235
Merchandise Marks Act, 19–20
midwifery, 299
milk, 181–4, 193, 208, 297, 303–4
minerals, in food, 181–2, 184–5, 208, 304
moodiness, 279; *see also* depression
mortgages, 78–9
motherhood, 288–96, 297–309
mumps, 201, 204, 210–11

nails, 182, 188
National Assistance, 236, 240
National Health Service, 197, 229–37, 240, 248, 297
National Insurance, 34–5, 47, 236, 247, 308
National Savings, 40–1, 58, 243
N.S.P.C.C., 258–62, 266–7, 306
nurseries, 301–2
nursery classes, 303
nursing
　home, 199–200
　mothers, 304

obesity, 203, 209
oil
　central heating, 165–9
　heaters, 164, 227
old people, 313
ophthalmic services, 233, 257
ovaries, 272, 275
Oxfam, 11, 267

painting, 124–6
parents, 88–90, 92–4; *see also* motherhood
Pasteur, Louis, 201
pasteurisation, 208
periods, *see* menstruation
personal relationships, 87–102
pituitary gland, 272
plastic
　bags, 220
　glue, 121

laminates, 133
padding, 120
play, 296, 301, 302
play groups, 302
pneumonia, 201, 203
poisons, 111, 219, 225
police, 241–3, 306
post-natal clinics, 300
Post Office Savings Bank, 40–1, 58
posture, 189
pregnancy, 208, 288, 295, 297–8
premature babies, 300
Premium Bonds, 42, 244
proteins, 180–1, 230
puberty, 186, 191, 272–7

quarantine, 210

Rambling Association, 98
rates, 238–40, 248
Red Cross, British, 98, 199, 214, 254–6, 266–7
refuse disposal, 158–61, 240
rent, 30, 32
rented accommodation, 70–6, 85–6
repairs
　electrical, 121–2
　general, 120–1, 122–3
rheumatism, 203, 209
rickets, 203
roughage, 183, 275
R.S.P.C.A., 263–7
rubbish, *see* refuse disposal

St. John Ambulance Association, 214, 256–8, 266–7
Sale of Goods Act, 18, 19, 52
salesmen, 54–7, 58, 311–12
Salvation Army, 69
Samaritans, 262–3, 266
Save the Children Fund, 267
savings, 39–60, 244
Savings Bonds, British, 40–2, 58, 243

scalds, 223–4
scarlet fever, 204, 210
School
  Health Service, 196, 198, 303
  Welfare Officers, 198, 306
Scouts, Boy, 99
scurvy, 203
security, of children, 195–6, 293–4
shingles, 202
shock, treatment for, 215
shoes, 189, 194
shopping, 3–27, 312
shyness, 91
signs, *see* labels
skin, 182–3, 190, 278
sleep, 179–80
smallpox, 201, 204, 206, 210
smokeless zones, 207
smoking, 122, 203, 209, 223
Social Security, Dept. of Health and, 191, 212, 229, 236–7, 297
solicitors, 82–3, 312
solid fuel
  Advisory Bureau, 175
  central heating, 165, 167–9
  fires, 162–3, 175, 221–3
spiders, 209, 292–3
Spectator, The, 313
stain removal, 116–18
stamps, trading, 10–11, 312
storage space, 150–1
strikes, 246
sub-letting, 73
superannuation, 36
supermarkets, 4–8, 26
Supply of Goods Act, 22

taxes, 34, 243–4
teenagers, *see* adolescence
teeth
  care of, 182, 188, 304–5
  decay, 203, 305
Teltags, 13–14

tetanus, 206
thyroid gland, 272
tickets, *see* labels
tiles, 128, 132–3
Town Planning, 312
toys, 302, 312
Trade Descriptions Act, 21
Trade Unions, 36, 244–9
travel agents, 311
tuberculosis, 202, 206, 212
typhoid, 204, 206

U-bend, 159
ulcers, 202
unmarried mothers, 297
uterus, 274, 275

vaccination, 205–6
vacuum cleaners, *see* cleaning equipment
V.A.T., 34
venereal disease, 202
ventilation, 171–3
virus diseases, 201, 203–5
vitamins, 180–4, 208, 230, 304
voluntary organisations, 251–67

wages, 31–2, 287
wallpaper, 121, 126–7
washing, 111, 113–14, 188–9
  machines, 110–12
  powders, 110, 111, 116–19
waste disposal units, 158
water
  hard, 110
  heating, 170–1
Weights and Measures Act, 21
Welfare Services, 197, 221, 247, 297–8, 301, 308
Which?, 18, 22–3, 25–6, 108, 132, 139, 140, 194, 312
whooping cough, 204, 206, 210
windows, 171–3

wood
  floors, 132
  repairs, 120
  treatment of, 135–6
  types, 135
woodworm, 79
working surfaces, 133–4, 142, 146–8, 149, 150

working wives, 285–6, 296
W.R.V.S., 64, 253–4, 266–7

youth
  clubs, 98
  Employment Office, 96, 199
  Hostels Association, 97, 98, 99
Y.W.C.A., 69